"In a post-pandemic age when design expertise is

Gregg, and Ralston-Berg offer the experience of working with an instructional designer to any faculty member. Written in an accessible 'workshop' tone, this book systematically guides instructors through 8 practical steps with hands-on design documents and faculty-ID collaboration scenarios. With the help of HIDOC, new and seasoned instructors can successfully take their online courses from inception to launch, using resources typically made available only through consultation with an ID. This text is a must-have for institutions, schools, and departments interested in scaling quality online course design."
—***Rae Mancilla,*** *Ed.D., Assistant Director of Online Learning, Office of Online Learning, University of Pittsburgh*

"What I love about the HIDOC model and this book is its flexible, adaptable, and pragmatic approach to designing online courses. The eight-step model can be applied incrementally, in an agile manner, or on an ad-hoc basis. This adaptability empowers you to create online courses quickly, focusing on the essential elements that will best support your students. The authors provide a plethora of practical examples to help guide the reader in designing their own online courses."
—***Wendy Tietz,*** *Ph.D., CPA, CMA, CGMA, CSCA, Professor, Ambassador Crawford College of Business and Entrepreneurship, Kent State University*

"Laid out in an easy-to-follow fashion with wonderful tips for the entire design process, HIDOC promises to be a great addition to anyone's library of 'how to' for online course design, whether you're a new or experienced online instructor. The book also does a wonderful job of differentiating true online course design from the 'emergency remote' courses that happened during the pandemic. One of my favorite parts, though, is scenarios at every step of the process between a faculty member and an instructional designer. The faculty/ID team is so crucial to successful course design, yet the roles are often misunderstood; these scenarios help clarify those roles and how to work together effectively."
—***Barbara W. Altman,*** *Ph.D., Associate Professor of Management, College of Business Administration, Texas A&M University–Central Texas*

"This is the book on online course design and development that you didn't know you needed, and that you should now never be without! It is immensely practical, and focused on how to accomplish an excellent, engaging online course with a new model drawn from research and best practice. The highly experienced authors have created a practical and pragmatic guided 'how to' that is sure to be used by faculty and students of instructional design alike."
—***Sasha Thackaberry,*** *Ph.D., Senior Vice President of Wave, D2L*

"The HIDOC handbook is a must-have for any instructor developing an online course. What makes this book unique is that it focuses on the design of online course instruction, using a model specific to the online format, and providing a solid pathway for the course development process. In addition, HIDOC is responsive to the current cultural context, with an emphasis on inclusive design. While this handbook is likely to be helpful to instructors of all disciplines, those teaching STEM in particular may appreciate the very organized, step-by-step process of how to create high-quality online education."
—***Sarah Zappe,*** *Ph.D., Assistant Dean for Teaching and Learning, College of Engineering, The Pennsylvania State University*

"Whether you're creating an online course for the first time, or wanting to improve the quality of your online teaching experience, HIDOC meets you where you are and guides you through the pedagogical planning of course design with added tips that will greatly enhance your teaching interactions and your students' learning experience. This research-based, but very practical guide, turns the challenge of designing a quality online course into an easily obtainable, and perhaps even enjoyable, experience. The book itself is a great fit for individual faculty, faculty cohort/collaborative design approaches, IDs and ID teams, as well as centers for teaching and learning. I also strongly recommend it for senior leadership who want to better understand the deep and challenging work of designing quality online learning."
—***Valerie Kelly,*** *Associate Vice-President, Kent State Online, Kent State University*

HIGH-IMPACT DESIGN FOR ONLINE COURSES

BLUEPRINTING QUALITY DIGITAL LEARNING IN EIGHT PRACTICAL STEPS

Bethany Simunich
Andrea Gregg
Penny Ralston-Berg

Access the HIDOC Course Blueprint, Design Documents, and other resources at: https://hidocmodel.com/

NEW YORK AND LONDON

First published 2024
by Routledge
605 Third Avenue, New York, NY 10158

and by Routledge
4 Park Square, Milton Park, Abingdon, Oxon, OX14 4RN

Routledge is an imprint of the Taylor & Francis Group, an informa business

ISBN: 9781032577951 (hbk)
ISBN: 9781032580654 (pbk)
ISBN: 9781003442370 (ebk)

DOI: 10.4324/9781003442370

Typeset in Times New Roman

Publisher's note
This book has been prepared from camera-ready copy provided by the authors.

Cover created by the authors with Canva
Icons licensed through The Noun Project

Access the Design Documents and other resources: https://hidocmodel.com/

For busy instructors and designers everywhere

Contents

Preface.....xv
Introducing HIDOC.....1

Section I - Designing Your Course with HIDOC
Step 1 - Learner Analysis.....19
Step 2 - Learning Outcomes.....31
Step 3 - Course Structure.....53
Step 4 - Assessments & Activities.....63
Step 5 - Instructional Materials.....87
Step 6 - Technology & Tools.....113
Step 7 - Online Learner Support.....129
Step 8 - Continuous Improvement.....161
Bonus Chapter - Design Execution.....187
Design Doc Library.....209

Section II – HIDOC-in-Action: Course Design Cases
#1: The Case of the Third-Party Tool and Technology Issues.....234
#2: The Case of Lab Kit Logistics and a Heavy Workload.....237
#3: The Case of Assignment Choice Leaving Too Much to Chance.....241
#4: The Case of a Hands-on Headache.....245
#5: The Case of Learner-Curated Content Complications.....249
#6: The Case of Copyright Complications and Tough Topics.....253
#7: The Case of Multimedia Simulation That's Difficult in Reality.....257
#8: The Case of High Anxiety and the Absentee Professor.....261
#9: The Case of the Peer Collaboration Calamity.....265
#10: The Case of the Dual-Mode Disparity.....269

Index.....275

Detailed Contents

Preface xv

This Book in Historical Context xv

Remote Teaching versus Intentional Course Design xvii

Your Virtual IDs xviii

Course Modalities xix

Face-to-Face xx

Fully Online Asynchronous xx

Fully Online Synchronous xx

Hybrid xxi

Dual-Mode and HyFlex xxi

Audience for this Book xxii

Instructors xxii

Instructional Designers xxii

Visual Notations xxiii

Design Docs & HIDOC Course Blueprint xxiii

Faculty-ID Collaborations xxiii

Inclusive Design xxiv

Examples xxv

Reminders xxv

Further Explanations xxv

Starting Where You Are xxvi

Let's Get Started! xxvii

Introducing HIDOC 1

Starting with the "Why" of HIDOC 2

Key Differences between F2F and Online Learning 2

More on the Development of HIDOC 4

The HIDOC Model 5

High-Impact Design Practices 7

Course Design Alignment 8

Being "Present" Online Starts with Design 9

More on Transactional Distance 10

Section I - Designing Your Course with HIDOC 10
Design Docs and HIDOC Course Blueprint 11
Section II - HIDOC-in-Action 13
Beyond Design: Development and Delivery 13
Design vs. Development 13
Design vs. Delivery 14

Section I - Designing Your Course With HIDOC

Step 1 - Learner Analysis 19
Learner Analysis in an Online Context 19
Respecting the Diversity of Your Students 20
Design Implications of Learner Analysis 21
Your Turn: Learner Analysis 23
Part 1: Key Course Details 23
Part 2: Learner Considerations 24
Faculty-ID Collaboration: *Considering Your Learners* 27

Step 2 - Learning Outcomes 31
Starting with the "Big Vision" 31
"Big Visions" by Discipline 32
CLOs as Foundation for Aligned Course Design 33
CLOs Should Be "Measurable" 34
More on Learning Taxonomies 36
CLOs Should Be Student-Focused 36
Clear 36
Specific 37
Focused on Mastery 37
Evaluating & Revising CLOs 37
Learning Outcomes FAQ 40
What if I have mandated CLOs? 40
What if I have "objectives" instead of learning "outcomes"? 41
Can I have too many CLOs? 41
Do learning outcomes differ by discipline? 42

Don't CLOs just invite students to "check the box"? 42
Do students even read them? 42
What does any of this have to do with online learning? 43
What about higher-level courses? 43
Do these learning outcome "rules" always apply? 43
Your Turn: Learning Outcomes 44
Part 1: "Big Vision" 44
Part 2: Draft Your CLOs 44
Part 3: Revise Your CLOs 45
Part 4: Check Your CLOs 45
Faculty-ID Collaboration: *Replacing "Understand"* 47
Faculty-ID Collaboration: *Using Student-Centric Language* 48

Step 3 - Course Structure 53
Modular Organization 53
Your Course Alignment Map 54
Your Turn: Alignment Map 55
Part 1: Module Brainstorming 56
Part 2: Module Planning 57
Faculty-ID Collaboration: *Importance of Structure & Organization* ...59

Step 4 - Assessments & Activities 63
Overview of Types 63
Summative Assessments: Learning and Mastery 63
Formative Assessments: Crucial Feedback 64
Learning Activities: Practice and Guidance 64
Examples of Learning Activities 65
Avoiding "Busy Work" 66
Connecting Assessments & Activities with Presence & Community ..67
Social Presence via Assessments and Activities 67
Ways to Promote Social Presence 68
Cognitive Presence and Authentic Assessments 68
Examples of Authentic Assessments 69
More on Online Exam Proctoring 69

Teaching Presence through Assessments and Activities..........70
More on Regular & Substantive Interaction............................71
Inclusive Assessments 71
Voice and Choice 72
Voice and Choice Options..72
Alignment: CLOs and Assessments..73
Your Turn: Assessments & Activities 74
Part 1: Summative Assessments 75
Part 2: Formative Assessments & Learning Activities 76
Part 3: Assessments and Learning Activities Check...............76
Part 4: Learning Outcomes Alignment 77
Faculty-ID Collaboration: *Feedback, Timing, & Engagement*.............80
Faculty-ID Collaboration: *Checking for Alignment*.............................82

Step 5 - Instructional Materials..87
Materials in an Online Context..87
"Overstuffed" Online Courses..88
Instructional Alignment...89
Inclusive and Accessible Course Content 90
Inclusive Instructional Materials 90
Accessible Instructional Material 92
Examples of Accessibility Practices 93
Sourcing Instructional Materials...94
Curating 95
Searching for Online Content 97
Creating...98
Instructor-Created Content 98
Your Turn: Instructional Materials.......................................100
Online Topical Lectures...102
Steps to Create an Online Topical Lecture 103
Lectures in Hybrid and Online Synchronous Courses...........106
Your Online Topical Lectures 107
Faculty-ID Collaboration: *Why Don't We Start with Content?* 108

Step 6 - Technology and Tools 113
Technology, Tools, and Your Context 113
Reasons to Use Institutionally Supported Technology 114
Types of Technology and Tools 115
Common Assessment and Activity Tools in the LMS 116
A Note on the LMS Discussion Tool 117
Minimizing Cognitive Load 119
Ways to Minimize Cognitive Load 119
Your Turn: Technology & Tools 121
Part 1: Technology Planning 121
Part 2: Technology Documentation 123
Faculty-ID: *Collaboration Choosing the Right LMS Tool* 125

Step 7 - Online Learner Support 129
Learning Online is Different 129
Create a Well-Designed Learning Path 130
Essential Module Elements 131
CLOs and MLOs 133
Your Turn: Detailed Module Layout 135
Part 1: Create a Draft of Your Module Overview 135
Part 2: Review Module Overview & Create MLOs 137
Part 3: Draft Your Module Summary and Next Steps 138
Actively Support Your Students on this Learning Path 139
Provide Thorough Assignment Explanations 139
More on Office/Student Hours 141
Your Turn: Assignment Prompts 141
Part 1: Key Segments of Assignment Prompts 142
Part 2: Check for Clarity 143
Intentionally Schedule, Scaffold, and Remind 144
Provide Course Supports Specific to Learners' Needs 145
Provide Helpful and Informative Materials & Activities 145
A "Start Here" Folder 146
An Instructor Welcome and Course Orientation 147
Syllabus with Policies Specific to Online Learning 148

Course Schedule Appropriate for an Online Course.............151
Course Space for Introductions & General Discussions........154
Content Descriptions 155
Activity That Allows Students to Share................................155
Faculty-ID Collaboration: *Importance of a Detailed Learning Path*..157

Step 8 - Continuous Improvement 161
Your Turn: Teaching Calendar...163
Considering the Student Perspective 164
Spacing and Rhythm...164
Student Workload..166
Balance of Types...166
Your Turn: Course Alignment...167
Planning for Future Improvements...169
Your Turn: Revision Roadmap 170
Collecting Student Feedback 172
Module-Level Survey Questions 173
Course-Level Survey Questions 177
Revision Triage: Prioritizing Improvements.......................................181
Fixes to Make While the Course Is Running........................181
Planning Revisions before the Next Run..............................182
Faculty-ID Collaboration: *Planning for Revision*..............................183

Bonus Chapter - Design Execution...187
Being Present in Your Online Course 187
Make Introductions...188
More on Cameras..189
Use Announcements to Keep Students Motivated.................190
Opportunities for Guidance and Connection 193
Make it Personal 194
Extend the Conversation...194
Your Course Timeline 195
Before Class Begins..196
Module Release: Staggered or All-at-Once? 196

First Week of Class 199
Early Weeks 200
Throughout the Course 201
Final Week 202
Your Turn: Active Teaching 203
Your Turn: Teaching Calendar 206

Design Document Library 209

Section II - HIDOC-in-Action: Course Design Cases

Welcome to HIDOC-in-Action: Course Design Cases! 232
#1: The Case of the Third-Party Tool and Technology Issues 234
#2: The Case of Lab Kit Logistics and a Heavy Workload 237
#3: The Case of Assignment Choice Leaving Too Much to Chance 241
#4: The Case of a Hands-on Headache 245
#5: The Case of Learner-Curated Content Complications 249
#6: The Case of Copyright Complications and Tough Topics 253
#7: The Case of Multimedia Simulation That's Difficult in Reality 257
#8: The Case of High Anxiety and the Absentee Professor 261
#9: The Case of the Peer Collaboration Calamity 265
#10: The Case of the Dual-Mode Disparity 269

Index 275

Preface

This book arrives at the intersection of a multi-century history of distance education (which includes online education) and a relatively recent global pandemic that forced educators worldwide to rapidly pivot to remote teaching and learning. The need for this book existed prior to the COVID-19 pandemic; however, it is even more urgent now. With the emergency shift to remote teaching, nearly every educator had some experience teaching at a distance. At the same time, this experience often took place without the necessary guidance to most effectively design those online offerings. This meant that for many, remote teaching during the pandemic reinforced, rather than challenged, problematic beliefs about the poor quality of online education. For those of you whose first "online experience" was during the emergency shift to remote learning, we applaud your heroic efforts! However, we also hope that through this book we can help you to never again feel confused, frantic, or unsupported when teaching online because you will have learned how to design high-quality online courses.

This Book in Historical Context

While the COVID-19 pandemic has certainly brought online learning into a new spotlight, online higher education was already a prominent learning modality with individual online courses, complete online programs, and fully online colleges and universities. In recent years, online learning has also been recognized as the primary driver for growth within higher education (Lederman, 2019). Enrollment in online courses has exceeded growth in enrollment in residential education since 2012 (Seaman et al., 2018). Additionally, its broader container of "distance education," defined as education when faculty and students are physically, and often temporally, separated has been around in different forms for centuries (Kentnor, 2015). Distance education modalities have included postal correspondence courses, radio and TV educational broadcasts, individualized computer-based training, early online text-based learning with limited opportunities for interaction, streamed courses, and, more recently, rich multimedia online courses with the integration of web conferencing (Anderson & Dron, 2011; Anderson & Dron, 2012).

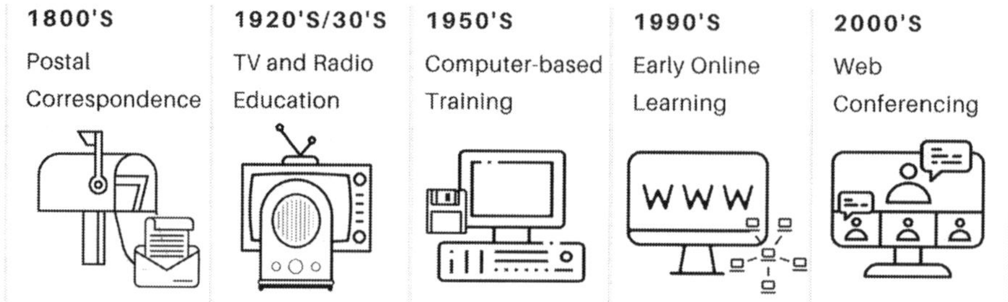

Fortunately, this progression of distance and online education has also been accompanied by a robust research base covering online learning theory, instructional design models, and empirical work in areas like the efficacy of online modalities, online instructor and student satisfaction, learning outcome achievement in online courses, and design and technology best practices and impacts. In addition to foundational texts and a multitude of scholarly journals, there are key research centers and accompanying research databases central to the field, which include comparison studies to F2F learning (e.g., No Significant Difference Database; Online Learning Efficacy Research Database). While conversations during the pandemic frequently referenced "when things get back to normal," the reality is that in the "new normal"—whether due to another global pandemic, weather disruptions that require campus closures, or the need for additional ways to reach students—online learning will continue to play a vital role in higher education.

> ***There is already a solid literature base for online and distance education. There is much we already know and plenty that we continue to investigate. Be wary of research that positions online learning as "new" or less effective, as well as research that conflates emergency remote learning with purposefully designed online learning.***

Remote Teaching versus Intentional Course Design

There are significant, impactful differences between a course intentionally designed for online learning versus a course rapidly transitioned for emergency remote instruction (Carr-Chelman, 2021; Hodges et al., 2020). Typically, remote delivery essentially attempts to replicate the classroom model as much as possible (e.g., moving from in-person lectures to Zoom lectures). In contrast, intentional course design relies on learning theory, empirical findings specific to online distance education, instructional design models, and the realities of learning at a distance within an online medium. Intentional design, then, attends to the whole course, identifying learning outcomes along with selecting the best aligned content, activities, and assessments, as well as strategically integrating appropriate educational technologies.

An intentionally designed online course also frequently involves collaboration between a faculty member who is a subject matter expert in the discipline and an instructional designer (ID) who is an expert in designing quality learning experiences and typically holds an advanced degree in fields like educational technology, learning design and technology, or learning experience design. Most IDs are also specifically knowledgeable about designing online courses and are skilled in using educational technology and instructional design to maximize the learning environment and educational experience to promote student success. (For more information on instructional design, please see the Further Explanations section toward the end of the Preface.) ***The challenge is that many instructors have limited or no instructional design support.***

Despite having taught remotely, many faculty haven't yet done intentional online course design. The remote teaching experience is not akin to a well-designed, quality online course—either for instructors or students.

Your Virtual IDs

Rest assured that, with this book and its companion website, you do have instructional design help! You can think of us as virtual IDs who will guide you through the process of designing your course, just as we would via a workshop or individual consultations. At this point, you may be wondering why you should invest your trust (and more importantly, your time) in us. Below, we summarize our collective professional experience relevant to leading busy instructors such as yourselves through online course design.

We have designed A LOT of online courses.

With a combined 60+ years of experience working closely with faculty members across all disciplines and levels, we have collectively collaborated on the design and development of over three hundred online and hybrid courses. Disciplines we have worked with include, but are not limited to, engineering, communication, sociology, business, math, education, lab-based sciences, English, computer science, health sciences, accounting, psychology, anthropology, religious studies, and history. Courses we've worked on range from remedial to advanced levels and include dialogue-intensive graduate seminars, project-based courses, writing-intensive courses, laboratory courses, dual-enrollment courses, and more. We have also hired, managed, and mentored dozens of instructional designers. Throughout our years of experience, we have developed and refined processes and accompanying worksheets to support faculty members as they create their online courses. The process and practices promoted in this book rely on this collective experience of what has worked and been most effective for a variety of faculty in developing high-quality online courses, across all disciplines and levels.

We are grounded in the research base of instructional design and online distance education.

We each have advanced degrees, have published and presented widely in the field of online learning, and currently hold professional positions that require our work to be research-supported. Where appropriate, we will reference supporting literature. Ultimately, though, this book is written to be a practical guide rather than an academic text or scholarly research. While the design practices we advocate here have solid theoretical and empirical support, you don't necessarily need all the academic backstory to be able to apply them. For those of you who might be interested, we do provide some key pieces of research and theory that can be explored more deeply on your own.

We believe in "learning first, technology second."
Collectively, we have taught online, hybrid, and in-person undergraduate and graduate university courses. We have also facilitated and led many faculty workshops and, therefore, understand first-hand the experience of transitioning from in-person to online teaching and learning. We believe that online education is, first and foremost, about learning, rather than the technology that supports it. After working with instructors to design online courses, we often hear from faculty that the design process made their in-person courses better as well. This is because much of the process requires clarifying teaching and learning intentions and aligning all the parts of the course, including content, activities, and assessments. While we emphasize this in the context of an online modality, the core design principles apply across settings.

We're excited to be your guides on this rewarding journey!

Course Modalities

Course modality refers to how a course is offered. While this book focuses foremost on fully online asynchronous courses, it is helpful to know all the different ways courses can be offered. We also realize that there is no universal definition for course modalities, and institutions (and faculty) can have different definitions for the same term. These are some of the important reasons we wanted to state and define the modality terms we'll be using in this book. If you or your institution uses different terms, that's absolutely fine—by using the definitions, you'll be able to "translate" information in a way that makes sense for you and your work.

Face-to-Face

We use the term face-to-face (or F2F) to reflect the traditional, classroom-based form of teaching and learning that takes place on a campus with students and instructors in the same physical space at the same time. Other terms to describe this modality that we use interchangeably are *on-ground, on-campus, or in-person.* A F2F course can also sometimes be "web-enhanced," meaning it is augmented with online learning technology—usually the LMS (learning management system) or a content repository. A F2F course that uses a flipped pedagogical approach would fall here, for example, if students watch instructional videos outside of class, then use class time for hands-on application. A traditional F2F class that uses the LMS for digital documents, to turn in assignments, and for an online gradebook would also fall in this category.

Fully Online Asynchronous

An online asynchronous course is 100% online—traditionally, there are no required live/real-time class meetings, whether F2F or synchronously, though some online degree programs may have an in-person inaugural session, for example. This has been the most common type of online course since the early 1990s. An online asynchronous course relies on a full and robust web-based design that is nearly always more time-intensive to create since it requires developing the complete course structure in the LMS and digitizing all course materials. It is, therefore, easier to adapt this design to other modalities by scaling back which aspects occur in the LMS. By designing an asynchronous online course first, regardless of what online modality you will be teaching in, you will be better prepared for any modality change or emergency.

> ***The big takeaway here is that we recommend as a best practice to design an asynchronous online course first whenever possible, as it is easiest to adapt that design to any other modality.***

Fully Online Synchronous

An online synchronous course is one in which the course is offered entirely online and includes regular, online class meetings that students are required to attend. The structure is similar to a F2F course, but the online modality strongly impacts design choices. Class meetings are most often held via web-conferencing software, such as Zoom, or collaboration software built into the LMS, and there are no required F2F meetings. The course structure is built in the LMS, which is also used for things like sharing digital materials and turning in assignments. An online synchronous class is NOT simply a remote in-person class and should be well-designed and purposefully designed for online learning.

Hybrid

A hybrid course is a hybrid or blend of F2F class sessions and asynchronous online instructional content and materials. The precise ratio of how much time students spend online interacting with materials compared to in-class can vary (and is often dictated by the state or institution), but a general gauge that reflects most hybrid courses is that at least 50% of the course is online. This course type is best designed as an asynchronous course, with consideration for where and when students will interact with course materials. If the pedagogical approach of a "flipped classroom" is used, students will interact with materials asynchronously and use the F2F class time for active, applied learning (a flipped F2F class is similar in structure, but hybrid students usually do not spend as much time together in person). If it's not designed as a "flipped" class, the students will spend their F2F class time listening to the instructor lecture and doing in-class activities and will do most of their applied work via the LMS.

Dual-Mode and HyFlex

A dual-mode course has two distinct audiences: both in-class students and students participating at a distance. Online students might be attending the class synchronously, through a live, streamed video conference of the F2F course, or asynchronously, based on a recording of the F2F class session. Students typically enroll in either the F2F or online section(s) and stay in their section for the term.

A HyFlex course is one in which each class session is offered in two or three distinct ways, and students can choose how they will attend each session. They can attend live, in-class; they can connect live, synchronously online; or they can participate in the class asynchronously online, if the course is offered in all three modalities (some HyFlex courses, however, offer only one online mode in addition to the F2F option; for more on HyFlex courses, see Brian Beatty's publicly available book on HyFlex courses, listed in the references for this chapter).

Both dual-mode and HyFlex courses soared in popularity after the Spring 2020 remote pivot re-introduced the synchronous modality to a new generation of learners, and faculty and students alike enjoyed the flexibility of teaching and learning in multiple modalities. Your institution may have different names and definitions for these multimodal online courses, including different requirements or registration options. While courses offered in multiple modalities provide best-fit options for students, it's vital to understand that designing and teaching a multimodal course is more complex in terms of technology, teaching, classroom management, and more. If you're newer to online teaching, we don't recommend that you dive head-first into teaching students in multiple modalities simultaneously.

Audience for this Book

Instructors

Put simply, this book is for any instructor designing an online course. Whether you are brand-new to online teaching or an experienced veteran, designing or revising your course with the HIDOC model will allow you to "step back" to gain a fresh perspective, reflect on the needs of your students, and consider the unique realities of designing a quality online course. Even very experienced online instructors will find a new idea, inspiration, or consideration! And for those who are adapting to online learning from an emergency remote teaching experience, this book will help ease the transition to creating a high-quality online course. The book is written "workshop style," with accessible information and advice that isn't technology-heavy. And while the HIDOC model is research-supported, and this book includes some select references, this isn't a literature review or a heavy, academic tome—we did our best to create a readable, welcoming experience for you.

Instructional Designers

A secondary audience for this book is instructional designers (IDs) who collaborate with faculty to design online courses. HIDOC provides IDs with a practical, research-based instructional design process to use in their own collaborative work with faculty. Additionally, throughout the book are "Faculty-ID Collaborations" that, while serving to answer common questions and illustrate some big takeaways for our faculty readers, also provide examples for our ID audience for modeling their own consultations. IDs can use the HIDOC framework and activity sheets as-is, or use them as inspiration to create documents that work best for the faculty with whom they work.

Visual Notations

We wanted this book to be friendly in both tone and layout; therefore, we've designed it with visual notations to distinguish key types of content you'll encounter throughout. Below are descriptions of these visual cues and icons.

Design Docs & HIDOC Course Blueprint

On our companion website—https://hidocmodel.com—you will find supporting documents for this book. We want to briefly draw your attention here to two documents that will be referenced throughout the book: **Design Docs** and the **HIDOC Course Blueprint.** These will both be explained in greater detail in the next chapter but in brief are the documents you will use to actually design your course. When you see either of the following notations in the book, it is a sign that you can find a downloadable version of the referenced document on the companion HIDOC website:

Faculty-ID Collaborations

All chapters in Part I have at least one dialogue featuring an ID and a faculty member. These were written based on our years of experience and many collaborations with faculty members on course design. They are meant to demonstrate HIDOC "in action" and illustrate how the steps make a practical impact on your course design. These collaborative consultations are called out specifically in the document with the following notation:

Faculty-ID Collaboration
Title

INSTRUCTOR PERSPECTIVE:

This icon and font represent the Instructor perspective.

ID PERSPECTIVE:

This icon and font represent the Instructional Designer (ID) perspective.

Inclusive Design

Throughout the book, we'll provide and highlight considerations and techniques for inclusive design to ensure that you are welcoming, representing, and recognizing all students. As a general definition, inclusive design means that your design (in this case, the design of your academic course) considers the robust, diverse range of people with respect to things such as culture, language, gender identity, sexual orientation, physical or learning differences or disabilities, family make-up, and physical attributes. In short…are you representing people like (and unlike) your students? Will all your students feel welcomed and supported? Have you tapped into ways to allow students to use and share their lived experiences? Does your course represent and promote diversity, equity (of access and opportunity), and inclusion?

Like several other topics in this book, however, inclusive design is deep, broad, and nuanced. Dedicated books on the subject are best able to help you fully understand it. Inclusive design ideas are also contained in Universal Design for Learning (UDL) models. Therefore, while we've included several Inclusive Design callouts in this book, understand that these callouts do not represent the entire breadth of considerations. For a deeper dive on this subject, see the resources in the references list (Brooks & Grady, 2022; Gunawardena et al., 2018; Jung & Gunawardena, 2014; Simunich & Grincewicz, 2018).

Throughout the HIDOC book, inclusive design callouts are highlighted with the following notation:

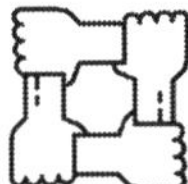

Inclusive Design

This notation will bring your attention to specific inclusive design practices and strategies.

Examples

Where appropriate, we have provided examples to illustrate the general principles we're describing. These will be notated with the following:

For Example…

This notation will be used whenever a concrete example of a general principle is given.

Reminders

Throughout the book you'll also see a few core concepts emphasized repeatedly. We note these with the following symbol of a string tied on a finger to signify "remember":

Don't forget to pay special attention to this notation.

Whenever you see this notation, it means a core concept is being (re) emphasized.

Further Explanations

Lastly, because this is intentionally a practical guide rather than a research text, we have tried to keep jargon and the underlying research to a minimum, though most chapters do have references. That said, we know that some of you will want to dig deeper. Therefore, where appropriate, we include boxes (like the one that follows) for those who want to learn more about a topic. Feel free to scan or skip based on your time and interest. For example, if you want to learn more about instructional design, you can read the following overview.

More on Instructional Design

Instructional design, also frequently referred to as learning design, is increasingly a discipline and practice central to education. As a process, it can be applied to any teaching and learning situation, in any modality, and at any level of instruction. Like many things in education, it has deep, historical roots and, as a methodology, has existed for 80+ years. During World War II, instructional design emerged as a process for rapidly developing high-quality training materials to meet very specific military needs (Reiser, 2001). The highly procedural instructional design model that came out of this time (and has remained very popular to this day) is ADDIE, which comprises the steps of: Analysis, Design, Development, Implementation, and Evaluation. New design models later emerged that align more with contemporary education and corporate training, both of which are rarely as structured and regimented as traditional military approaches (for example, see Allen, 2012).

Starting Where You Are

The amount of time you have to spend working on your online course can vary tremendously, as can your starting points with online learning:

- You may be starting from scratch, with a successful history of face-to-face teaching but disappointing experiences with remote teaching during the COVID-19 pandemic.
- You may be an experienced online instructor who wants to revise a course you already teach online and is especially keen to discover new ideas or insights.
- You may have had your doubts about online education but had surprisingly successful remote teaching experiences during the pandemic and want to build on those positive experiences to teach online moving forward.

- Perhaps you're an adjunct instructor and are typically asked to develop and teach online courses with little time to prepare, but you'd like to be better prepared for those "just-in-time" scenarios.
- You may have been assigned to design an online course and even given a course release or some other incentive to do so but are unsure how to best spend your time.
- Some of you may have the luxury of a semester (or more!), while others may have only a few weeks or even a few days to improve or design an online course.

We believe that any time and attention dedicated to enhancing the online teaching and learning experience through intentional instructional design will always be superior to no time. So, for whatever time you can spend with us now...

Let's Get Started!

References

Allen, M. (2012). Leaving ADDIE for SAM: An agile model for developing the best learning experiences. American Society for Training and Development.

Anderson, T., & Dron, J. (2011). Three generations of distance education pedagogy. *The International Review of Research in Open and Distributed Learning,* 12(3), 80–97. https://doi.org/10.19173/irrodl.v12i3.890

Anderson, T., & Dron, J. (2012). Learning technology through three generations of technology-enhanced distance education pedagogy. *European Journal of Open, Distance, and E-Learning,* 15, 2–14.

Beatty, B.J. (2019). Hybrid-Flexible course design (1st ed.). EdTech Books. https://edtechbooks.org/hyflex

Brooks, R., & Grady, S.D. (2022, May 03). Course design considerations for inclusion and representation. *Quality Matters.* https://www.qualitymatters.org/qa-resources/resource-center/articles-resources/course-design-inclusion-representation-white-paper

Carr-Chellman, A. (2021, June 09). Let's stop confusing what just happened with true online learning. *The Campus.* https://www.timeshighereducation.com/campus/lets-stop-confusing-what-just-happened-true-online-learning

Gunawardena, C., Frechette, C., & Layne, L. (2018). Culturally inclusive instructional design (1st ed.). Routledge.

Hodges, C., Moore, S., Lockee, B., Trust, T., & Bond, A. (2020, March 27). The difference between emergency remote teaching and online learning. *Educause Review.* https://er.educause.edu/articles/2020/3/the-difference-between-emergency-remoteteaching-and-online-learning

Jung, I., & Gunawardena, C.N. (2014). Culture and online learning: Global perspectives and research (online learning and distance education) (Illustrated ed.). Stylus Publishing.

Kentnor, H.E. (2015). Distance education and the evolution of online learning in the United States. *Curriculum and Teaching Dialogue.* 17(1&2): 21–34.

Lederman D. (2019, Dec. 11). Online enrollments grow, but pace slows. *Inside Higher Ed,* https://www.insidehighered.com/digital-learning/article/2019/12/11/more-students-study-online-rate-growth-slowed-2018

No Significant Difference Database (n.d.). Distance Education and Technological Advancements (DETA) Research Center. [online database] https://detaresearch.org/research-support/no-significant-difference/

Online Learning Efficacy Research Database (n.d.). eCampus Research Unit, Oregon State University. [online database] https://ecampus.oregonstate.edu/research/projects/online-learning-efficacy-research/

Reiser, R.A. (2001). A history of instructional design and technology: Part II: A history of instructional design. *Educational Technology, Research and Development,* 49(2), 57. https://doi.org/10.1007/BF02504928

Seaman, J.E., Allen, I.E., & Seaman, J. (2018). Grade increase: Tracking distance education in the United States. Bason Survey Group. https://eric.ed.gov/?id=ED580852

Simunich, B., & Grincewicz, A. (2018). Social presence and cultural identity: Exploring culturally responsive instructional design in the online environment. In K. Milheim (Ed.), *Cultivating Diverse Classrooms Through Effective Instructional Design.* (pp. 136–162). IGI Global.

Introducing HIDOC

High-Impact Design for Online Courses

(the acronym is pronounced as "high dock")

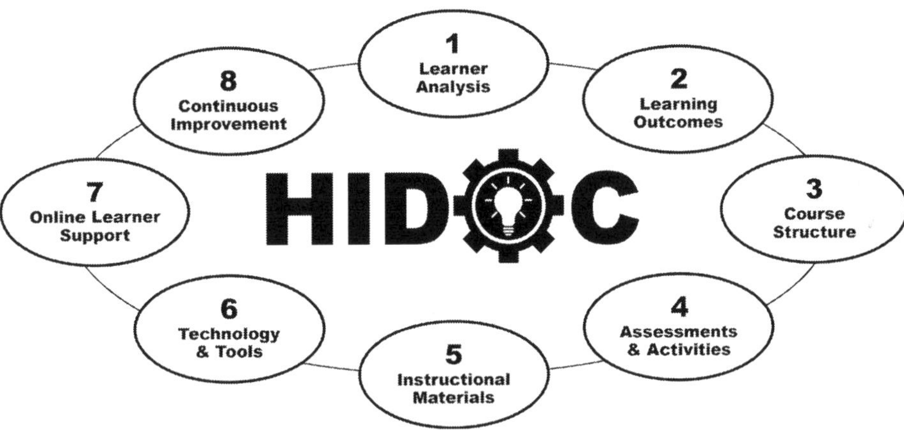

Our goal in this book is to help you develop the best online course possible given the time you have available. To do this, we have packaged the key steps for online course design in a straightforward and streamlined way, all focused on designing a quality online educational experience for your students. ***High-Impact Design for Online Courses, or "HIDOC," is a robust and flexible 8-step design process that attends to all the unique aspects specific to online learning.*** The model is systematic and covers the entirety of the online course design process in a linear fashion, from considering your potential learners well before the course launches, to making revisions after the course has run. The model can also be applied in an incremental, agile, or ad-hoc manner, adapting to your time constraints and immediate design needs. In other words, the HIDOC instructional design model provides you with a sequential, holistic approach that is specific to online learning and also provides you with the flexibility to create an online course quickly, focusing first on the most crucial elements that will best support your online students.

Starting with the "Why" of HIDOC

We spoke in the Preface about the important ways in which courses rapidly transitioned for remote delivery differ from courses intentionally designed for the online environment. Here we address the more specific question of ***why we need an instructional design model specific to online teaching and learning.*** In short, we need this model because online design and teaching are different from in-person design and teaching. There are existing books focused on teaching online as well as those targeting instructional designers and curriculum developers (more information below); ***HIDOC, however, is the only step-by-step model specifically targeting instructors and tailored to designing online courses in a higher education context.*** Other design models and processes either do not attend to these key differences or do not fully address them. A well-designed online course should parallel a well-designed in-person course in that learners should achieve the same learning outcomes and have comparable, but often not identical, learning experiences. Achieving learning parity for any online modality requires an understanding of the differences between face-to-face (F2F) and online learning, and how to design with those differences in mind. Let's take some time to define those key differences.

Key Differences between F2F and Online Learning

The crucial difference to account for when designing an online versus a F2F course is the physical separation of learners and their instructor. This "distance" impacts how you communicate and interact with students, as well as how they interact with the course. It also requires designing ways to be "present" in an asynchronous online course, where students and their instructor are separated by time in addition to distance. And all of this requires forethought and purposeful planning during the design, which takes place before the course begins. Because most of us have done most of our learning in physical classrooms and with F2F instructors, we don't have much (if any) personal experience to incorporate into our design planning. Even if you have learned online, chances are good that you've taken fewer quality online classes than F2F classes and may not have had faculty role models for effective online teaching. Most faculty develop their teaching strategies and pedagogical approaches via "teaching how they were taught," modeling their practice on experiences with effective instructors.

However, if you've never taken an online course, let alone a good online course… *where do you begin?*

Additionally, many faculty have not had the benefit of instructional design training or coursework, and far fewer have had design training specific to online courses. In classroom-based course design, also, many crucial design elements for the in-person classroom are largely invisible because of their familiarity. As an example, students in a F2F class are aware simply by the nature of being together in person that they are having a shared educational experience with other students. In contrast, an unfortunate but not uncommon feeling expressed by online learners is that they are "learning in isolation." When we design for online learning, we have to make all of those invisible elements visible and account for the physical and psychological separation, as well as the mediating role of educational technology in the digital classroom.

Below are some distinct ways online learning differs from classroom-based/F2F learning:

- Students are physically distanced from the instructor, and creating rapport and connection takes work. Connection and communication do not happen organically.
- Student engagement takes place differently and focuses on cognitive engagement that is facilitated by an instructor and student interaction.
- Assessment strategies differ for online learning, impacted by factors such as technology, computer-mediated communication, the absence of non-verbal cues to indicate confusion, and a heightened focus on academic integrity.
- A faculty-centric design approach can potentially be effective in a campus-based course but is rarely a good learning experience for students in an online course.
- Online learning relies on technology and digital learning in a way that F2F courses do not have to.
- Students are often unprepared for the different (and greater) responsibilities they have as online learners, including a higher degree of time management, required minimum technology skills, and being

more proactive in both their learning progress and their communication with the instructor.

- For online learners, an asynchronous online course in the Learning Management System is their campus, classroom, instructor, and peers all at the same time.
- Content functions differently online, and an easy error to make is "stuffing" an online course with content to demonstrate its rigor.
- Participation looks different and happens differently online…so does engagement.
- *And more...*

These are some of the most salient reasons that online learning—*and online course design*—require a robust, holistic approach like HIDOC that reflects the unique design considerations for online teaching and learning.

More on the Development of HIDOC

There are many existing instructional design models and approaches, including ADDIE (Branch, 2009), the Dick and Carey nine-step model (Dick et al., 2015), and Backward Design (Wiggins & McTighe, 2005). However, while crucial to the field and very useful for design, these instructional design texts do not address the practical needs of busy faculty who need a doable design process, nor are they specifically focused on designing online courses for higher education. There are also several quality texts dedicated to teaching online that we recommend to faculty who are new to teaching and learning in this modality (e.g., Boettcher & Conrad, 2010; Darby & Lang, 2019; Linder & Hayes, 2018; Riggs, 2020). A crucial difference between these books and the one you are currently reading, however, is that HIDOC emphasizes the pedagogical planning and work that takes place before the course starts.

HIDOC is grounded in facets of longstanding instructional design models; reflects established best practices for online course design; is supported by research in instructional design and online learning; and, perhaps most importantly, is a design model that attends to the unique and specific needs of an online learning environment, as well as the greater effort it takes for faculty to create an online course. The eight steps of HIDOC, in this order, with the accompanying Design Docs and Course Blueprint you'll learn about soon, have been "field-tested" via the hundreds of instructors, instructional designers, and courses that we've collectively worked with over the years.

The HIDOC Model

The eight steps in our HIDOC model have been synthesized and boiled down to the most basic elements necessary to design a quality online course. When worked through systematically, these practices will impact how you think about your teaching as well as the strategies and methods that you'll use while teaching, whether in person, online, or in a blended modality.

Who are your potential students?

In Step 1, you'll analyze your cohort of learners before you begin your course design. This involves considering your students holistically, including the knowledge, competencies, and misconceptions they will (likely) bring to your class. Often overlooked or assumed, this is an essential first Step that focuses your design, from the start, on your anticipated learners.

What will they be able to do by the end of the course?

In Step 2, you'll write clear and observable or measurable learning outcomes that represent the major skills and abilities students should be able to demonstrate when they successfully complete your course. Creating good course learning outcomes provides the foundation for your design and ensures that everything in the course supports student learning.

How will the course be organized?

In Step 3, you'll determine the macro-level view of how your course will be organized and when different topics will be covered. In doing so, you'll begin to organize your course into discrete, aligned learning modules (a.k.a. units or lessons) to sequence learning and facilitate the creation of a learning community as students move through these modules with each other and with you.

4 Assessments & Activities

How will you assess & engage learners?

In Step 4, you'll design summative assessments that best evaluate your course learning outcomes, formative assessments that provide feedback to you and your students on their learning progress, and learning activities that allow students to practice their learning and check their knowledge.

5 Instructional Materials

Where will they get the information they need to succeed?

In Step 5, you'll create and/or curate relevant instructional materials and content to support student learning and, specifically, to give students the information they need to do well on assessments and activities.

6 Technology & Tools

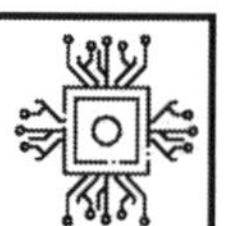

What technologies & tools will support their learning?

In Step 6, you'll select and plan to effectively use technologies and tools, including and in addition to the learning management system (LMS), that support student learning and your own pedagogical goals without adding unnecessary complexity to your course.

7 Online Learner Support

How will you support learner success?

In Step 7, you will structure your course to ensure a clear and supported online learning path, allowing you to proactively guide and help students. Scaffolding, sequencing, and organizing your course in the LMS, as well as including additional student support aids, many of which are unique to the online classroom, will help to ensure an ideal teaching and learning environment.

8 Continuous Improvement

How will you collect feedback & prioritize course revisions?

In Step 8, you'll plan for continuous improvement of your online course by collecting student feedback along with your own observations from throughout the design process and as the course is running ("Derek Bok Center," n.d.). This will give you the data you'll need to prioritize and implement changes when you eventually revise your course.

When applied systematically and in an iterative and recursive manner—meaning that you allow the work of later steps to impact the revision of earlier design work, if appropriate—these steps will lead to a higher quality online course, as well as a change in how you think about your online (and likely in-person) teaching. Taken together, these High-Impact design practices prioritize instructional alignment so that all elements of the course exist with purpose and intentionally connect to support your specific learners and your intended course learning outcomes.

High-Impact Design Practices

"High-Impact" is a central part of the HIDOC model. Here we describe what we mean by the term. High-Impact Practices, or "HIPs" as they are often called, are well documented and researched teaching practices and learning experiences shown to significantly impact a student's educational experience, staying with them long after they graduate. Top-referenced HIPs include First-Year Experiences; Common Intellectual Experiences; Learning Communities; Writing-Intensive Courses; Collaborative Assignments and Projects; Undergraduate Research; Diversity/Global Learning; ePortfolios; Service Learning, Community-Based Learning; Internships; and Capstone Courses and Projects (Kuh, 2008; Kuh &

O'Donnell, 2013). We are big fans of HIPs! And, luckily, when it comes to online teaching and learning, there is already a great book that shows you how to translate HIPs from in-person experiences to online settings (Linder & Hayes, 2018).

While the traditional HIPs refer to practices in student learning, our reference to "High-Impact" is distinct in that it applies not only to online student learning, but also to you, as the designer and teacher. As we mentioned, we have collectively designed hundreds of online courses and worked with at least as many instructors, and the vast majority of individuals who worked with us mentioned during (or, more commonly, after) the design process something to the effect of: "working through this systematic practice has really changed how I teach online and in the physical classroom, and also changed how I think about teaching in general." So, while the HIDOC process model is designed to create a quality online course (Reigeluth & An, 2021) that will positively impact your students, it also takes you through a process of deep reflection about your own teaching philosophy, practices, and approaches, which frequently carries over to your in-person teaching as well.

Course Design Alignment

Throughout the book, we emphasize the importance of alignment. An aligned course is one in which all the parts work together and support each other. Students will never have "busy work," for example, because the correct application of the HIDOC model ensures that assessments are always focused on the learning outcomes and that instructional content supports your assessments. In other words, students will be using all the materials they interact with by applying their new knowledge and skills to show their learning progress and achievement.

Alignment is a simple concept to understand but a difficult goal to achieve. It can be easy for instructors to "fill in the blanks" mentally because there are no gaps in their expert-level knowledge; without careful attention, therefore, it's also easy to inadvertently leave "gaps" in the course design from the student perspective. As instructional designers, one of our primary responsibilities is to help you take a purposeful look at your course from the student perspective. This contributes significantly to alignment and allows you to focus your students' time and effort in deliberate ways by, for example, privileging application-based activities over the passive intake (i.e., reading, listening, watching) of multiple pieces of content.

Being "Present" Online Starts with Design

You may already be familiar with the concept of online "presence," but you might not know that it's grounded in design. Online presence is embedded in the Community of Inquiry (CoI) framework (Garrison et al., 2000). When research on CoI first emerged, the authors were investigating how computer-mediated communication (which, at the time, was a very text-based environment) impacted the educational experience. The seminal article presented a conceptual framework that showcased three necessary elements for a successful online educational experience: social presence, cognitive presence, and teaching presence.

Social presence allows your online learners to feel connected to one another, present themselves to their peers as a "real person," and become (and feel that they are) a part of an online community. Social presence is related to the rapport and trust that builds when students interact in positive, meaningful ways and serves to reduce the inherent feelings of "distance"—both the physical distance and the emotional or psychological distance (Moore, 1993) that is often felt when students are not physically present with their instructor and one another. On the other hand, cognitive presence is a vital component of critical thinking and speaks to the learning that happens when students engage with new topics and questions, exchange information, and connect and apply new ideas. It is how they "...are able to construct meaning through sustained communication," which takes on a new challenge in a technology-mediated environment (Garrison et al., 2000, p. 89).

However, it is the third part of the framework, "teaching presence," that is most important to our discussion here because teaching presence **begins with design** and continues through to the facilitation of the course. Think of it this way: in an asynchronous online course, your direct instruction is (mostly or entirely) completed prior to the course beginning. By selecting content, creating assignments, and organizing the course in a web-based format, you have made strategic pedagogical choices at each step that communicate to students what you think is important, what they'll learn, what they'll do, and how the educational experience will unfold for them. Before your active teaching even begins, students have a clear idea of who you are as an instructor just by logging in on day one, when they see and interact with your design. Teaching presence is also what facilitates the other elements of the CoI framework—without your teaching presence, social and cognitive presence are unlikely to occur. Throughout the

HIDOC process, we'll guide you to consider all three facets of presence in different ways, which will positively impact your students' learning.

More on Transactional Distance

While physical distance is an obvious difference in distance education, psychological distance is also paramount. In Moore's (1993) theory of transactional distance, he argues that "[i]t is the separation of learners and teachers that profoundly affects both teaching and learning. With separation, there is a psychological and communications space to be crossed, a space of potential misunderstanding between the inputs of the instructor and those of the learner" (p. 22). The HIDOC design model aims to reduce this distance through purposeful design efforts that promote presence and interaction, as well as effective and meaningful online communication.

Section I - Designing Your Course with HIDOC

This book is made up of two sections: *Designing Your Course with HIDOC* and *HIDOC-in-Action: Course Design Cases*. While you can read through the first section just to understand the HIDOC process, what makes this book unique is that it's both an "information" book and an "activity" book, where you can read about the Step, then actually work through that part of the design process on your own course. Think of it as a faculty development workshop hosted by us! We'll introduce the "what" and "why" of the Step, then walk you through the related design work (the "how"). **The goal of the first section of this book is for you to have a complete, well-aligned course design, which you will use to then develop and build your online course in the LMS.**

Design Docs and HIDOC Course Blueprint

DESIGN DOCS

To help you with the thinking and drafting necessary to design a high-quality online course, we have created specific documents, or **Design Docs,** that you can download from the companion website or reference in the **Design Doc Library** section of the book. We describe the design process for each Step within the text itself, so you are also, of course, welcome to create your own versions of the design documents. You can think of these Design Docs as the "rough draft" of the different elements of your course design with much of the information feeding directly into the **HIDOC Course Blueprint.**

HIDOC COURSE BLUEPRINT

The HIDOC Course Blueprint is the living document for your actual course design. The Blueprint is "living" because, as we emphasize throughout the book, the process involves revisions and improvements. For example, as you work on a later HIDOC Step you may realize you need to make adjustments to the design elements from a previous Step. These adjustments should be made in the HIDOC Course Blueprint so that this Blueprint document always has the most updated course design information.

The HIDOC Course Blueprint includes two major parts:

1. **The Course Alignment Map:** This is the macro-level view of your course design and the primary way you will check to ensure that your various course components support one another holistically. The final version of your Course Alignment Map can also be shared directly with students to give them a literal "map" of their journey throughout the course, including the different topics they'll explore, the work they'll do, and the knowledge and skills they will gain.

2. **Detailed Module Layout:** This is the micro-level view of your course, module by module, and is what you will use to actually develop your course in the LMS. (More on course development below.)

Much of the draft work you do in the Design Docs will feed directly into your HIDOC Course Blueprint.

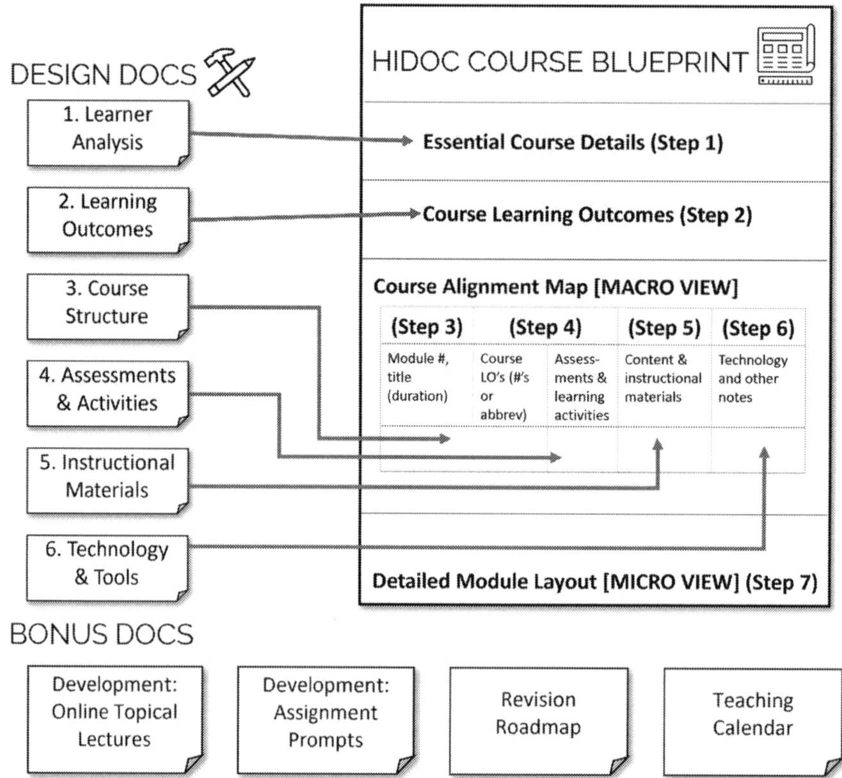

As mentioned in the Preface, whenever you see the following notations, that's a sign to go to the companion website (https://hidocmodel.com) or Design Doc Library in the book for the accompanying documents.

Your [Design Doc name]

1. Access the **[Specified Design Doc]** from the companion website, use the version in the Design Doc Library section of the book, or create a version that works for you.
2. Work on the parts as specified above.

Your HIDOC Course Blueprint 

1. Open the **HIDOC Course Blueprint** from the companion website, use the version in the Design Doc Library section of the book, or create a version that works for you.
2. Work on the parts as specified above.

Section II - HIDOC-in-Action

Each of the chapters in Section II corresponds to a design case from across our collective experiences and portrays fictionalized courses that have mixed success in terms of the design. These design examples represent a variety of disciplines, and we have pulled out the key lessons learned so that you can make use of this information when working on your own course. Cases are structured to give you both the instructor's plan, students' experiences, and how the HIDOC model could be used to revise the course.

Beyond Design: Development and Delivery

Design vs. Development

In key places in the book, we refer to "development," but what do we mean when we say "development," and how does it differ from design? Design is all the strategic thinking and planning you do to blueprint a course that reflects your pedagogical approach and vision, and it is the primary focus of this book. Online course *development,* on the other hand, is the additional hard work that happens *after* you've designed your course. Development, also commonly referred to as "building," includes creating (or curating) content that meets accessibility requirements, quiz and exam questions, activity and assessment prompts, course documents such as the syllabus and schedule, your instructor introduction video, and more. Development also includes creating the organizational structure in the LMS, laying out your modules, appropriately uploading content and assignments, and organizing your course navigation.

We include two "bonus" Development Docs for key pieces of your course in both Step 5 (Online Topical Lectures) and Step 7 (Assignment Prompts), but for now, we just want to remind you that development is a time-intensive process and to plan for this additional work. Many faculty ask why it's not best practice to develop materials while designing. In short, if you do so, there is a strong possibility that you will invest time developing materials and components that you will discover you don't need, or will need to re-do, by the end of the design process (this is especially true with instructor-created videos or lectures). Developing your course without first fully designing it and reviewing it for alignment and other factors often wastes time in the end, and we're here to help you work smarter, not harder! Additionally, moving from a more macro, holistic view of your course to the micro-level detail necessary to, for example, create dozens of exam questions or a rubric for a research paper, can easily take you out of both the student perspective and that "bird's-eye view" that you want during design.

Design vs. Delivery

Design, as mentioned, includes the strategic, pedagogically based decisions you make *before* your course begins. Delivery, then, is the execution of this course design and is the active teaching you do *after* the course begins. Because we know that many faculty have questions about online teaching, and that many design decisions are connected to teaching strategies, we also include a "Bonus Chapter" in this book at the end of Section I that gives you some top tips and strategies for executing your design via your active teaching. As we discussed earlier, the quality of your teaching presence begins with your design. Online, you must *plan and design* opportunities for your active teaching. Nothing happens organically, spontaneously, or by chance in an asynchronous, online environment. If you want students to interact, you must design it into the course, just as you must *design* opportunities to interact with your students. Speaking of students…it's time to start Step 1: Learner Analysis!

Summary and Next Steps

To sum it up...

High-Impact Design for Online Courses (HIDOC) is the 8-step course design model used throughout this book that was created specifically to address the needs of instructors designing online courses in higher education. The eight steps of HIDOC are: (1) Learner Analysis, (2) Learning Outcomes, (3) Course Structure, (4) Assessments & Activities, (5) Instructional Materials, (6) Technology & Tools, (7) Online Learner Support, and (8) Continuous Improvement. HIDOC promotes aligned course design, in which course components, such as learning outcomes, assignments, and content, serve to support, reinforce, and reflect one another. Designing an online course differs importantly from designing an in-person course. For example, creating a learning community requires more time and effort, the LMS plays more of a central role in the teaching and learning experience, and students in an online course need to be more self-directed.

This book is both an "information" and an "activity" book, and if you work through each of the steps and the corresponding design activities, you should have a completed course design at the end of the first half of the book!

Looking ahead...

In the next chapter, we start with the first step of HIDOC: Learner Analysis. Get ready to put learners (and learning!) at the forefront of your course design as we work through this vital step.

References

Boettcher, J.V., & Conrad, R.-M. (2010). The online teaching survival guide: Simple and practical pedagogical tips. John Wiley & Sons.

Branch, R.M. (2009). Instructional design: The ADDIE approach. New York, NY: Springer. https://doi.org/10.1007/978-0-387-09506-6

Darby, F., & Lang, J.M. (2019). Small teaching online: Applying learning science in online classes. Jossey-Bass.

Derek Bok Center for Teaching and Learning, Harvard University. (n.d.) Putting evidence at the center. https://bokcenter.harvard.edu/assessment-types

Dick, W., Carey, L., & Carey, J.O. (2015). Systematic design of instruction (8th ed.). Pearson.

Garrison, D.R., Anderson, T., & Archer, W. (2000). Critical inquiry in a text-based environment: Computer conferencing in higher education. *The Internet and Higher Education,* 2(2-3), pp. 87–105.

Kuh, George D. (2008). High Impact educational practices: What they are, who has access to them, and why they matter. Washington, DC: Association of American Colleges and Universities.

Kuh, George D., & O'Donnell, K. (2013). Ensuring quality & taking High Impact practices to scale. Washington, DC: Association of American Colleges & Universities.

Linder, K.E., & Hayes, C.M. (Eds.). (2018) High Impact practices in online education: Research and best practices. Sterling: Stylus Publishing.

Moore, M.G. (1993). Theory of transactional distance. In D. Keegan (Ed.), *Theoretical Principles of Distance Education* (Vol. 1, pp. 22–38). New York: Routledge.

Reigeluth, C.M., & An, Y. (2021). Merging the instructional design process with learner-centered theory: The holistic 4D model. Routledge. https://doi.org/10.4324/9781351117548

Riggs, S. (2020). Thrive online: A new approach to building expertise and confidence as an online educator. Stylus.

Wiggins, G., & McTighe, J. (2005). Understanding by design (2nd ed.). Association for Supervision and Curriculum Development.

SECTION I

DESIGNING YOUR COURSE WITH HIDOC

1 Learner Analysis

The HIDOC model's learning results-focused approach stands in contrast to a content-focused approach. In a content-focused course design approach, the instructor typically begins with selecting the content, such as the textbook or lecture materials, and then creates assignments to support that content—often without paying specific attention to the alignment of students and goals. Conversely, beginning with a consideration of your learners and learning goals allows you to align the design realistically to your students and the level of mastery you want for them. This step also removes some of the surprises you might otherwise experience (e.g., "I assumed they already knew how to do this…" or "My online students, as working professionals, seem to have much more experience in this area than my F2F students.").

Learner Analysis in an Online Context

Because of the mediated nature of online learning, especially asynchronous online learning, you have limited ability to adapt your teaching "on the fly." In an asynchronous course, you have the entire course built before it begins, making it difficult to change content or assignments. In a F2F class, your lectures or assignments might change based on student questions or what you observe from your students' non-verbal behavior—whether confusion, boredom, or something else. Even in a live/synchronous web-conferencing lecture, you don't get the same degree of feedback, as any non-verbal cues are limited to faces of students who have their cameras on. This means that being prepared in advance is crucial, and thinking critically about who is likely to take your course is the first step.

We can share with you that nearly every faculty member we've worked with who has gone through the step of considering their learners has found it valuable and one of their favorite steps...and not just in terms of how it informs the design of the course. Your students are individuals who are juggling many things in their lives—school being just one of the balls in the air. (Yes, even the "busyness" of your students matters! It can play a role in various design decisions discussed further below.) Emergency remote learning aside, students who choose to take online courses come to your course from different life situations, cultural and socioeconomic backgrounds, and geographic locations (Friedman, 2017). They may have full-time jobs, military duties, parental obligations, or other responsibilities to balance, and are attracted by the flexibility of online learning. They might also be in a different time zone or country or could be a returning adult student who last took an academic course several years ago. Students taking individual/discrete online courses are often campus-based students who need scheduling flexibility, while there's a greater chance that fully online students (such as those in online degree programs) are working professionals who are not located close to campus.

Respecting the Diversity of Your Students

A student's background and culture can be a heavy influence on their education for many reasons. For example, cultural dimensions such as power distance (Hofstede, 2001) can influence interactions with both instructors and peers. Power distance describes how people from a particular culture might view a power relationship, such as superior/subordinate or teacher/student. Students from high power distance cultures, such as many Asian cultures, can be more reticent to reach out for individual help due to these culturally based influences. Students may be hesitant to reach out for other reasons as well, such as anxiety issues or individual neurodiversity. Add to that the fact that online students in general are less proactive in asking questions (it's much easier for some students to raise their hand in class than email a professor they've never met in person), and you are now aware of a potential problem. Knowing this, however, you can address it proactively. We'll talk in greater detail about these strategies in later chapters; briefly, though, we'll say that some options are to allow students to anonymously ask questions in an all-course discussion; provide anonymous surveys for feedback on lingering confusion; or create some small-group assignments that allow students to learn from each other and ask questions as a group. These strategies benefit all students, while particularly attending to those students whose cultural backgrounds or individual differences reduce their inclination to reach out.

Our important reminder here, though, is to not make assumptions or generalizations about students' backgrounds, capabilities, and lived experiences. You can invite (not require) students to share information about themselves or their background that they'd like you to know. This might be in a student introduction assignment or private journal, and students might share their country of origin, familial culture, gender, ethnicity, race, age, sexual orientation, religion, physical or learning disabilities, neurodiversity, and even military/Veteran status, which may call for greater trauma-informed approaches. Keep in mind that sharing personal information should be the choice of the student—ethnic background, place of origin, gender identity, or religion may not be things a student wants to discuss. The inclusive design strategies we highlight throughout this book are intended to benefit all students, though, even when you don't know the makeup of a specific student cohort.

Design Implications of Learner Analysis

In most cases, you cannot choose or change who enrolls in your class. Additionally, maybe you know that students are commonly underprepared for your course, but you might feel helpless to address that issue. However, information such as this is more valuable than you think, because while you can't prevent some of these issues, you can plan for them by taking them into account in your course design. While it is true that we don't always know the student cohort that will enroll—because it's a new course or you have an "outlier" or uncommon cohort—you should still be able to come up with some concrete information to use as a starting point. For example, you can find out more about typical student demographics in the program or department. Or, you might have a colleague who's previously taught the course (or a similar course) and is willing to share their insights with you. At a minimum, refer to the course description and note any prerequisites and other characteristics, such as whether it's a course that can be taken by non-majors and/or as a general education course.

Here are some examples of design implications of learner analysis. We discuss all of these in greater detail in later Steps. Here we just want to show some of the key ways that doing this crucial first step directly informs later design decisions. When you anticipate that your cohort will include...

- **A diverse demographic of students in terms of geographic location, employment status, and family responsibilities,** simple things like being explicit with time zones and having clear policies on attendance/participation and late work can be quite helpful.
- **A mix of majors and non-majors, or first-year and upper-level students taking your course,** it might be beneficial to include optional content in your course—this can benefit both less knowledgeable students as well as those who are more advanced.
- **Working professionals in the field,** such as in a graduate-level nursing course or a course in a business program, scenario- and case-based activities can allow students to combine their professional experience with their newfound course knowledge and also enable them to learn from each other's "real-world" experiences.

Positioning your students in a holistic way, by considering their preconceived ideas (and misconceptions!), existing knowledge, and life experiences and beliefs, will help you make the curriculum more directly applicable to them. For example, you can:

- **Anticipate and address misconceptions about your subject matter.** You might survey students at the beginning of your course about expected misconceptions and/or ask them to do a web scavenger hunt for where these misconceptions appear. Together, you can find information that is factually correct to debunk these problematic beliefs.
- **Design for relevance.** While all students (including you and us!) seek relevance for what they're learning, instructors often fail to consider how relevance can inform their course design. Adult learners especially seek relevance as they want to be able to apply what they are learning (Sogunro, 2015). You might ask the students to identify ways that course information is relevant to them beyond the classroom and also emphasize that relevance in your teaching.
- **Offer support for "non-content skills."** Even if your course technically does not have any prerequisites, you might realize that it requires a lot of "non-content" skills—such as knowing basic algebra, having a minimum writing proficiency, or even using certain technologies. "Non-content" skills are those unrelated to course content but nonetheless required for

success in the course. While you're not going to teach these skills (nor are students prevented from enrolling in the course if they don't have these skills), you can provide resources to help students develop them on their own.

Now that we've highlighted a few of the ways you can use the information gleaned from reflecting on your student cohort, it's time for you to conduct your own learner analysis.

Design Docs and the HIDOC Course Blueprint are where you will draft and revise your course design.

The first Design Doc, Learner Analysis, begins below. Your Design Docs are where you'll do your thinking and drafting. Much of your Design Docs will be moved to your Course Blueprint, which is what you will use to eventually create and develop your course within your Learning Management System (LMS) or similar type of educational website. Your most current course design should always be in the HIDOC Course Blueprint. Remember that you can download the Design Docs and Course Blueprint from the companion website, use the version in the Design Doc Library section of the book, or create a version that works for you.

Your Turn: Learner Analysis

In this section, we guide you in conducting Step 1, your Learner Analysis. This Step can become vital to your course design, as it allows you to really think about and center your students from the start.

Part 1: Key Course Details

Conducting your learner analysis begins with gathering some key course details. Your answers to the following questions will begin to naturally inform the likely characteristics of your potential students:

1. What is the course name and #?

2. What is the course level (e.g., graduate, undergraduate)?

3. What is the length of the course (e.g., number of weeks)?

4. How many credits is the course?

5. What is the expected enrollment range?
6. Is the course taken to fulfill a degree requirement, or as an elective?
7. What, if any, are the course prerequisites?
8. What, if any, are the courses that follow?
9. What is the course modality (e.g., face-to-face, web-enhanced, hybrid, HyFlex, online synchronous, online asynchronous)?
10. Are there any other relevant details, such as whether the course is cross-listed, writing-intensive, a diversity requirement, or required for a particular major?

Part 2: Learner Considerations

Below is a list of questions to ask yourself about your students. Answer each question based on the students who commonly take the course that you're designing. For a course you've never taught, try to think about similar courses you've taught and/or speak with colleagues who can potentially provide insight. The point of the activity is not to get the "correct" answers but to help you anticipate learner needs, motivations, and likely misconceptions you'll need to proactively address.

Who typically takes your course?

Think about who your students are likely to be: for example, majors and/or non-majors; undergraduates and/or graduates; taking the class as a core requirement, elective, or course for their major; domestic and/or international students; year in school; working adult professionals and/or "traditional"-aged college students living on campus. (While we use the terms "traditional" and "non-traditional," keep in mind that at many institutions, the demographics are changing and there is no longer a "traditional" age for post-secondary education.) Answers to these questions will help inform things such as the skills and constraints students might bring to the course. Also consider the diversity of experience related to things like cultural background, nationality, ethnicity, race, neurodiversity, physical or learning disability, and veteran status. Even if you cannot get clarity on demographics, focusing on the inclusive design strategies we highlight will ensure that all students feel welcomed, represented, heard, and respected.

What knowledge and experience do students typically bring into the course?

Consider prerequisite knowledge, professional experience, and other experiential knowledge, as well as likely past coursework in high school or lower-level classes. If you have time, it can be very helpful to look at the syllabi of any course prerequisites and speak with instructors who teach those courses.

What misconceptions, misunderstandings, or preconceived notions do students often have (or are likely to have) about the course and its concepts?

Consider if there are misguided beliefs or false claims that students might be exposed to in news reports, interpersonal conversations, or social media, for example, or if there are common misconceptions about your field or course-specific topics. You will need to address and overcome these things early on.

What are some things students frequently struggle with in your course?

If you've taught the course before in any format, you will likely have a sense of where students run into challenges, whether it is in understanding a particular theory or topic, doing hands-on or technical work, or completing a certain assignment. If this is a new course, you can focus on the concepts or topics that are difficult in the field and plan to provide extra time or materials for those topics.

How is this course and its topics and activities relevant to these students?

Consider how students can use course information, knowledge, and skills in their current or future educational endeavors, their current or future professional lives, and/or in their social or everyday life. What parts of the course do you see as relevant to even non-majors? Ask yourself: "If I weren't teaching this course or inherently interested, why would I care? Are there small ways I could use this information in my daily life? Are there professional payoffs to learning these things and completing these assignments? Can any of the work I do in this course be used for job applications or ePortfolios?" Making sure your students understand how the course is relevant to their lives can heavily impact motivation and effort.

What "non-content" skills must a student have to succeed? These are skills that students must have to do well in the course but that you won't be teaching as part of the course curriculum. They might include skills in reading, writing, or math, as well as technical skills related to using a particular piece of software or the LMS. Identifying these "non-content" skills allows you to be transparent about them with students, as well as source content that can help students get up to speed if necessary.

Your Learner Analysis

1. Open the **Learner Analysis** Design Doc from the companion website, use the version in the Design Doc Library section of the book, or create a version that works for you.
2. Work on the **Key Course Details** and **Learner Considerations** sections discussed above.

Now that you've conducted your learner analysis, it's time to move the key information to your HIDOC Course Blueprint.

Your HIDOC Course Blueprint

1. Open the **HIDOC Course Blueprint** from the companion website, use the version in the Design Doc Library section of the book, or create a version that works for you.
2. Fill in the **Key Course Details** (Step 1) at the top of the document (you can pull this information from the **Learner Analysis** Design Document).

As we talked about in the Introducing HIDOC chapter, we have included Faculty-ID Collaborations to demonstrate each HIDOC step through the lens of a faculty member and an instructional designer collaborating on course design. Our first Faculty-ID Collaboration follows.

Faculty-ID Collaboration

Considering Your Learners

I'm excited to finally be creating an online course! I've brought with me my syllabus and the content I use in the face-to-face version...what else do I need to provide?

That's great! I'd love to review with you all of these materials. Before we begin designing your course, though, I want to first learn more about the course itself and the students who typically take it.

Well, I don't know that I've thought a lot about the student cohort because all students, regardless of who they are, have to master certain things in the course.

Absolutely—all students will need to meet your learning outcomes. Knowing about student demographics, though, can often cue us in to important design considerations early on so that all students are supported. Let me ask you this: do all students typically come into your course with the same existing knowledge level of course topics?

Oh, absolutely not. In fact, I usually have a mix of majors and non-majors in this course, so it sometimes feels as though I'm teaching two different cohorts.

That's really helpful to know! Tell me more about that. For example, how do you effectively teach both of those groups in your face-to-face class?

Well, I do a few things. For example, when students discuss or work in groups, I purposefully pair up majors and non-majors. I also suggest extra content for students who need more help with the fundamental ideas.

This is exactly the kind of information we'll need to make sure we design your online course so that it works well for all of your students. Tell me more about your students...aside from having different levels of preparation and maybe interest, do you have students at all levels, from first year to senior, for example?

Typically, yes. This is an introductory-level course on web design, so many students see this as a valuable skill to have, whether they are going into web design or not. So, I have students at all levels, but they don't all have the same level of technical skill.

OK, that's important to know as well. Let's start making a list of the following items, and then we can appropriately incorporate them into the course design so that all your students are supported.

1. *Technology skills that students need to come into the course with.* These are skills that they will need to have to do well, and they may or may not be related to institutional prerequisites. We will incorporate these skills into the outcomes, activities, and assessments and make sure that students understand from the first day that they'll need these to be successful.

2. *Skills that would be helpful for students to have but are not required.* These might be things that you'll discuss in the course but that will give students with existing knowledge an advantage on certain assessments. For this area, we can provide extra and optional content, build in some practice activities, and also sequence and scaffold assignments so beginning-level students aren't disadvantaged.

3. *Things students typically struggle with.* We can make sure we have good, clear content for these items, as well as provide examples and practice opportunities.

Oh! OK. That all makes sense now—I can see how analyzing these things will help us cater the design to the specific students who enroll in my course. I think I do a lot of this naturally face-to-face—such as pairing up specific students for peer feedback—but I hadn't thought about purposefully including these considerations in the design.

Exactly. Many faculty have already thought through these items and attend to these considerations during their in-class teaching. Online, however, we need to consider everything proactively, rather than "in the moment," and reflect these important considerations and analysis in the design of the online course.

Yes, I can see that. OK, so one technology skill they should come in with would be basic-level skill in HTML. What I teach in this course is intended to build on some basic knowledge, but I have review pieces I could share for students who need to get up to speed.

For skills that I will teach in the course, but that some students already have, I'd include having practice with visual design elements and user experience design in that category. For this one, we could probably include more examples to even the playing field for all students.

Lastly, you had asked about things students typically struggle with. This might include choosing fonts, colors, or layout, or deciding on/creating appropriate content for a website. Whether or how students struggle with these items depends on a number of factors, including natural abilities they might have for visual composition, as well as previous experience or related coursework/training. This is another place where sharing more examples would be helpful, as well as providing options for early or additional feedback—even feedback from peers.

Exactly! Those are all great ideas that we'll incorporate into the design.

Summary and Next Steps

To sum it up...

Instead of starting by diving right into content, the HIDOC model first asks you to consider the students who take your course by reflecting on aspects such as background knowledge, demographics, and motivation. In Step 1, you also identify skills students will need to be successful, areas of likely challenge, and typical misconceptions. Later, this information informs course design decisions such as providing supplemental resources, addressing misconceptions, and emphasizing relevance.

Looking ahead...

In the next chapter, you will establish the foundation for your course design by articulating your course learning outcomes. Everything else in your design will stem from these learning outcomes, so it's crucial to think through them. Your learning outcomes should reflect your pedagogical goals, institutional or program competencies or requirements, as well as your student cohort.

References

Friedman, J. (2017, April 4). U.S. News data: The average online bachelor's student. U.S. News & World Report. https://www.usnews.com/higher-education/online-education/articles/2017-04-04/us-news-data-the-average-online-bachelors-student

Hofstede, G. (2001). Culture's consequences: Comparing values, behaviors, institutions and organizations across nations (2nd ed.). Sage Publications.

Sogunro, O.A. (2015). Motivating factors for adult learners in higher education. *International Journal of Higher Education,* 4(1), 22–37. https://doi.org/10.5430/ijhe.v4n1p22

2 Learning Outcomes

While all the steps in the HIDOC model are important, Step 2 provides an essential foundation for the rest of your course design and ensures your students will know from day one what they'll be learning and doing. Completing this Step enables you to confidently answer the question: "At the end of your course, what should your students be able to do?"

Starting with the "Big Vision"

Before you define your specific course learning outcomes (CLOs), it can be helpful to ground yourself in the bigger picture of your course, including the big topics and ideas and cognitively intriguing questions surrounding them. Here we invite you to step back, slough off any preconceived ideas or lived experiences you might have related to the course, allow a fresh perspective, and tap into your passion! This process of starting with the macro-level "big vision" and later going to a more granular level of CLOs (and, later still, to a detailed micro-level of module outcomes) ensures you're grounding the design in the most crucial topics and takeaways. And having a clear, motivating "big vision" of your course from the start best enables you to create and share that vision with your students, via design. Most faculty are so busy designing and teaching that they rarely allow time to re-ground themselves in their love for their discipline, and to share that love with their students. So, take a moment and just allow yourself some space to reconnect with your "why." Step back and consider:

Why do you love your field? Why are you excited to teach this specific course? What is your vision for this course and the students who take it? What are the big takeaways of the course? What are the significant ideas or provocative questions that drew you in and will draw students in?

Think about ways to pique students' curiosity so that they're excited about course topics from the start. In their book, Understanding by Design, Wiggins and McTighe (2004) describe "essential questions" and explain that "[they] are provocative questions that foster inquiry, understanding, and transfer of learning." These can be philosophical and promote reflection or serve to spark a debate and promote information-seeking and attitude changes. Enthusiasm is contagious and motivating, and the components that draw your attention and interest are often excellent to focus on, as you'll naturally draw students in with your excitement.

"Big Visions" by Discipline

Anthropology: What does it mean to be human?

Literature: Is an author's view privileged in determining the meaning of a text?

Philosophy of Law: What is justice?

Math: How well can pure mathematics model messy, real-world situations?

Nutrition: How does what I eat impact my health?

Rhetoric/Communication: How does language construct reality?

Technical Writing: How does technical/engineering/scientific writing differ from other types of writing?

Thermodynamics: What is energy? What are its limits?

First-year Seminar: How do I survive and thrive in college? Where can I make a difference?

A beginning dance course for non-majors might focus on these big ideas: understanding the importance of dance to our lives, the benefit of dance to the body, and learning & performing basic moves for several dances.

A graduate-level course on effective online teaching might focus on these big ideas: understanding the different roles of both the instructor and student online, elevating presence and creating an online learning community, and creating digital materials for direct instruction and engagement.

A history class might cover several significant historical periods or events and analyze them in three major ways: socio-cultural, political, and economic.

An introductory accounting course might focus on these big topics: How can basic accounting principles help our everyday lives? How do we use financial data to plan and make decisions?

CLOs as Foundation for Aligned Course Design

Following the big vision and major goals for the course, we get more specific with the CLOs that inspire students to engage with those big ideas. As mentioned briefly in the chapter introduction, CLOs describe what students should be able to do by the end of the course and as such provide the pedagogical foundation for aligned course design. From the CLOs, you can create applied, relevant assessments that allow students to show they've met the desired outcomes, activities to gauge and grow their knowledge, and instructional content to provide information and inspiration. Additionally, CLOs inform how we will interact with students and how they will interact with one another and the course. We must also decide how to support these pedagogical choices with appropriate technology and tech tools, such as the tools available in a learning management system. CLOs may also serve as design tiebreakers down the road. For instance, if you can't decide between two student activities, revisit the outcomes to evaluate which activity provides better evidence that students have met one or more of your CLOs.

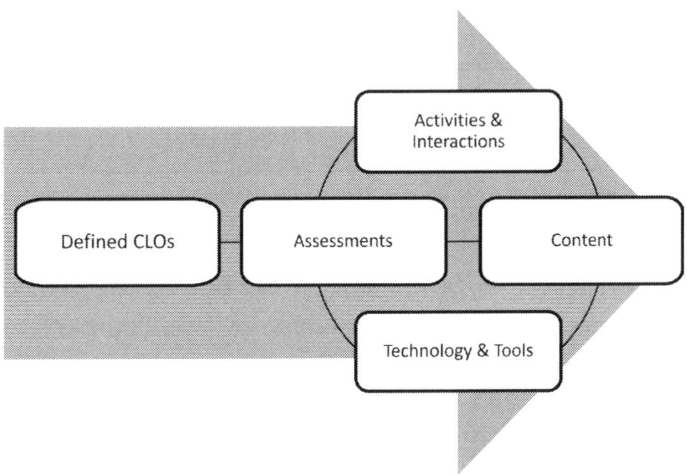

And...good news! Your CLOs stay consistent through any course format or modality, so you do not need to completely rewrite them simply because you are designing an online course. However, you may need to tweak a few words if something will be done virtually instead of in person, such as recording a presentation. But the intent of the CLOs should remain the same regardless of modality so that you have educational equity between all course offerings. If you have existing learning outcomes from a face-to-face course, you will still want to work through the activities in this chapter to review them and ensure they are specific, observable, and understandable by your students. We encourage you to step back, see your course holistically with a fresh perspective, and design it *purposefully for the online environment* with your online learners in mind. Remember that it is never a best practice to simply migrate or transfer the face-to-face version online.

CLOs Should Be "Measurable"

Now that you're ready to think about your CLOs, the first thing to discuss is making them "measurable" or "observable." This is crucial because you cannot assess something that you can't measure or observe. To be measurable or observable, learning outcomes must use active verbs. Active verbs stand in contrast to verbs such as "know," "understand," or "learn." Of course, we want our students to "know," "learn," and "understand," but we cannot assess if students "know" something or if they have "learned" something unless they do something with their new knowledge to demonstrate their learning, such as "write," "define," "evaluate," "describe," "speak," "solve," or "build."

The active verbs you select for your CLOs need to align with the level of learning you intend for your students to accomplish. While there are multiple taxonomies for conceptualizing levels of learning, Bloom's taxonomy is widely known and used, intuitive to understand, and easily applicable, and so it is the taxonomy we have chosen to highlight in this chapter (Bloom, 1956). We are using the revised version (Anderson & Krathwohl, 2001) as it is the most up to date in terms of recognizing creating something new as the highest level of learning. (See the Learning Taxonomies callout below for more information.)

Bloom's revised taxonomy identifies six distinct levels of learning, starting at the lower end, with recall and summary, moving through application and critical analysis, and ending with evaluation and the creation of something new. Lower levels of learning allow students to grow their knowledge, but it's also vital that students have many opportunities to apply what they're learning. Our brains process and retain new information best through application rather than recall. Therefore, be sure to review the verbs used in your outcomes to ensure students also have opportunities to apply what they're learning. Below, you can see a sample list of active verbs that reflect each domain level.

Examples of Active Verbs Using the Revised Bloom's Taxonomy

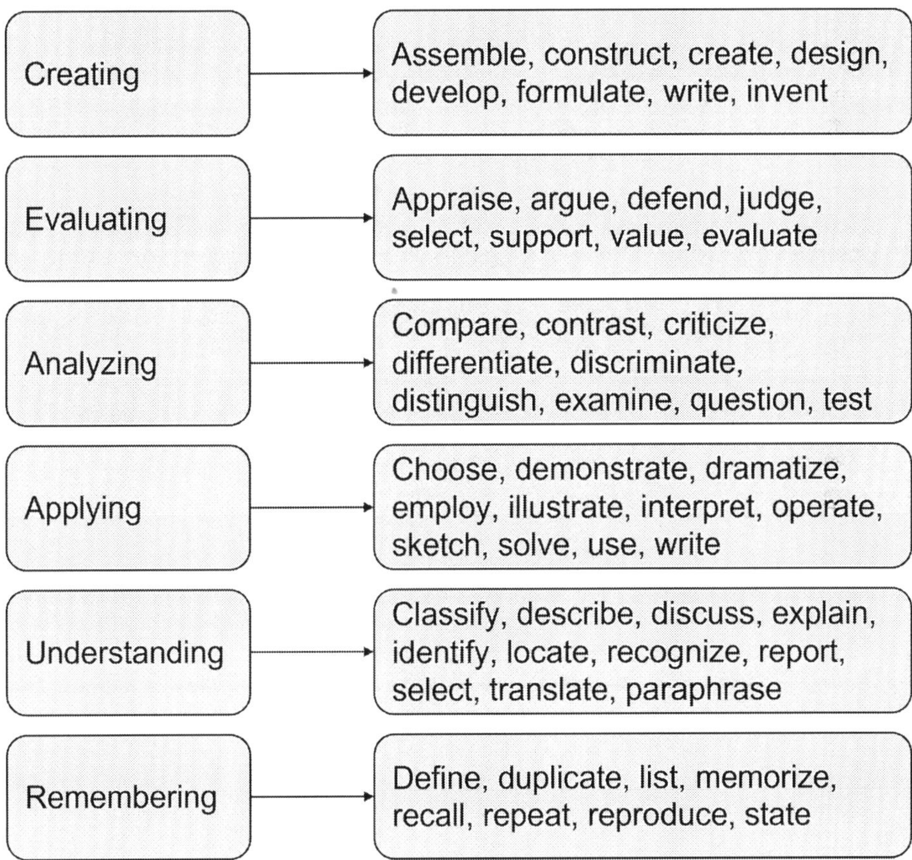

While most disciplines focus on the cognitive domain, there are three distinct domains in Bloom's taxonomy: 1) psychomotor, relating to manual or physical activities; 2) affective, relating to attitudinal and self-awareness; and 3) cognitive, relating to mental skills and knowledge. Here are some guiding questions to help think about desired outcomes: Will students be required to demonstrate manual or physical skills? If so, you are in the psychomotor domain, and example active verbs include perform, add, draw, exercise, demonstrate, and measure. Will students demonstrate a change in attitude, feelings, or sense of self? If so, you are in the affective domain, and active verbs include advocate, reflect, adopt, accept, and reject. Especially for verbs in the affective domain, you may need to think more deeply or creatively about how you will evaluate student work.

More on Learning Taxonomies

Bloom's taxonomy is considered a seminal work in writing learning outcomes. Benjamin Bloom, an educational psychologist who was very interested in students reaching higher levels of learning, created his taxonomy in 1956. Anderson & Krathwohl updated the taxonomy in 2001 to account for creation, rather than evaluation, as the highest level of learning. Churches revised the taxonomy again in 2008, calling it Bloom's Digital Taxonomy (Churches, 2008). Aside from Bloom's, there are other taxonomies you can explore, including the Six Facets of Understandings (McTighe & Wiggins, 2012), Dee Fink's Taxonomy of Significant Learning (Fink, 2003), and the Depth of Knowledge Framework (Webb, 2002). No matter the taxonomy you use, focus on selecting the most appropriate active verbs for the level of your learning outcome.

CLOs Should Be Student-Focused

In addition to being measurable or observable, your CLOs should be student-focused, which means they also need to be clear, specific, and focused on mastery.

Clear

Students should understand from the first day of class what they'll be able to do by the end of the course, which means CLOs should be written in student-centric language so that they are understandable by new students in the course. Too often, we construct CLOs that are understandable to us and our expert colleagues rather than to the students themselves.

This is one of the first big connections to your Learner Analysis from Step 1. Who are your learners? Will they understand the CLOs from the start? Obviously, this will look different if you're teaching a graduate-level course versus an undergraduate course, or even an advanced course for majors versus a general education course taken by non-majors. Many faculty ask if they can use terms in their CLOs that students won't understand when they begin but will understand by the end of the course. The answer is: it depends. If students can glean the meaning based on the rest of the CLO, then using a brand-new term in your outcome might be fine. However, your CLOs are generally not the best place to introduce new or complex terminology.

Specific

Additionally, CLOs should be specific, giving students a concrete image of what they'll be able to do by course's end. But, be careful that CLOs aren't so long that they read like a prompt for the required assignment(s).

Focused on Mastery

CLOs should be written so that students can conceptualize the level of knowledge-backed performance they're aiming for. You might think of this as the level or degree of learning you expect students to achieve by the end of the course. Mastery and specificity are often deeply connected. For example, is the objective to "write a paper?" Or is the focus on learning to "write and organize a paper well"? In the case of the latter, the better learning outcome is to "write a well-organized essay relevant to various course topics." Both convey the same general idea that students will be able to write some type of paper by the end of the course, but the revised CLO gives students a preview that the focus here is on good organization, as well as relating and applying their essay topics to ideas and themes in the course.

Evaluating & Revising CLOs

We have now discussed the importance of learning outcomes being:

- Measurable
- Clear

- Specific
- Focused on Mastery

In what follows, we evaluate three different CLOs all focused on writing a paper. Only one of them successfully meets all the necessary criteria of being measurable, clear, specific, and focused on mastery.

Example One: "At the end of this course, students will be able to write a paper."

- *Measurable?* Yes, "write" is an active verb which can be observed.
- *Clear?* Yes, this is something that students could easily understand.
- *Specific?* No, this doesn't specify whether the paper is an essay, research paper, argument paper, literature review, or something else.
- *Focused on mastery?* No, no degree of mastery is referenced, so it is unclear if any paper will suffice or if it should be of a particular quality.
- *Overall evaluation?* The biggest issue with this learning outcome is that students could write any type of paper, and even do a poor job, and still have met its specifications.

Example Two: "By the end of this course, students will be able to write a literature review with an introduction, body, and conclusion, which reflects the five C's and appropriately cites at least ten scholarly sources using APA style."

- *Measurable?* Yes, "write" is an active verb which can be observed.
- *Clear?* No, the "five C's" is an example of jargon and would not be meaningful or clear to incoming students even with context clues. This CLO could instead list the actual Five Cs, but that would make it too lengthy. Depending on the course, students might also not know what APA style is.
- *Specific?* Yes, but it is so specific that it has ceased to be a CLO and instead acts as an assignment prompt.
- *Focused on mastery?* Yes, but it is ultimately too much information.
- *Overall evaluation?* Whereas Example One was not sufficiently specific nor focused on mastery, this example swings the pendulum too far

in the other direction by giving too much detail. This CLO is a run-on sentence and nearly a complete assignment prompt. Its length and content load could be especially difficult for high-anxiety students and could negatively impact learning.

Example Three: "At the end of this course, students will be able to write a well-organized literature review, using properly cited scholarly sources."

- *Measurable?* Yes, "write" is an active verb which can be observed.
- *Clear?* Yes, this is clear in that even if students do not know exactly what a literature review or a scholarly source is, they'll understand that they'll be writing a paper that reviews research on a topic.
- *Specific?* Yes, it makes clear that the type of paper being written is a literature review using scholarly sources.
- *Focused on mastery?* Yes, it makes explicit that it needs to be well-organized and use properly cited sources.
- *Overall evaluation?* This is a good learning outcome that meets all four criteria and that students can achieve only if they (a) understand the components of a literature review and know how to organize it well, and (b) also understand what a scholarly source is, how to summarize it appropriately, and how to cite it correctly.

Below are two additional examples, adapted from Felder and Brent (2016), of how you might revise your learning outcomes to use active verbs for measurability while also using clear, student-centric language, being appropriately specific about the skill/action, and referencing the level of mastery that students will be aiming for.

- *Original CLO:* "By the end of this course, students will learn how to do experiments."
- *Revised CLO:* "By the end of this course, you will be able to design and carry out several simple experiments and effectively analyze the data that is produced."
- *Revision Explanation:* The revised version replaces "learn" with "design," "carry out," and "analyze." All students would have a basic

understanding of what the revised CLO means in this introductory-level science course. The word "students" becomes "you" to use more student-centric language. "Do experiments" is made more specific by saying: "design and carry out." Finally, mastery is attended to both by the changes for specificity and by adding that students will not just analyze the data from the experiments but be able to "effectively" do so.

Let's check out another example.

- *Original CLO:* "By the end of this course, students will understand the requirements of teamwork."
- *Revised CLO:* "By the end of this course, you will be able to function effectively as a team member on a multidisciplinary project, as determined by instructor observations, peer ratings, and self-assessment."
- *Revision Explanation:* In this example, the fuzzy verb "understand" is made measurable with the active verb "function." "Students" is replaced with "you" for a more student-centric tone. "Requirements of teamwork" is made more specific by revising to "function effectively as a team member of a multidisciplinary project." Finally, mastery is attended to via "effectively," referring to their functionality as a member. Additionally, students understand how this effectiveness will be evaluated—via instructor observations, peer ratings, and self-assessment.

Learning Outcomes FAQ

We have found in our collaborations with faculty that learning outcomes, perhaps more than other elements of course design, can raise several good questions. Listed below are some frequently asked questions and our responses.

What if I have mandated CLOs?

You may already have CLOs mandated by your program, institution, or accrediting body. While these mandated outcomes typically reflect important course topics or skills, they may not be suitable for serving as the foundation of your course design or as clear guideposts for your students' learning. The issue with mandated CLOs is often that they are not measurable and/or not written in student-friendly language. If you have mandated outcomes, you can continue to list those in your syllabus and also ensure that the core ideas behind them are reflected in the course. Many faculty list the mandated outcomes in their syllabus and then add a simple statement, such as: "These outcomes ensure that by the end of this course, you will be able to…," and then list their new, measurable, student-centric, performance-based learning outcomes. In other words, you, as the expert, know what the mandated outcome means and are simply translating that into something on which you can build your design and effectively communicate to your students.

As an example, if your institutionally mandated outcome is, "Understand the scientific method," your revised version for design purposes might become: "List and describe each step of the scientific method and apply it to various contexts and problems." You would then design your assignments and create or curate materials to align with your "rewritten," measurable objective. You would still list the mandated outcome in your syllabus, followed by your rewritten version.

What if I have learning "objectives" instead of learning "outcomes"?

"Learning outcomes" are also commonly referred to as "learning objectives," "instructional objectives," or "course competencies," and many faculty or institutions have a preferred term or a required term. There are differing linguistic implications for "outcomes" versus "objectives," but that discussion is not relevant for this book. While we refer to them as "learning outcomes" or "CLOs," we invite you to use whatever term you (or your institution) favor.

Can I have too many CLOs?

As mentioned in the introduction, we generally see between five to nine CLOs for a course. If you have significantly more than that, it might reflect the fact that some of them are actually more appropriate for the module or lesson level (more on this in Step 7) or that you have multiple outcomes around the same idea that can be combined. While CLOs reflect the key ideas in a course, CLOs should not be an exhaustive list of everything students will do throughout the term.

Do learning outcomes differ by discipline?

Yes and no. Some of your desired outcomes may be directly tied to your subject matter, and those outcomes may not be appropriate for other courses. However, some skills commonly apply across disciplines. For example, outcomes and active verbs related to skills such as effectively supporting an opinion with evidence, demonstrating critical thinking, and proposing a solution or solving a problem can apply across disciplines.

Don't CLOs just invite students to "check the box"?

Unfortunately, because of external requirements and a lack of knowledge about the purpose of CLOs for course design, some students (and instructors) do experience them as "checking the box" or something to do simply because "it's required." We remain excited about learning outcomes, however, because when you start with them, you create a firm foundation for your course. You can then design your assessments, activities, interactions, and content, all to support students in achieving and demonstrating your outcomes. In short, learning outcomes serve a crucial function in design and learning.

Do students even read them?

We posit that many students disregard learning outcomes largely because they typically aren't aligned well with the assessments, activities, and materials and aren't referenced by the instructor throughout the course. They do not connect the skills and knowledge that students are acquiring to the usefulness of those new skills and knowledge. If CLOs are well-written and properly aligned, however, they become much more meaningful to both you and your students. Additionally, when you incorporate outcomes in your design and teaching throughout the course, they can be part of the useful feedback and discussions you have with students about their learning progress and achievement. In other words, use them actively in both your design and teaching!

What does any of this have to do with online learning?

Great question! Writing quality learning outcomes (and, more importantly, aligning them with assessments, activities, and course materials) is good practice for any modality. However, online learning is unique in many ways, one of them being that students see your design. Alignment gaps or a disorganized learning path that might be less apparent and/or easily compensated for in an in-person class become glaringly obvious in an online course. If online courses are not easily accessible and organized into the course site/LMS in a meaningful way, students will notice, and their investment in the class will be affected. Additionally, CLOs inform your thinking about how students will interact with you, with one another, and with the course in unique, online-specific ways. Most importantly, however, if you are designing a fully online course and fail to start with good CLOs, you will inevitably spend more time throughout the process revising and adjusting your design—in other words, it pays to put in this time at the beginning before moving to your assessments, activities, and content.

What about higher-level courses where I co-create learning outcomes with my students?

For most faculty, co-creating an asynchronous online course with students is not feasible given workload and time limitations, as well as online practicalities (like making sure all digital components are accessible, even when creating them as the course is running). This sets up a situation like the "designing while you're teaching" scenario, which is always more difficult and makes it harder for you to be present as an instructor. In future chapters, though, we have included several ideas to promote flexibility and student choice in your design, especially for content and assignments.

Do these learning outcome "rules" always apply?

If you are working on interior design for your house, there are general color principles that should be applied. Are they rules that can never be broken? No, absolutely not. Are there exceptions to these general rules? Yes, of course. But do those general color principles apply to most design of most houses? Yes. Just like most artists first learn the fundamentals (e.g., painting a lot of fruit) before "breaking the rules" and becoming masters, HIDOC is a faculty-tested design model for online courses that provides fundamental guidelines. Once you've gone through the process, though, we encourage you to incorporate your own creativity and teaching philosophy. No design model will 100% apply to 100% of courses; rather, these are best practices distilled from our decades of experience designing online courses and are written to be helpful to the majority of faculty in a wide variety of disciplines. Our hope is that you find the design process empowering, not restrictive. In the end, choose what resonates with you, your course, and your students, and leave behind what does not.

Your Turn: Learning Outcomes

In this section, we walk you through Step 2 so that you can draft and revise your Course Learning Outcomes. This Step takes you through the macro-level view of your course, focusing on your Big Vision and ideas, then moves you to a more detailed level of what you want students to learn and know, and ends with specific, measurable learning outcomes that reflect how they'll apply that new knowledge, and the skills and abilities they'll gain in your course.

Part 1: "Big Vision"

We've included space on the Design Doc for you to draft some notes and ideas you have for the course. Here is where you can list big topics or takeaways, make some notes for questions that will promote cognitive inquiry, or even sketch out the larger vision you have for the course. This is a "Free Think Space" for you to use before moving to the more granular level of drafting your CLOs. Consider your vision for this course. What are its big takeaways? What are the significant ideas or provocative questions that drew you in and will draw students in?

Part 2: Draft Your CLOs

Now that you've thought about the big ideas, big picture, and big questions for your course, you can build off that work to draft your learning outcomes. Begin by considering the course description and the purpose of the course. What do you want students to know or understand by the end of the course? We are inviting a "draft" here because it can sometimes be hard to start thinking about your outcomes while also focusing on active verbs. It's often easier to start with the understanding or knowledge you want for your students and revise later. So, in this draft, you can use "fuzzy" verbs that can't be measured, such as "know," "understand," "learn," or "appreciate," to begin your thinking, or you can choose to dive right in with using active verbs. Think of this as freewriting in a no-judgment zone.

Part 3: Revise Your CLOs

Next, revise your draft outcomes for measurability and student-focus (i.e., specific, clear, focused on mastery). How do you know that students "know" something, have "learned" about something, or "understand" something? Because they can do things such as "describe," "analyze," "solve," "design," "execute," or "evaluate." Clarify your learning outcomes with an active verb and describe, in specific and jargon-free terms, what students will be able to do by the end of the course.

Part 4: Check Your CLOs

After you've drafted and revised your CLOs, take a moment to review them objectively. Sometimes, it helps to leave a little time between revising and checking so that you can see them with a clearer perspective. You might also ask a colleague to review them from the student perspective.

Do the course learning outcomes you've written meet the following criteria?

They begin with an active verb and describe what students will do to demonstrate their learning.	[YES/NO]
They avoid fuzzy verbs such as "understand," "know," or "learn," or any verb that cannot be measured or observed.	[YES/NO]
They are written in clear, student-centric language so that incoming students can understand what they mean.	[YES/NO]
They give students a general idea of what they will be learning and doing in the course.	[YES/NO]

They are broad enough to reflect major outcomes for the course (i.e., they cover significant course concepts and represent either a major theme/topic or ones which are touched upon in prominent ways throughout the course).	[YES/NO]
They are specific without being an assignment description.	[YES/NO]
They relay the desired degree of mastery/proficiency.	[YES/NO]

For any of the areas you answered NO to above, return to the Revising Your Course Learning Outcomes section on the Design Doc and continue to improve them. Remember that you'll have future opportunities to revise and refine your CLOs, so they do not have to be perfect at this stage. In fact, nothing, at any point in the design process has to be (or will be) perfect! That's one reason why it's wonderful that design is iterative—we have an entire step dedicated to continuous improvement, so don't waste precious time now on pursuing perfection.

Your Learning Outcomes

1. Open the **Course Learning Outcomes** Design Doc from the companion website, use the version in the Design Doc Library section of the book, or create a version that works for you.
2. Work on the **Big Vision**; **Draft Your CLOs**; **Revise Your CLOs**; and **Check Your CLOs** sections discussed above.

Now that you've conducted your learner analysis, it's time to move the key information to your HIDOC Course Blueprint.

Your HIDOC Course Blueprint

1. Open the **HIDOC Course Blueprint** from the companion website, use the version in the Design Doc Library section of the book, or create a version that works for you.
2. Copy the **Revise Your CLOs** part of the Design Doc to the **Course Learning Outcomes** (Step 2) section of the HIDOC Course Blueprint.

Faculty-ID Collaboration

Replacing "Understand" with Active Verbs

I teach argumentation and rhetoric, and one of the things I want my students to understand is how to form an argument. So, for example, I have a learning outcome that is: "Students will understand how to form an argument." Why is "understanding" not the goal here?

Understanding is the goal! But explain to me how you will know that students understand, for example, how to form an argument. Can you describe for me some activities that students are doing, or could do, to demonstrate they understand?

Well, I teach students about the Toulmin model, which breaks an argument down into six main parts, including asserting a claim and providing evidence to support that claim. So, for example, if students effectively show that or include that in their argument, I know they understand.

Perfect! OK, so that is a great example of the evidence that you will be assessing for your students, and we can formulate that as an outcome for their learning. All that means is translating "understanding" into performance or application so that a student's degree of understanding can be assessed. In this case, a learning outcome based on what you just explained to me might look something like: "By the end of this course, you will be able to construct a well-reasoned argument that makes a claim and provides appropriate evidence to support that claim." Is that something that students will be doing in the course and that they will need to do well in order to demonstrate understanding of the subject matter?

Yes, that makes sense... students will be completing several assignments that will allow them to practice using the Toulmin model, so this definitely should be a course learning outcome, as it's not just one small assignment. And I like the inclusion of "well-reasoned" in the outcome because that's a foundational part of argumentation and speaks to the level of mastery that I'd be looking for from students. I also like that we're putting a qualifier around the evidence because I do a whole section on finding quality supporting evidence using scholarly sources and even how to vet sources.

Excellent! I think we've hit the mark, then, with just a small but important edit for this outcome.

Faculty-ID Collaboration

Using Student-Centric Language

I see here that one of your current CLOs is: "By the end of this course, you will be able to write an expository essay." That makes sense to me for sure. But do your students know what an expository essay is?

This is a College Writing I course typically taken by freshmen. So, no, most students haven't heard of an expository essay before taking the course, but they will know what it is by the end. They will have to write an expository essay, so why is that not the learning outcome I want here?

Good question! You are right… that is an outcome for your students. But we want to make sure that they also understand what that goal is, even if they haven't yet completed the course. So, let's see if we can just tweak it a bit. Can you explain to me what an expository essay is, just as you would explain it to a typical freshman?

Sure! An expository essay presents a balanced analysis of a topic using facts, statistics, and examples. They can be of different types, for example, a compare & contrast essay or a cause & effect essay.

OK, so there are different types of expository essays, and students will be using facts and data to analyze a topic in a balanced way. Where will they get these facts? For example, do they need to provide citations in this paper?

Oh, yes. They need to provide citations, and for a lot of students, this is really one of the first times they'll learn how to appropriately include quotations and paraphrases and also cite sources using APA style. That is a key part of this assignment.

That's good to know. What else is "new" and perhaps difficult for most students in writing this type of essay?

Well, for most of them, this is the first time that they've had to research a topic, find good, reputable sources, and use those sources to explain the topic. Many students mistakenly turn it into an opinion piece or persuasive essay.

OK, this is all great information that will help us edit the outcome. So, what if we rewrite it as:

"By the end of this course, students will be able to write a well-researched essay that explains a topic to an audience and is supported by properly cited scholarly sources.

I like that! That explains to them very clearly what they're going to do, and it also speaks to the level at which I need them to be.

Yes, exactly! You described some important facets of the assignment, such as using scholarly sources and citing them properly, that speak to the level of mastery that you're looking for. In other words, you don't want students to simply "Write an essay"; you want them to write a college-level essay that demonstrates important skills, such as their ability to research a topic, locate appropriate source material, and use that material appropriately to explain something to their audience.

Summary and Next Steps

To sum it up...

Course learning outcomes are important for both you and your students.

For you, the instructor: CLOs form the basis of your aligned course design by setting the stage for the activities and assessments students will complete in the course. This is why you want to:

Write the learning outcomes so they reflect both the larger ideas in the course and the actual things that students will do to demonstrate learning achievement.

For them, the students: CLOs serve as a "learning guidepost" or "learning lighthouse," steering and guiding them towards the level of mastery they'll need with the new knowledge and skills they are acquiring. This is why it is important to also:

Write the learning outcomes in understandable language so that students have a clear idea from the start of the course what they will be able to do by the time they finish.

Looking ahead...

In the next chapter, we'll continue our macro view of the course and begin to lay out the course structure. You should expect this structure to evolve (and the modules you identify in Step 3 to be revised) as you get more specific with your design in later Steps.

References

Anderson, L.W., & Krathwohl, D. (2001). A taxonomy for learning, teaching, and assessing: A revision of Bloom's Taxonomy of Educational Objectives. Longman.

Bloom, B. S. (Ed.). (1956). Taxonomy of educational objectives: The classification of educational goals. Handbook I: Cognitive domain. McKay Publishing.

Churches, A. (2008). Bloom's digital taxonomy. https://www.researchgate.net/publication/228381038_Bloom's_Digital_Taxonomy

Felder, R.M., & Brent, R. (2016). Teaching and learning STEM: A practical guide. John Wiley & Sons.

Fink, L.D. (2003). Creating significant learning experiences: An integrated approach to design college courses. Jossey-Bass.

McTighe, J., & Wiggins, G. (2012). Understanding by design framework [Whitepaper]. Association for Supervision and Curriculum Development.

Webb, N.L. (2002). Depth-of-knowledge levels for four content areas. http://ossucurr.pbworks.com/w/file/fetch/49691156/Norm%20web%20dok%20by%20subject%20area.pdf

Wiggins, G., & McTighe, J. (2004). Understanding by design (2nd ed.). Association for Supervision & Curriculum Development.

3 Course Structure

By the time you reach Step 3, you've thought deeply about your students and the big ideas of the course. You've also identified where you want your students to be, in terms of their abilities, by the end of the course. We're going to stay in that "big picture" thinking to sketch out your high-level course structure, which is also the architecture for how you will organize and build your course in the learning management system (LMS). Course modules, also referred to as units or lessons, are the discrete segments that make up your course and create a learning pathway for students. The content for this Step is much briefer than the others, but while you will be spending less time reading, you'll be spending more time thinking and creating in your Design Doc and HIDOC Course Blueprint.

Modular Organization

Throughout the book, we refer to organizing your course as creating a "learning path." What we mean by that is that the structure of an online course serves as the sequence of what students learn and when, but is also a literal, visual framework that you will develop in your LMS. It is both the cognitive journey your students will take and the actual web-based path they will follow. Especially in an asynchronous online course, the explicit structure that you create before the course begins is a primary way that you will guide students through the course, and it is a vital component of your teaching presence.

At this point in the process, you are starting to identify key landmarks and topics that will be organized into modules that will house your assessments, activities, and instructional materials. If you are working on a brand-new course, this will be your first attempt at mapping it out in its entirety. Alternatively, if this is a course you've taught before, you have an opportunity to reflect on previous offerings and determine if a reorganization is in order. You might also have insights from student feedback related to areas such as workload, alignment, and sequencing. Below is an example of how a fully online Thermodynamics course is laid out in the LMS in terms of its high-level course structure.

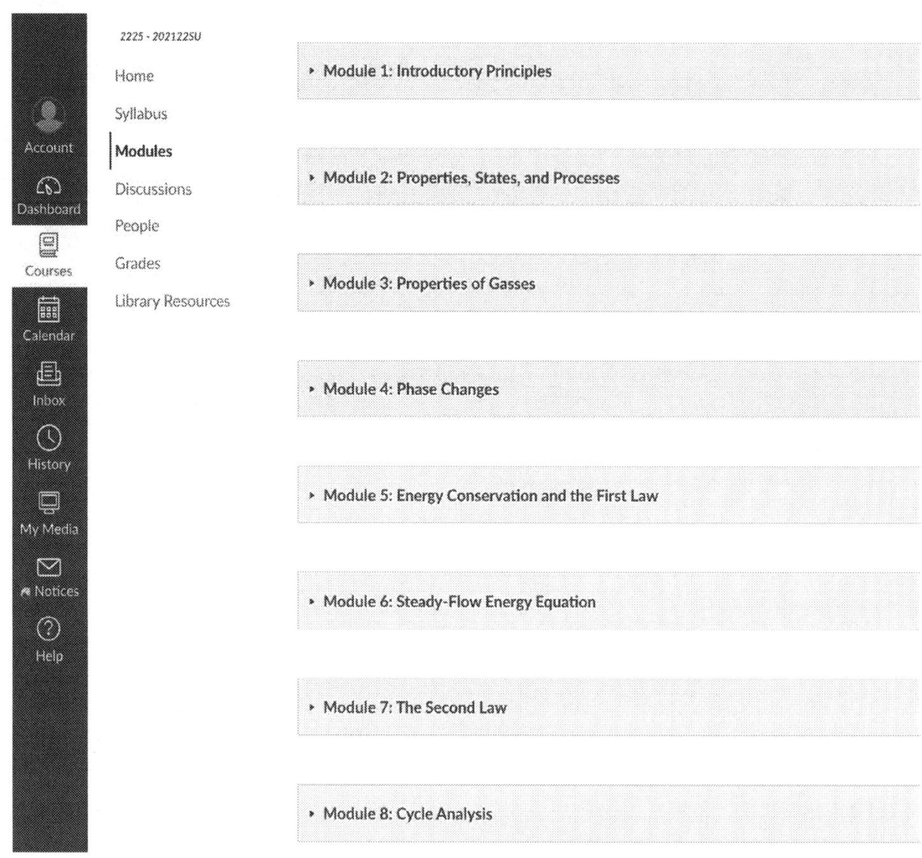

Your Course Alignment Map

Your Course Alignment Map is the macro view of your course that enables you to evaluate whether all elements are instructionally aligned. After you develop the first draft of your course structure, you can start working on your Course Alignment Map, or "Course Map" or "Alignment map" for short.

Instructional alignment is key.

Instructional alignment means that: (1) all your course learning outcomes (CLOs) are covered and assessed in the course; (2) you don't have any major course elements that are not addressed in your CLOs; (3) your assessments evaluate your CLOs at the same cognitive level; and (4) your instructional materials enable students to perform successfully on those assessments.

In addition to allowing a clear window for you to evaluate alignment, the Course Alignment Map also gives you a holistic view of your course before you start to build it in the LMS and is a document that will be added to and revised throughout the rest of your design process. You can review it at the end for gaps, redundancies, and balance of content and assessment types. (We'll return to these ideas in Step 8: Continuous Improvement.) In Step 3, after drafting your Course Structure, you will be ready to start identifying in which modules your CLOs will be addressed. A given module might address one or several CLOs, and a CLO might be addressed once or in several places throughout the course.

> ***Your Course Alignment Map is an essential part of the design process. It allows you to evaluate alignment and reveals gaps, redundancies, and imbalances in your design.***

Your Turn: Alignment Map

Keep in mind that this is your first draft of modular organization, and it will continue to be revised as you clarify other elements of your course design. It's okay if you have some gaps or uncertainties; nothing has to be "perfect" at this point. As mentioned before, throughout this process we encourage you to update your Design Docs and HIDOC Course Blueprint as you improve your design. Also, it's important to note that while we use the term "module" throughout the book, we recognize that you may use other terms to organize your curriculum, such as "lesson," "unit," or simply "week." Use whatever term you prefer. For this Design Doc activity, you'll first think through the progression of students' learning while also considering pragmatics such as how many weeks the course spans. Then, you'll begin sketching out your modules, including title and length.

Part 1: Module Brainstorming

Brainstorm your learning path.

You've just done the hard work to write CLOs that reflect what you want your students to have achieved by the end of the course. So, begin with that end in mind: to achieve those CLOs, what do students need to learn first, and should the weeks progressively build? What topics naturally connect, or are typically addressed together? What sequence best allows you to ramp up from easier to more complex ideas and applications? Does your course naturally lend itself to a specific order, such as chronological, novice to expert, or beginning to end of a process? This is also a good time to consult your notes (or the Design Doc) from Step 1, as answers to those questions might impact how you begin to organize your modules. For example, graduate students, those with professional experience, and those in the major will likely start out with advanced knowledge and skills, so they might begin with a review of foundational concepts.

Consider the length of your course.

If you are currently teaching a shortened version of a course that you know will also be taught as a full-term course, we suggest mapping it out first as a full-term course. It's often much easier to contract a course schedule than expand it, and you want to ensure that versions of a course varying by length are equal in terms of content, assessments, and rigor. A shortened version of a course needs to be restructured, but it cannot be reduced, in terms of learning.

Focus on your first and final week.
Will the first week include some "introductory" material? Will the final week include some type of reflective activity? Some instructors use the first week as a "prep" week to review relevant material and do introductions, and then start new course material at the start of the second week, so think about your teaching philosophy and the "rhythm" of the course.

Part 2: Module Planning

Once you've worked through the questions above, it's time to do a first draft of your course structure. Think of this as sketching out your course—including what students will learn and do first, and how their knowledge will build throughout the course. Don't forget that we're still at our high-level view. In Step 7: Online Learner Support, we'll begin to narrow down to a more detailed view of each module, but for now you don't need to know all the specifics; we're just aiming for the title and a general, sequenced structure.

Provide the module #.
Number your modules sequentially so that you can start to create the learning path for your students.

Give each module a title.
The title should generally identify or describe what the module is about. Remember that it can always be edited, so consider this a tentative title. When you develop your course in the LMS, though, the title will be used as a label for the module and also in digital documents, such as the course schedule. The title can be a simple name or short description of the content for that lesson, an essential question to promote cognitive inquiry, or something more creative and fun. Right now, you can start off with a simple title that generally describes what the module is about, such as "Week 4: Photosynthesis," "Module 2: Cell Structure or Function," or "Lesson 3: Writing for the Technical Fields."

Indicate the length of the module.

After you title each module, you then need to decide how long each one will be. If your sequenced topics are amenable to a weekly structure, that's ideal. It provides a consistent rhythm for the course that can be helpful to online students who don't meet in class each week on the same day and time. However, sometimes learning just doesn't fit neatly within a 7-day window. In that case, give the module and its topics the time they deserve. Denote each module's anticipated length, whether it is one week, two weeks, or some other length.

Capture additional information.

Make any notes for yourself about topics you might cover in the module, or if you know of associated assessments or activities that will take place within a certain module or at a certain time in the course. These are notes that will guide you in brainstorming content and assessment ideas, and you can also revise and refine these notes later for use as a module introduction.

Your Course Structure

1. Open the **Course Structure** Design Doc from the companion website, use the version in the Design Doc Library section of the book, or create a version that works for you.
2. Work on the **Module Brainstorming** and **Module Planning** sections discussed above.

The work you did above in the Course Structure Design Doc will now inform the Course Alignment Map—which is the Macro View in your HIDOC Course Blueprint. Because your Course Map does a lot in a relatively small amount of space, we suggest using abbreviations and shorthand for some things, such as your module titles. If the abbreviations make sense to you, they work! Your Course Map will ultimately have five columns, but at this point in the process, we will focus only on the first, which will include the module #, title, and duration that you drafted in the Design Doc for this Step.

Your HIDOC Course Blueprint

1. Open the **HIDOC Course Blueprint** from the companion website, use the version in the Design Doc Library section of the book, or create a version that works for you.
2. Go to the **Course Alignment Map [MACRO VIEW].**
3. Fill in the first column using shorthand or abbreviations that make sense to you, pulling relevant information from the **Module Planning** part of the Design Doc: Module #, title, duration (Step 3).

Faculty-ID Collaboration

The Importance of Structure and Organization

OK, so I have my syllabus, content, and assignments all ready to go on this flash drive...can you load this up into folders for me in the LMS?

That's great! Did you have in mind a way you want to organize everything? I want to get a better sense of your thoughts on organizing your online course.

Oh, I'd just envisioned we'd create a "Content" folder, upload all of that, and then create an "Assignments" folder and upload all of the assignments. I figure if we add my syllabus, it's pretty much done, right?

If this were a F2F class, yes, that's probably all you'd need to do. But when you teach online, you have to do something that you don't have to do F2F—you have to create a well-organized, easy-to-navigate, web-based structure so that your online students have a visual learning pathway.

I don't think I know what you mean. I don't know how to do web design or anything...do I have to know that to be a good online instructor?

Thankfully, no...most learning management systems (LMSs) are pretty easy to navigate and use to create your course—you don't need to know coding or web design, for example. Also, our institution also offers an LMS template that you can fill in and adjust as needed in terms of layout. And, we can rely on the great research we have now regarding the layout and organization of online courses.

In general, we want students to follow a path of learning that you plan via your course design, where you create individual modules, or learning units, for them to work through sequentially. If we put all the content in a single folder and all the assignments in another folder, it's easier and less time-consuming for us, but it's very confusing for students. Each week, they'll need to sift through a huge list of things to find what they should focus on, read, and do, and they may not even know why they're doing it because they aren't clear on how it connects to your learning goals for them.

Oh! Well, I never thought of it like that. I was kind of thinking about it similar to how I organize the desktop and folder structure on my computer.

Absolutely—that's a very natural assumption. When we build your course in the LMS, though, think of it more like setting up a learning space, or online classroom, for your students, rather than the discrete, digital materials and components that we'll put in the classroom.

Good structure and organization allow you to interact with your students in a regular and substantive way and to set the pace and "rhythm" of your course, so you can guide students as a learning community.

OK, I think I understand what you're saying now. So how do I start thinking about how to structure my online class?

For now, set aside what you already have—don't worry, we'll come back to it—and let's use the learning outcomes you have in the syllabus to think through how you want to structure your course. A common approach is topically and by week, but we'll let your pedagogical goals and learning outcomes guide this part of the process.

Summary and Next Steps

To sum it up...

Your modules (or units, lessons, or topical weeks) give organization and structure to your course. They should be sequenced in a way that best supports student learning and aligns with your assessments and activities. The start of this course map (which will also be used to help build your course in the LMS) will continue to evolve and be refined as you work through the HIDOC process.

Looking ahead...

In the next chapter, you'll start planning your activities and assessments. We'll help make sure that each activity and assessment aligns with at least one of your course learning outcomes and that each of your CLOs has at least one assessment evaluating it.

4 Assessments & Activities

How will you know that your learners have actually achieved your CLOs? How will students know throughout the semester what they understand and can do well, and where they need to improve? How will students practice their skills and use your feedback to improve? The answer is through course assessments and learning activities that align with your CLOs, and that is the focus of Step 4.

Overview of Types

Specifically, this chapter focuses on three distinct assignment types: summative assessments, formative assessments, and learning activities.

Summative Assessments: Learning and Mastery

In brief, summative assessments are typically large, culminating assessments. Their primary purpose is evaluation; they allow students to demonstrate a level of mastery that should correspond to one or more of your CLOs. Students' learning achievement and performance are frequently showcased in summative assessments, such as exams, papers, projects, portfolios, and presentations. You might have several summative assessments in your course or a single summative assessment at the end. As one example, when a course has two major exams—a mid-term and a final—each of them is a summative assessment in that each exam is primarily meant to measure students' cumulative knowledge at a point in time. The final submission of a semester-long paper is another example of a common summative assessment.

Keep in mind that feedback on summative assessments is often of limited use—for example, a student typically cannot use feedback from their final exam to retake the test. Feedback, however, both for your students and for you as an instructor is essential to quality online learning. Consider, when students are interacting with you in an in-person learning environment, how you know when they don't understand something. An expression of confusion on a student's face is usually as easy to recognize as a raised hand. Online, however, (especially in an asynchronous teaching environment), we have no such non-verbal cues. Additionally, asynchronous online students can't pause a recorded lecture and ask questions in real time. This is why both formative assessments and learning activities are crucial to provide students with opportunities for feedback and improvement, and to give instructors (and students themselves!) necessary information about where students might be struggling.

Formative Assessments: Crucial Feedback

Formative assessments usually take less time and are worth less than summative assessments. In contrast to measuring and evaluating students' abilities at a point in time, the primary purpose of formative assessments is to provide helpful, robust feedback as students are working with their new knowledge and provide students an opportunity to do better on a related summative assessment. Formative assessments often build up to a summative assessment. For example, a topic submission, outline, and paper draft are all corresponding formative assessments that culminate in a final semester paper. Or, a presentation script and slide outline can serve as formative assessments culminating in a summative course presentation. Quizzes can also be formative assessments that lead up to summative exams.

As discussed above, formative assessments are crucial in an online setting because they let both the instructor and students know where problem points might be, problem points which can be less apparent online. Timing here is key. Students need to receive feedback early enough to improve their learning and performance moving forward. For instance, if an online student has taken two graded quizzes leading up to a mid-term but hasn't received feedback on the quizzes, they will not have the chance to refine their knowledge before the exam.

Learning Activities: Practice and Guidance

While summative assessments are typically higher stakes and contribute heavily to students' grades, and formative assessments are often smaller portions or building blocks to the summative assessments, learning activities are often used as a way for students to practice what they are learning. As an example, if a final exam is a summative assessment, and a short, graded, timed quiz is a formative assessment, then an ungraded quiz that students can take multiple times and even use course materials for is a great example of a learning activity.

Quizzes, whether implemented as low- (or no-) stakes learning activities or more formal formative assessments, are most effective when they include feedback for each question. LMS quizzing tools allow the addition of your automated comments and notes for correct and incorrect answers, so this is something good to spend time setting up during development. Ideally, each incorrect answer in an auto-graded quiz includes auto-generated feedback guiding students to review specific information and try again (correct answers can have kudos or even suggested ways to deepen their knowledge). You might also use question pools that present a random selection of questions each time the student takes the quiz to give more opportunities for practice. With multiple or unlimited attempts, students can see improvements. Providing auto-feedback for each quiz item is also a much less time-consuming way to provide feedback for large-enrollment classes.

When designing learning activities, challenge your students but use "safety nets" by making the activities low- or no-stakes or giving students opportunities for remediation and improvement.

Examples of Learning Activities

Below are some additional examples of learning activities.

- Knowledge-check activities they can engage with multiple times
- A chance to revise a draft
- Partial credit if they re-answer a question correctly
- Interactive activities, such as drag-and-drop or mini-quizzes, immediately following an online lecture or other piece of content
- Practice homework problems (even done collaboratively)
- Breakout room activities in synchronous online classes
- Discussion forums in the LMS where students discuss homework problems, post their thoughts about content, and ask general course-related questions

- Short essays or blog posts where students explain key concepts in their own words, ask questions, and share examples
- Rough outlines or sketches (possibly with peer feedback)
- Short, reflective journal questions or 3-2-1 responses following a lecture (where students indicate three things they learned, two things confirming what they already knew, and one question they still have)

In some cases, it may not be immediately clear if something is an assessment or an activity. Discussions are a good example of an assignment type that might be either an assessment or an activity, depending on the intent, depth, or point value. To make the determination, ask yourself: Is the primary intention here to assess learning progress or give students a chance to practice with little or no "penalty"?

Avoiding "Busy Work"

It's important to keep in mind that your learning activities and formative assessments are not "busy work" (Schaffhauser, 2021) but instead purposefully designed to help students practice and improve. When first designing an online course, it's common for instructors to feel that since we aren't physically seeing students multiple times a week, we need to add assignments to ensure that students are "busy." There's also a sense that since we aren't delivering direct instruction live, students need more work to make an online course equivalent to a campus-based course. We often add additional assessments and activities (and content) to online courses with a false sense that more readings and assignments translate to a rigorous course. However, this often serves to increase only workload, not learning achievement. Ultimately, course learning activities and formative assessments should serve students by affording them opportunities to practice their learning, connect with peers in their learning community, and interact with you for crucial guidance and feedback.

Connecting Assessments and Activities with Presence and Community

In the Introducing HIDOC chapter we talked about how presence online stems from your course design and that the three key elements of a community of inquiry are social presence, cognitive presence, and teaching presence. In an online context, interaction does not happen organically, however...it must be purposefully designed into the course. This is why it is important to include assessments and activities designed for interaction, which fundamentally helps establish this learning community. Promoting interaction via online assessments and activities happens in three ways:

1. When students interact with one another (also called student-to-student or peer interaction, which relates to social presence)
2. When students interact with instructional materials (known as student-content interaction, which refers to cognitive interaction and engagement and relates to cognitive presence)
3. When students interact with their instructor (called student-instructor interaction, which relates to teaching presence)

Here we explore each of these elements in more depth.

Social Presence via Assessments and Activities

Recall that social presence is what allows your online students to feel as if they are part of a real learning community, rather than being isolated behind a computer, psychologically separated from their peers and professor. Social presence also relates to the rapport and trust that is built when students interact with each other (and their instructor), and provides the necessary foundation for cognitive exchange, authentic discussion, and the vulnerability embedded in asking for help. In general, assessments and activities that encourage personal reflection, disclosure, connection, and collaboration can enhance social presence. Social presence-elevating peer interaction also happens in course activities that may not be as obviously connected to learning, such as self-introductions done in the first week that help students get to know one another.

Ways to Promote Social Presence

Additional examples of assessments and activities that promote social presence and peer interaction include:

- Online synchronous breakout sessions for brainstorming or think-pair-share activities
- Engaging asynchronous discussions that promote critical thought and dialogue
- Group work done via wikis or other collaborative software
- Peer feedback and peer-to-peer teaching
- Role-playing and debate done through the discussion board
- An individual blog that students keep throughout the course where they post thoughts or reactions (usually in response to a prompt), and where peers can interact through comments or questions

When done well, these assessments and activities also promote cognitive engagement and cognitive presence in addition to social presence, so it's a win-win!

Cognitive Presence and Authentic Assessments

When we talk about students engaging with assessments, activities, or instructional materials, we're referring to cognitive engagement, which is related to cognitive presence, another key element of the Community of Inquiry framework. Both career-focused students and currently employed professionals are seeking relevance in their coursework, which is a primary way to heighten the cognitive appeal of an assessment or activity. Relevance can often be found through cognitively engaging "authentic assessments"—also referred to as performance, alternative, or direct assessments—which ask students to participate in activities that are worthwhile, significant, and meaningful, and focus on actions and artifacts relevant to their professional or personal lives. Authentic assessments differ from common assessments, like quiz or exam questions, in that they are less focused on a single, objectively correct answer and instead focused on effectively performing an authentic task and explaining or justifying the solution and barriers. Even if there is a single correct answer, authentic assessments are centered around multifaceted tasks that introduce complexity to problem-solving. They don't rely on remembering discrete pieces of information but instead are at the level of Application or above on Bloom's Taxonomy.

Examples of Authentic Assessments

Authentic assessments are frequently unstructured, complex problems that may have multiple solutions and require students to perform discipline-specific activities or procedures, drawing on a wide range of knowledge and skills. Some examples are:

- Well-designed lab experiments
- e-Portfolios
- Reflective writing
- Oral interviews
- Project-based work

For the instructor, authentic assessments provide diagnostic information about the ability of students to integrate and apply knowledge in various complex tasks and contexts. As well, online faculty often turn to authentic assessments to avoid proctored exams, which can be both expensive and stressful for students. (For more on exam proctoring, see the callout box below.) Keep in mind, though, that because of this complexity, authentic assessments often take more time to grade and should be well-timed so that students have future opportunities to hone their skills and performance. For more examples of authentic assessments, explore Jon Mueller's Authentic Assessment Toolbox referenced at the end of this chapter and on the HIDOC website.

More on Online Exam Proctoring

Online proctoring is typically done by third-party providers and ranges from automated options using artificial intelligence to live options where a proctor live monitors the student.

During the pandemic-induced Emergency Remote Learning of 2020–2021, proctoring became a hotly debated topic. Many students shared that they were unfairly targeted for cheating and that proctoring heightened their already elevated stress.

> Additionally, research shows proctoring might not be an effective aid for learning (Daffin & Jones, 2018; Prince, et al., 2009).
>
> However, we also know that many programs and professions require proctored testing, that many institutions use (or require) proctoring for academic integrity, and that it can be hard to avoid proctored exams in large-enrollment online courses. If using proctoring, then, be sure to tell students at the start of the course if there are any associated fees that they will need to pay, if they will need any special hardware or software (such as a webcam), and which exams are proctored. Additionally, share screenshots, make a screencast, or describe exactly what will happen during a proctored exam so students know what to expect, and explain to them how their privacy will be protected.
>
> To increase academic integrity on exams without utilizing proctoring, you can design timed exams and create a test bank, so students receive random questions and not one, set question list. Ultimately, you know your students and the discipline best and can decide if authentic assessments might offer an attractive alternative to ensure original student work without incurring the expense and stress of proctored exams.

Teaching Presence through Assessments and Activities

As mentioned previously, a primary function of formative assessments and learning activities is to provide opportunities for feedback and guidance. In doing so, they also provide one of the most vital ways that you will interact with your online students and, therefore, elevate your teaching presence. You might also record a short video discussing an upcoming assessment, create a screencast that walks students through an exemplar, or provide video, audio, or screencasted feedback. Providing feedback on coursework, responding to student questions, and facilitating an online discussion related to course content are all additional ways you interact with online students and are also crucial to federal policies related to instructor-student interaction in distance education.

More on Regular & Substantive Interaction

"Regular and substantive interaction" or "RSI" is an important Department of Education regulation that distinguishes a distance education course from a correspondence course—it also has big implications for federal financial aid. In short, RSI means that online instructors should be interacting with their students proactively, promptly, and on a scheduled basis, by providing direct instruction, feedback, information, or engaging in other instructional activities. We mention it here, as providing feedback is one of the most common and visible ways to interact with online students in a regular and substantive way.

If an instructor cannot demonstrate RSI, the course is classified as a correspondence, not a distance education, course. The financial impact is that the institution would have to return the federal financial aid received for that course, as the aid was predicated on it being an interactive distance education course. A different loss, however, is experienced by the student, who has taken an online class with a professor who never really showed up, engendering feelings of "students teaching themselves" and opinions that "online learning isn't good." Without you interacting with your students, everyone loses.

WCET, a national leader in policy for distance education, has covered this topic extensively. A link to RSI-related information is available in the references list (Downs, 2021), with additional resources available on the HIDOC website.

Inclusive Assessments

As an inclusive design strategy, also consider allowing for voice and choice in your activities and assessments whenever possible.

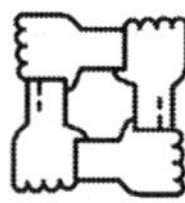

Voice and Choice

"Voice" refers to student empowerment in contributing opinions, ideas, and perspectives based on past experiences, frames of reference, and knowledge or interests. Voice is also related to social presence as it allows students to show up as their authentic selves and share their unique experiences and perspectives. A discussion prompt that promotes student voice, for example, might begin with phrases like: "Think about a time when you [felt like the character in the novel] or [had communication issues with someone you disagreed with] or [faced or observed workplace harassment] or [dealt with a difficult patient]." Voice activities also include journal assignments in which students reflect on and/or react to course materials, and learning activities where students identify topics they need additional help with, such as "Muddiest Point" activities or self-rating their level of understanding or confidence after completing a small task or sample problem.

"Choice" refers to opportunities within the course where students are able to make decisions about their learning, such as an assignment that provides three options for completion—a paper, a presentation, or a multimedia piece. Voice and choice are both enveloped in a presentation, essay, or research paper assessment where students can choose their topic or focus area. Incorporating voice and choice in course assignments and materials can provide students with learner agency and help to personalize learning—all of which can increase engagement. Voice and choice activities also recognize the diversity of your students—in terms of cultural background, skill set, thought/perspective, lived experience, and more—and allow them to choose how they demonstrate their learning achievement and mastery.

Voice and Choice Options

Below are some additional examples and ideas for incorporating voice and choice with activities and assessments:

Give options for how students complete assignments. For an assignment on a specified topic intended to have students to demonstrate that they can communicate factual information in meaningful ways, give students options for how to complete the assignment. They could, for example, write an essay, create a peer lesson designed to teach others, record an informative speech, or prepare a visual representation, such as a timeline or concept map.

Give options for artifacts to analyze. A prompt for writing an essay or research paper might allow for a student's choice of material, such as choosing the novel for an essay or choosing a course-relevant but individualized topic for a research paper.

Give options for how to answer exam questions. Allow students to choose different types of questions on an exam, such as multiple-choice, fill-in-the-blank, or essay. You might include instructions, for example, where they can select a certain number of questions from each type or choose a mix of questions that add up to a given number of points. Alternatively, you could provide a choice between two exam types: multiple-choice or essay.

Give options for types of exams. You could also have students submit quiz or exam questions and collaboratively create a question bank.

Give options for the look-and-feel of projects. In a design project, you might constrain materials while letting students determine the look and feel of the physical artifact or, similarly, provide parameters for the final product but give freedom as to the materials used to create it.

Alignment: CLOs and Assessments

While each CLO will be connected to at least one assessment, multiple CLOs can connect back to a given assessment, and multiple assessments may tie back to a single CLO. A common alignment challenge is CLOs that are not assessed or assessments that are not tied to any CLOs. This may indicate conflicting perspectives on the course design and a need to review the pedagogical goals. Another common type of misalignment between learning outcomes and assessments is when the CLO is relatively ambitious while the assessment for it measures a lower level of thinking/doing. For instance, if your learning outcome is "students will be able to critically analyze how themes of religion in Hamlet apply or do not apply in contemporary society," and your only related assessment is a few multiple-choice quiz questions on religious themes in Hamlet, then that is a misalignment. In this example, the relevant quiz questions might be considered a formative assessment, and you might choose to create a summative assessment that reflects the mastery level indicated in the CLO. Fortunately, you will rely on your Course Alignment Map, introduced at the end of Step 3, throughout the HIDOC process to ensure that you have design alignment.

Your Turn: Assessments & Activities

You've already done the hard part in determining what students should be able to do when they leave your course (Step 2), and you've identified a starting modular structure for your course (Step 3). It's time now to start to identify the formative assessments, summative assessments, and learning activities (collectively "assignments") at a macro level that align with those learning outcomes so students can work with their new knowledge and skills, receive feedback and support, and ultimately demonstrate their achievement and mastery. You will also continue the process of course design alignment. As you are working below, if you start to feel frustrated thinking certain assignments can't be done online, think about what makes them so effective and/or engaging in person and what learning outcomes they are tied to. It's often helpful to go back to your pedagogical goal: What do you want students to do, and why? Why is it important? Why is it relevant or useful to them? Thinking about the learning experience you want to create can help you avoid getting bogged down in specific logistics. Nearly all classroom-based activities and assessments can be done online in some fashion. Students can have discussions, write papers, explore case studies, complete problems, work on group projects, take quizzes, use wikis, create a blog, do public or private journals, create mind maps, have debates, role play, interpret results, interact with simulations, view or create graphics and videos, play educational online games…and more. As you go through the following steps, know that you aren't yet fully developing your assessments and activities, just writing a brief description of them.

The HIDOC process is recursive.

As you work on each Step, you will notice things that need to be tweaked or updated from earlier steps. Don't panic; this is to be expected. (We'd be more concerned if you made no edits as you went along!) In completing Step 4, for example, you may realize you need to revisit your CLOs and edit some of the active verbs you used to ensure that at least some of the outcomes ask students to apply their new knowledge in some way. You will revise accordingly as you continue to complete your Design Docs and Course Alignment Map.

Part 1: Summative Assessments

Reference your most updated module information and revised CLOs.

Your most updated list of course modules will be in the HIDOC Course Blueprint in the Course Alignment Map [MACRO VIEW] section, and your revised CLOs will be near the top of that same HIDOC Course Blueprint document in the Course Learning Outcomes (Step 2) section. If it is helpful, you can copy over the most updated module information to the Assessments & Activities Design Doc; otherwise, simply reference it. (Your CLOs are there for reference for now.)

Describe, or simply list, each of the summative assessments you think will be in the course.

Considering summative assessments within the course module structure is a natural starting place. It also helps to reference your revised CLOs, as those summative assessments will ultimately tie to one or more of your CLOs (and your CLOs will ultimately tie into one or more of your summative assessments). Start by determining where each summative assessment falls in the context of your course modules. Remember, these are typically larger assessments that happen at crucial times (e.g., mid-term and final) or after covering crucial topics. Examples of summative assessments include exams, cumulative reports, and project presentations. If you have a sense of where in the course structure you want to have a summative assessment but are unclear as to what the assessment should comprise, return to your CLOs to inform that decision. In some cases, the active verb that you used will suggest the type of assignment(s) you may need to have as evidence of outcome achievement.

For example,

- If students will be able to “identify” or “define,” you might consider exams.
- If they will be able to “apply” the information or “create” something new with it, they may be designing artifacts or writing project reports.

Part 2: Formative Assessments & Learning Activities

Now that you’ve identified your summative assessments, it’s time to identify the corresponding formative assessments and learning activities. Remember, it’s important that students get enough feedback from their formative assessments and enough practice from their learning activities to prepare them for their high-stakes summative assessments. In each module (or each week), students should be completing some type of formative assessment and/or learning activity, as this is a key part of RSI.

Describe, or simply list, each corresponding formative assessment.

Here, think in terms of scaffolding assignments and remember that types of formative assessments include timed quizzes, discussions, homework assignments, reflective essays, and individual components of larger projects. In identifying your formative assessments, make sure that students have sufficient opportunities to be evaluated with feedback that will help them prepare for their summative assessment.

Describe, or simply list, each corresponding learning activity.

To help determine some necessary places for learning activities in your design, reflect on assessments or even concepts that students often struggle with (or places you anticipate they’ll struggle if you’re designing a new course). Then, include more practice learning activities in these areas to provide additional guidance and instruction.

Part 3: Assessments and Learning Activities Check

Given your list so far of summative assessments, formative assessments, and learning activities, it’s time to think about both voice and choice and opportunities for interaction. For each summative assessment, formative assessment, and learning activity:

Identify which assignments could provide elements of voice and choice.

This can relate to students' ability to determine the type of assignment they do (choice) and/or opportunities for them to present their authentic selves within the assignment (voice).

Identify which assignments could be made interactive.

Having a learning community students feel connected to is vital. In an online course, more than in an in-person course, you will need to create opportunities for interaction and for elevating social presence. If you're designing a synchronous course, look at options for breakout room interactions. If you're designing an asynchronous online course, consider discussions, blogs, wikis or Google docs, or even reflective journals that allow for interaction between you and your students. If students currently submit a problem explanation to you, consider having them pair up and explain the problem to each other; paper drafts could become a great opportunity for peer review. And, as a learning activity, rather than students submitting assignment-related questions directly to you, consider making assignment-based threaded discussions where they discuss relevant topics with each other.

Brainstorm new possibilities for assignments that might lend themselves to voice and choice and/or interaction.

This is especially important to do if you do not have any (or many) items that lend themselves to voice and choice and/or interaction.

Part 4: Learning Outcomes Alignment

Ultimately you want to be sure that there is alignment between your summative assessments and your CLOs. Each CLO should be assessed by at least one summative assessment, and each summative assessment should align with at least one CLO.

Can you say yes to each of the following?

Each of my CLOs is assessed by at least one summative assessment.	[YES/NO]
Each of my summative assessments is aligned with at least one CLO.	[YES/NO]
The cognitive level of the active verb(s) in each CLO matches the cognitive level of the corresponding assessment(s).	[YES/NO]

If you could not answer yes for any of the items above, revise your CLOs and/or assessments accordingly. (Remember, if your CLOs are institutionally mandated, your only option may be to change your assessments.) If you are struggling to revise your CLOs and/or assessments so that they align, here are some additional tips and reminders:

- If you were unable to come up with good ideas for activities and assessments for a given outcome, it could be that the outcome needs to be deleted or modified.
- Likewise, if you have an assignment that you really feel needs to be in the course but is not aligned to any CLO, then you might need to create or modify a CLO.
- You might also find that some of your current CLOs are too detailed to be at the course level or that you have activities and formative assessments that align with the outcome but no summative assessments. In this case, consider if the current CLO is too detailed or most relevant to a "small," rather than big idea. These CLOs might end up being best suited for a module-level outcome (we'll talk more about module outcomes in Step 7), so delete them as a CLO, but save them for later.

Your Assessments & Activities

1. Open the **Assessments & Activities** Design Document from the companion website, use the version in the Design Doc Library section of the book, or create a version that works for you.
2. Work on the **Summative Assessments; Formative Assessments & Learning Activities; Assessments and Learning Activities Check;** and **Learning Outcomes Alignment** parts in the Design Doc, as discussed above.

You are now ready to fill out the second and third columns of your Course Alignment Map within the HIDOC Course Blueprint. This will be based on the work you did in both Step 3 and Step 4 to determine how your CLOs, modules, course assessments, and learning activities all connect. In Step 3, you identified a modular structure/layout for your course; now you will indicate which CLOs will be attended to in those modules, along with their accompanying assessments and learning activities.

HIDOC Course Blueprint: Course Alignment Map

Indicate which CLOs are addressed in each module.

In the second column of your Course Alignment Map, list only the CLOs (use the corresponding # to make things fit) that will be attended to in that module. Don't overthink this Step—if you are covering a topic or assigning work that relates to a CLO, then that CLO is aligned, even if it is not fully addressed. Most often, CLOs are attended to in more than one module, as students learn and practice various pieces.

Indicate which assessments and learning activities are in each module.

For each module, you now want to identify the summative assessments, formative assessments, and learning activities assigned. Use abbreviations that will make sense to you.

Your HIDOC Course Blueprint

1. Open the **HIDOC Course Blueprint** from the companion website, use the version in the Design Doc Library section of the book, or create a version that works for you.
2. Go to the **Course Alignment Map [MACRO VIEW].**
3. For each module in your course, fill in the second column, **Course LO's** (#'s or abbreviations) addressed (Step 4) and third column, **Assessments & learning activities** (Step 4).
4. If you made any edits to your CLOs, be sure to revise them in Step 2 of your **HIDOC Course Blueprint.**

Faculty-ID Collaboration

Feedback, Timing, and Cognitive Engagement

My assessments are the traditional mid-term and final, plus some quizzes leading up to each of those exams. I don't spend a lot of time on feedback because students don't actually read it. So, with the type of course I teach, I think my assessments are already defined and done.

You said something very interesting: your students don't read feedback. Tell me more about that...did you, for example, have different assignment types in the past, but felt students didn't get as much out of them?

Yes. I teach a course with a lot of terms that students need to know, so that's what they're tested on. This course is a prerequisite to the next course in the program, and students still seem to forget these terms by the next class, so I instituted more quizzes. In the past, I had them complete some different activities, but I found little difference in their exam scores, so providing feedback on them wasn't fruitful. Now they have the quizzes, which give them an instant read on how they're doing, which prepares them for the exam.

Ah, OK…this is all helpful history for me to know. Sometimes students do not put your good feedback into practice because they don't have the opportunity to do so. We can make sure that your assignments are spaced out well during the course so students have time to use your feedback for the next assignment. We can also work to ensure your assignments build on your students' growing knowledge in a sequential manner, which can sometimes give greater weight to your feedback—students will have multiple opportunities to show their gradual mastery of course topics.

You also mentioned that your course has a lot of terms and is a prerequisite for a more advanced class. Very often, I hear from instructors that students are not retaining knowledge from one course to the next, and I understand how frustrating that can be because you know that students learned and were assessed on that lower-level material, right? It makes it even more important that you have assessment types that really ensure lasting learning.

How would some types of assessments do that more than others, though? With terms, you're very limited in the types of assessments you can create, and I prefer objective measures that tell the student if they're providing the correct definition, for example.

One of the tactics we can employ for your assessments is asking students to do something with the terms—to apply them in some way or within some context. We can even incorporate this into quizzes and exams, building on the work you've already done. By applying the terms, however, students have a better chance to move the information from their working memory into their long-term memory, and that's what will help it "stick" for the next course they take in the sequence.

What are some assignment examples where they can apply terms, though? And what type of feedback would be meaningful? I'm not sure why they never used my feedback before. In the past, for example, I'd have some short-answer essay questions on the quizzes, which were not auto-graded, but students didn't seem to improve based on the feedback from those questions.

While it's true (and unfortunate) that some students don't utilize feedback, there are some things we can do with the type and timing of assessments to help encourage their engagement with feedback. Let's think first about the large amount of terminology in your course. Assignments that ask students to choose the correct definition from a list, for example, really tap those lower cognitive levels. We're asking, in a sense, if they remember the definition, but that doesn't necessarily mean they can apply the term in a meaningful way...and our goal is the latter. We can still create multiple-choice assessments, however, that are more application-based by starting with a scenario and asking students to apply the term in context, as one example. We can also introduce some engaging learning activities, so students have more opportunities to practice defining and applying terms in various contexts.

Let's talk first about types of activities and assessments that are cognitively engaging and also better help students retain information.

Faculty-ID Collaboration

Checking for Alignment

Can we talk about one of my learning outcomes? I'm teaching a public speaking course, and one of my learning outcomes is: By the end of this course, you will be able to put into practice the skills of active listening. How can I, or they, determine if they're practicing effective and active listening?

Great question! Tell me...how have you chosen to assess that outcome in the past?

I incorporate questions on both a quiz and their mid-term exam about what active listening is and how to be an active listener.

OK, that's great that you already have some relevant questions around active listening. But I understand your question even better now—being able to define and explain active listening is not the same as practicing active listening.

As an expert in active listening, how would you know if someone has that skill?

Well, they would effectively engage with all five stages of the listening process. Also, they would provide helpful feedback to the speaker, preferably at the "Reflecting" level, and be able to restate the speaker's message using their own words. It also involves paying attention to and appropriately interpreting the body language of the speaker.

That's fantastic! So it seems as though there are a few keys you're looking for in order to assess student mastery of active listening. First, you noted that "effectiveness" of their active listening skills is crucial, and you also broke it down into smaller, important components, such as: engaging in the 5-stage process, providing feedback where they can effectively render the message in their own words, and also appropriately interpreting speaker body language.

So, first, how about we tweak your learning outcome using the goals that you just outlined for me. Are you comfortable editing the outcome to read something like: By the end of this course, you will be able to define and demonstrate the process of active listening, including speaker analysis and listener feedback.

Yes! That sounds a bit more like what I need to see them actually do to demonstrate their active listening competency.

Great! Now let's identify some well-aligned activities and assessments for this outcome. Your existing quiz questions on active learning could be put into a low-stakes quiz that they could take multiple times if they'd like, with targeted feedback for incorrect answers that would guide them to re-engage with the relevant material.

For a formative assessment, one suggestion here would be to have them watch a speech and work in small groups to complete short-answer essay questions that would allow them to restate the message in their own words, analyze the speakers' body language, and respond to the message they received. Done as group work, that provides some great interaction and is also a way for students to discuss this new topic amongst themselves.

Finally, we could meet the needs of the summative assessment by including a "video question" on the mid-term or final. We could embed a short speech and then have short-answer essay questions where students could respond to demonstrate their competency in active listening. Additionally, or alternatively, we could build in active listening to speech evaluations and, depending on the depth and scope, this could be a formative or summative assessment. Do any of those sound like good ideas that would work well for you and your students?

Wow, absolutely! I love these ideas...I especially like the idea of including active listening as part of their peer evaluations for the three speeches each student has to give. I think the low-stakes quiz is a great idea to ensure they understand the definitions, usefulness, and general fundamentals of active listening. Then, let's use the speech evaluations as a method of formative assessment, and I'll use the "group work" idea as a class session since this is a hybrid course—that would be a great small-group activity to do together, as we could then debrief as a class as well.

Summary and Next Steps

To sum it up...

Assessments and learning activities are crucial in your course design to ensure you have identified the best assignments to measure your students' achievement of your CLOs, and to give students opportunities to practice their learning as well as get helpful feedback on their performance in order to improve. Remember, you want a mixture of summative assessments (high stakes, measuring performance), formative assessments (lower stakes, enabling students to get feedback on how they are doing and giving you feedback on areas they might be struggling with), and learning activities (low- or no-stakes, giving students practice learning opportunities). You also want to consider cognitive engagement and interaction, neither of which will spontaneously happen online and must be purposefully considered during design.

Looking ahead...

In the next chapter, we will discuss the different types of instructional content and materials for online courses, as well as determine when to "curate or create." Waiting until Step 5 to focus on content enables better course alignment and favors application and engagement over large amounts of material.

References

Daffin, Jr., L.W., & Jones, A.A. (2018). Comparing student performance on proctored and non-proctored exams in online psychology courses. *Online Learning,* 22(1), 131–145. doi:10.24059/olj.v22i1.1079

Downs, L. (2021, August 26). Regular and substantive interaction refresh: Reviewing & sharing our best interpretation of current guidance and requirements. WCET. https://wcet.wiche.edu/frontiers/2021/08/26/rsi-refresh-sharing-our-best-interpretation-guidance-requirements/

Mueller, J. (n.d.). Jon Mueller's Authentic Assessment Toolbox. http://jfmueller.faculty.noctrl.edu/toolbox/tasks.htm#types

Prince, D.J., Fulton, R.A., & Garsombke, T.W. (2009). Comparisons of proctored versus non-proctored testing strategies in graduate distance education curriculum. *Journal of College Teaching & Learning (TLC),* 6(7), 51–62. https://doi.org/10.19030/tlc.v6i7.1125

Schaffhauser, D. (2021, April 9). Students complain: Too much (busy) work in online classes. *Campus Technology.* https://campustechnology.com/articles/2021/04/09/students-complain-too-much -busy-work-in-online-classes.aspx

5 Instructional Materials

Step 5 focuses on strategies for instructional content and materials. Your course content should support your learners in doing well on your assessments, which also means that the content will align with your CLOs. Additionally, we encourage you to think about instructional content and materials in terms of higher levels of cognitive engagement (just as we discussed with your CLOs, assessments, and activities). This means that you want to think about your instructional materials as things that students "use" and "apply" rather than things they passively "consume" or "receive." Online instructional materials can include instructor-created material like topical lectures, screencasts, and process diagrams, as well as text-based content, such as digital handouts, study guides, and narratives or notes. However, you don't have to create every piece of content yourself and can utilize textbooks, publisher materials, journal articles, videos, websites, blogs, podcasts, film, photographs, diagrams, simulations, games, and more. You have an immense amount of vetted, high-quality digital content available, whether in the form of Open Educational Resources (OER), publisher materials, or publicly available educational content, such as educational videos and presentations on YouTube or TED-Ed.

Materials in an Online Context

Designing a course that privileges active learning over the passive receipt of content involves designing deliberate opportunities for interaction and presence (King, 1993). Providing engaging, aligned content elevates cognitive presence, especially when combined with application-based activities and assessments. Additionally, content selection is related to teaching presence—the content you select reflects your pedagogical approach while the content you create is unambiguously direct instruction from you. When selecting content for your online course, it first helps to understand some of the major ways in which the role of content differs online and to be alert to the risk of "overstuffing" your online course with instructional materials or links to other resources.

"Overstuffed" Online Courses

Direct instruction looks and happens differently in an online course, especially an asynchronous course. Your teaching is no longer organized around a discrete section of class time, and you're no longer physically present with your students as you deliver information and provide guidance. (Even if you are teaching an online synchronous course, you do not want to fill the entirety of that time with a passive "Zoom lecture.") Instead, you create and curate content that supports your activities, assessments, and CLOs.

And here is where many online instructors take a bit of a wrong turn—without the familiar schema of delivering direct instruction live, new online instructors focus on uploading or linking to large amounts of content, mistakenly thinking that this is the work of good online teaching and that this is what makes an online course rigorous (Schwegler, 2019). This tendency is due in part to an innate passion for the discipline (and its content), combined with the ease of being able to upload or link additional content in the LMS, all without being time-bound by the constraints of the in-person class. Additionally, it's natural for subject-matter experts to underestimate how long it will actually take students to read, watch, and listen to everything since they themselves can get through it so much more quickly.

Notably, though, the "overstuffing" tendency is also due to the reality that most of our teaching models and practices were (and still are) based in the on-ground modality. In the F2F classroom, direct instruction often takes the form of a lecture, which is frequently interspersed with student questions, examples, class discussions, and other activities. In an asynchronous online course, however, any "lecture" type of material is created and uploaded to the LMS prior to the course beginning. For faculty new to online teaching, this can bring questions (and anxiety) about their role: "If the bulk of my direct instruction is created and uploaded to the LMS prior to the start of the course, what is my role once the course begins? What does active teaching look like online if it doesn't include the commonly known and practiced strategies that require live lecturing, real-time Q&A, and discussion?"

You'll be happy to know that effective online teaching is not just grading and answering questions. You are the value-added portion of a high-quality online course. Active teaching (which we'll talk more about in the Bonus Chapter on Design Execution) includes the robust ways you'll interact with students as the course is running, such as providing timely, helpful feedback and additional guidance. Over the years, online student feedback and related research have shown that learners have a clear desire for a deeper connection to their professor rather than "more content" (Tanis, 2020). Students ask for more support and guidance and even express a longing for faculty-student mentoring and the type of relationship that they frequently receive in the in-person classroom. In fact, a frequent complaint by students in an online course that is not well-designed is "I feel like I'm teaching myself." What students are communicating here is that they miss you. They tend to feel this way when content is seen as something to just "upload" rather than something that is strategically chosen to support online student learning. Focusing on alignment can help you avoid this trap.

Instructional Alignment

First and foremost, your content selection should start with what your students will need to know to do well on your summative assessments. We specify summative assessments here because if you have instructional alignment between your summative and formative assessments and your learning activities, as well as your CLOs, then it is really only necessary to identify the instructional materials needed for your summative assessments at this point. Notice we said "needed."

Focusing on need-to-know items first is the best support you can give students for doing well, and also means that you have taken the time to prioritize the most important materials for them. When the amount of content exceeds the workload for the course, students either make tough decisions for what to leave behind or they try to do it all, which can lead to burnout and a heightened cognitive load that affects their learning and performance. Content that falls in the outer two rings is always a great fit for a folder of optional content that is relevant to that learning unit or for the overall course.

> ***When "need to know" instructional materials are not clear, students triage and make their own decision on what to read and what to skip. The danger in this is they might inadvertently skip something that is foundational or crucial.***

Inclusive and Accessible Course Content

Inclusivity and accessibility warrant attention in both in-person and online course environments. How they are approached, however, differs in the online class.

Inclusive Instructional Materials

When selecting and creating instructional materials, always keep inclusion and representation in the forefront of your mind. This may be more or less applicable, depending on your discipline—a history course referencing an ancient battle, for example, might not have representative aspects. However, consider (and investigate) if there was diversity at the time and whether it hasn't been acknowledged, represented, and discussed, whether in relation to marginalized peoples, ideas, or perspectives. For other courses, representation might come solely from the images and people you use in examples such as case studies, scenarios, or even visuals for digital slides. Below we discuss common instructional materials which can be made inclusive and representative.

Images

When using images for your online course, ensure that you're not portraying just one type of person or group. When choosing icons, photographs, and other visual elements, try to vary the gender, race, age, physical ability, and body type of people who are represented. When selecting images of couples or families, represent the full spectrum of families. It's not only important that all students see themselves represented, but also that they see others who aren't like them. So, while you can continue to use the image databases that you may already be familiar with, we encourage you to purposefully search for and use images that represent the diversity of the world we live in.

Authors/Scholars/Guest Experts

Also consider all the ways that course content can introduce diverse perspectives and examples, as well as demonstrate the diversity of scholars in the field. You yourself might not have been exposed to varied material based on the potential limited perspective or bias you received in your own program of study. It may take you seeking and exploring new and less-mentioned scholars or perspectives to offer a wider variety to your own students. This is also a great opportunity to reflect cultural inclusivity by sourcing and sharing work from minoritized cultures within the United States, as well as cultures and communities around the world.

Examples and Anecdotes

Many of us provide examples, create scenarios, or relay anecdotes as part of helping students better understand an idea or theory in practice. When doing so, be sensitive to the diversity of your students and their experiences by creating scenarios or stories that reflect various backgrounds and cultures. Move beyond frequently used generic names, such as "John" or "Jane," and expand to reflect culturally inclusive names, people, and experiences. Similarly, when referencing STEM practitioners, we encourage you to not always reference, for example, the hypothetical engineer or scientist as "he," even though, at present, most practitioners in your field might be male. Examples and anecdotes serve to portray "what is" but also help our students envision "what could be." If you must include content that shows stereotypes or is problematic in some way, acknowledge the shortcomings of the piece, and try to find or create improved content for the future.

Voice and Choice

We talked about voice and choice in Step 4: Assessments & Activities, and those concepts apply to content as well. Consider opportunities for students to choose what they learn or explore, such as ways in which they might source their own content (as part of their work). Here you would give options and guidance for curating and applying content, and any related parameters (such as using only scholarly sources, determining the source and bias of the work, and providing appropriate citations).

Content Warnings

Content warnings can help students prepare for, or avoid, interacting with material that is connected to past traumatic experiences for them. For example, a history course using a realistic and graphic re-enactment scene of a specific battle might include a warning for active or veteran military students who may be dealing with PTSD related to war. Similarly, detailed text or graphic visual depictions of sexual or physical assault can include warnings that are important for students who have been victims of domestic violence or rape. Content warnings do not change or dictate the content you provide—they merely allow students to mentally prepare to engage with materials that potentially pose a risk to re-igniting brain-based trauma. Some students may also use content warnings to drop courses that discuss topics that are too traumatic for them, or to proactively reach out to their instructor to discuss possible alternatives to certain content items.

Student Contributions

You might also include your students in the important work of finding and sharing inclusive and diverse content. Ask students to think critically about the content, especially on how it relates to their own experiences. Student-submitted content can be an optional or required activity or integrated directly into assessments, especially if you have learning outcomes related to critical thinking and relating topics to real-world situations and experiences.

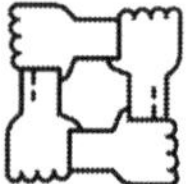

Accessible Instructional Material

Accessibility is, of course, not unique to online learning, but creating an accessible online course with accessible digital materials is. Just as in F2F courses, online courses are required by law to provide accessible materials to all students. In online, asynchronous courses, however, accommodations such as an in-class American Sign Language (ASL) interpreter aren't an option. We need to create or curate accessible materials from the start and be as proactive in that endeavor as possible. Remember: you cannot provide material to one student that is not accessible to all students. There are cases of online courses in which the instructor, due to content accessibility issues, was forced to re-design their course mid-term, when a student was unable to fully participate in the course.

If you build your course around non-accessible material, such as hours and hours of videos without closed-captioning or a publisher website that can't be read by a screen reader, you will need to either make that content accessible or remove it if you receive an accommodation request (which can happen at any point in the term). Even without an accommodation request, providing non-accessible material does not meet federal policies. If you are unsure how to approach this, reach out to your campus resources, such as the student accessibility services office. For more on accessibility for web-based content, explore the Web Accessibility Initiative (Education and Outreach Working Group, 2022). While you cannot anticipate every accommodation a student might need, you can attend to common accessibility facets as you're designing and developing your course.

Examples of Accessibility Practices

- Using explanatory alt-tags for images or long descriptions for complex graphics
- Providing access to larger versions of images
- Not using color to convey meaning
- Avoiding low-contrast visuals or text, or small font size
- Using built-in accessibility checkers like those in MS Word to ensure appropriate headings that can be read by a screen reader
- Not using html tables for content formatting
- When using tables to display data, having clearly identified headers and captions
- Using explanatory text for web links
- Providing videos that are closed-captioned
- Adding chapter markers to longer videos covering more than one topic
- Providing audio files with transcripts

Online learning has been especially powerful for students with certain disabilities because, in some cases, it has given them more educational opportunities than in-person classes. However, in addition to benefitting students with physical disabilities, such as blind or deaf students, accessible materials also benefit students with learning and/or psychological disabilities, which actually make up the majority of individuals seeking accommodations. These might include neurodiverse students, such as autistic individuals or those with ADHD or dyslexia; students with learning disabilities, such as audio-processing disorders; as well as students with anxiety or depressive disorders or PTSD.

Accessible material is also a fundamental part of inclusive design and educational equity. Rather than seeing accessibility as "one more thing to do," though, instead choose to view accessibility as a great opportunity to make course materials more helpful for all students. For example, an audio file might be used by a blind student and a student with dyslexia, but also by a working student who listens to the recording during their morning commute. In addition, the transcript for the audio file would be used both by students who are deaf or hard of hearing as well as students who prefer to annotate or highlight while listening to the material. Providing materials in different formats gives students options, so they can decide what works best for their physical, mental, and even lifestyle needs.

Accessible materials benefit all learners and are an issue of equity and inclusion. By law, content in your online course should be accessible. If you receive an accommodation request as your course is running, you must either make the content accessible or remove it from your course. Therefore, be proactive when designing your course and create or source accessible digital materials.

Sourcing Instructional Materials

When considering your online content, think both in terms of "curating" (finding and using created content) and "creating" (developing your own content), focusing on content that aligns with your CLOs and related assessments. The balance between curated and created content is often influenced by available time (creating your own content for every module will take much longer), plus the availability of quality, usable content. Today, the latter is much less of an issue than in the past, and there is plenty of curated content that is vetted, freely available, and accessible. An additional and important consideration is the cost of materials to students. To continue to increase affordable education options for students, choose quality materials that meet your needs and are free or low-cost whenever possible.

Consider the total time you want students to spend reading, listening to, and watching content in each module, as well as the total time you want them to spend on activities and assessments, and exploring, reflecting, and reviewing/comprehending (Beer, 2019). If you traditionally gave lectures in-person that summarized or repeated the textbook or other material, now is a great time to consider breaking that mold. If you source content that meets information needs, you can spend your time augmenting that content to add value via your knowledge and expertise. You can provide examples, walk students through problem-solving and critical thinking, or link the information to other course topics or real-world scenarios. Lastly, don't forget the benefit of "optional" or "supplemental" material, which can be grouped in a folder for interested students to explore further.

Curating

Curating content means exploring and examining existing digital content for use in your online course. Just as you might have previewed several textbooks before selecting one for a F2F course, becoming a curator of online content allows you the opportunity to explore vetted, free, and available content, which you then select and organize within your course. In what follows, we provide suggested steps for curating content for your online course.

1. ***Clarify what you are looking for.*** First, narrow down your search to keywords or topics. You might also be looking for a specific type of content, such as a multimedia or audio piece for a very text-heavy course.

2. ***Use databases and search engines to find appropriate and relevant content.*** Below we list some places to explore and also recommend you work with your institutional librarians, as they can provide expert help in sourcing content specifically for your course topics.

3. ***Evaluate content.*** When examining a piece of content, ask yourself if it is:
   - On-topic, meaning addresses the information you need students to know?
   - Aligned with your outcomes and assessments?
   - Cognitively engaging? Is the information presented well and in an interesting and easily understood manner? Does it also provide relevance?
   - A type of content you don't have a lot of? Look to balance text-based pieces with other forms, such as multimedia.
   - Easy to access and use? Anything students will have to create an account to access might be a barrier (or a security risk).
   - A cognitively digestible amount, or can it be "chunked" up? You can also assign short segments of longer pieces.
   - Accurate and vetted? Many states and organizations have available course content that has been vetted by academic instructors and subject matter experts.
   - Accessible? If it is screen-based text, ensure that it can be read by a screen reader. Use captioned videos and accessible websites and images. If you're unsure, check with your institutional office for student accessibility.
   - Inclusive or expansive? Does it represent the diversity of people and thought on the topic, or does it introduce a new or diverse perspective?

4. ***Make sure you have permission to use.*** Look for a Creative Commons license, for example, and/or check in with your library for copyright information. Note the citation that will go along with the content, as you will need that when you begin to develop your course in the LMS. Unless you have created the material yourself, work with your librarian to determine if you need to explicitly cite it. Most sourced content elements, including images, need a citation unless your source allows it to be used without attribution. In general, even if you are explicitly

allowed to include someone else's material without citation, it is best practice to acknowledge the source.

5. ***Save the content.*** If you discover good content as you are thinking through your course design, save it, ideally organized and/or named by the module in which students will use it. Be sure to also keep track of web links that you plan to include. (Keep in mind that for any content that exists only as a web link, you will need to check that the link works every time you teach the course. Because links frequently break, having a backup in mind is often useful.) This will save you a lot of time when you then move to develop your course in the LMS; saving files with the name that will appear in the course can be a timesaver as well. It is a good idea, however, to not derail your design process by trying to source all your content at this time; save most of that work for the development phase. You might waste time finding content, for example, that you will end up not using. It's also very easy to fall down the "rabbit hole" of interesting content and delay finishing the design of your course.

Searching for Online Content

Here are some common places to search for online instructional content.

- Open Educational Resources (OER) from sites such as OER Commons
- Publisher materials that often include test bank questions, presentation slides, handouts, and links to other web-based materials
- Articles from academic journals
- Articles from relevant newspapers and magazines
- Discipline-specific websites or groups
- E-books and e-textbooks
- Films, TV, and video
- Interviews
- Museum websites
- Podcasts

- Ted talks/TED-Ed talks
- YouTube videos
- How-to and instructional content from sites such as LinkedIn Learning, Khan Academy, MERLOT, and PHET (great for STEM)

Creating

Creating content means creating content yourself, usually from scratch. Instructor-created content is typically in one of five forms: narrated presentation/video lecture, screencast, webcam video, audio file/podcast, or text-based document. Some content will be multimedia and include more than one of these forms.

Instructor-Created Content

Here are some common examples of instructor-created content.

- An online "lecture," often consisting of narrated, recorded presentation slides, uploaded as a video file for students to watch
- Screencasts demonstrating a process, solving a problem, or using a piece of software
    - Screencasts use software that records your computer screen and your voice and can even record your mouse movement. Common types of screencasting applications include Screencast-O-Matic, Camtasia, and Kaltura.
- Recorded interviews with subject matter experts and/or practitioners
- Documents created as study guides, takeaway handouts, or reading guides
- Audio files that students can listen to from anywhere—like a podcast for your online course! This is a great option if there are no relevant visuals for what you're talking about or if you want to provide commentary on other material in the module.
- A short webcam video for your instructor introduction or very short videos that add on to course information as it's running

- Weekly announcements and module introductions as short videos
- A combination of these methods, such as lectures with embedded screencasts

Below is a visual that shows the most common types of instructor-created material, crossed with the most common usages of material in online courses. Some of these usages, such as assignment feedback, are not content you'd create prior to the course beginning, but are included here to demonstrate additional uses for content types. You can see that most boxes are checked—the overall message here is that there are a variety of types and uses for instructional material, as well as a select few cases in which a certain type should not be used.

	Course & Module	Lecture Materials	Announce-ments	Assignment Feedback	Assignment Overviews
Short webcam video (<5 min)	✓		✓	✓	✓
Audio	✓	✓	✓	✓	✓
Screencast	✓	✓		✓	✓
Video lecture (<15 min)	✓	✓			✓
Text-based content	✓	✓	✓	✓	✓

We'd also like to note here that uploading a "talking head" (webcam) lecture recording is usually not the best option. Research shows that students have less focus and more mind wandering for webcam lectures versus a lecture format that includes at least some slides that show visuals and text to reinforce what you're saying, or a presentation that shows slides plus your thumbnail image, in a "picture-in-picture" style. Uploading a recording of you delivering a lecture to a F2F class is generally not a best practice either, as it can suggest to your online students that your teaching is largely focused on your F2F students. It can also showcase in-person interactions between you and your F2F students when there are no similar opportunities for your online learners. While some online students may be used to this "recorded live lecture" approach and not mind it, we encourage you to consider augmenting any long videos of you teaching to your in-person students with at least some material that is specifically created for your online learners. Additionally, if you are going to post a recorded lecture from a previous F2F class, it's best practice to at least include markers or pause points, so students can more easily go back and review certain sections.

Your Turn: Instructional Materials

At this point in the process, you'll start to identify which instructional materials will best support learning throughout the course. Remember the idea at this point in the process is not to create or curate these materials but to identify and describe in more detail what types of materials are needed.

Reference your most updated modules, assessments, and activities.

Your most updated list of course modules, assessments, and activities will be in the HIDOC Course Blueprint in the Course Alignment Map [MACRO VIEW]. If it is helpful, you can copy over this information; otherwise, simply reference it.

Describe the learning function of the content/material that students need to be successful in this module.

Here you are not selecting where you will get the material (e.g., "textbook") but instead the types of instructional material they will need to be successful in this module. (e.g., "description of photosynthesis," "overview of the first law of thermodynamics," "worked examples of evaluating limits," "transcript of King's 'I have a dream' speech")

③ ***Provide specific information about the source for this content.***
Do you already have a piece of content that meets the need, do you need to find/curate it, and/or do you need to create it? Be as specific here as possible, e.g., if you already know the chapter, have a link to an OER, or have the lecture slides.

④ ***Evaluate content inclusivity.***
In terms of representation, examples, and sources, is this material inclusive? If not, is there a way to curate or create more inclusive content?

⑤ ***Evaluate content accessibility.***
Is this material already accessible, or can it be made accessible with transcripts or other additional elements?

Your Instructional Materials

1. Open the **Instructional Materials** Design Document from the companion website, use the version in the Design Doc Library section of the book, or create a version that works for you.
2. Work on the **Instructional Materials** part in the Design Doc, as discussed above.

Now that you've identified your instructional materials and content corresponding with your assessments and modules, it's time to move the key information to your Course Alignment Map in the HIDOC Course Blueprint.

Your HIDOC Course Blueprint

1. Open the **HIDOC Course Blueprint** from the companion website, use the version in the Design Doc Library section of the book, or create a version that works for you.
2. Go to the **Course Alignment Map [MACRO VIEW].**
3. For each module in your course, fill in the fourth column **Content & Instructional materials** (Step 5).

Online Topical Lectures

While online lectures are technically not part of course design since they pertain to the actual development of materials, let's pause to have a brief discussion about how you can rethink and retool your F2F lectures for your online classroom. Most of us have slides or notes created for our classroom-based lectures, and it's very common to want to simply record an hour-long lecture using those slides, upload it to the LMS, and call it done. However, listening to a lecture in person typically does not mean listening to an instructor talk for an hour…non-stop. It's common practice to pause, ask for questions, give additional clarification, provide examples, or insert a class discussion or other activity. This is why watching a lengthy recorded lecture online is wholly different from interacting with an instructor during a classroom-based lecture. In addition to pretty much ensuring students have a passive learning experience, lengthy lecture videos have other issues online as well, such as technology problems with streaming long videos, accessibility issues if videos are not closed-captioned or have poor audio, and brain-based learning issues, as the adult brain is not efficient in dealing with large/long pieces of new information without pausing intermittently to do something with that information. Does this mean that you need to simply scrap those in-person lectures and start completely from scratch? Thankfully, no! Ideally, though, you'll have time to storyboard out your lecture and then create or select the slides that fit your vision. We suggest your topical lecture videos be less than 15 minutes.

Steps to Create an Online Topical Lecture

The strategies below will help you rethink and retool your lecture approach (including rethinking your presentation slides) for the online classroom. We encourage you to read through this process but not get derailed by it by trying to re-envision your classroom-based slide decks right now. Remember that we're still at a more macro-level as we design the pedagogical blueprint for your course… Creating discrete digital items right now is not a good time investment until you've finished your Course Blueprint and know what items you absolutely need to create. Instead, return to this section of the book when you begin developing materials.

1. ***Determine the topical focus of the lecture.*** Start by thinking about your online topical lecture as a short video that is focused on a discrete topic. You might have one topical lecture per module, more than one, or none at all if relying solely on sourced material for that module.

2. ***Decide on key points.*** List 1–5 main points or sub-topics that you want to cover, and think of these as the discrete takeaways you want for students. Establish a clear learning goal for a block of learning, and make sure you are adding information, explanation, or clarification instead of summarizing or repeating other content in that module. If you are paring down a long lecture, think of it as "chunking"—break the lecture into smaller, discrete, topically focused bites that are easier for a brain to digest.

3. ***Sketch it out.*** Next, sketch out your slides, storyboard-style. You can use the Bonus Development Doc we walk you through below, or even use several sticky notes, each representing one slide. Borrowing from the Beyond Bullet Points and visual storyteller approach by Cliff Atkinson, each slide should ideally focus on a single idea. You want to break information into a logical sequence of small, connected units. Sketching and sequencing your slides before you create them can save you a lot of time, trial, and error, as you'll go into the creation with an organized plan.

4. ***Write a script.*** Then, write a script for each slide (if you're using MS PowerPoint, you can use the Notes section below the slide for this task and can also, then, export the slide with the Notes script as a PDF so students can use it for review). Many faculty are very resistant to the idea of writing a script as they fear they'll sound rehearsed, and maybe

they already feel confident in their extemporaneous speaking abilities honed after years in the F2F classroom. But recording a video for online direct instructional purposes is really nothing like speaking "live." Writing a script serves four very important functions: (1) It reduces filler words like "um," "uh," or "and," which can leave you sounding unsure or unprofessional. (2) Since each video lecture is short, it allows you to say precisely what you want to say. Writing, reviewing, and editing a script gives you a new perspective of the organization, flow, and conciseness of your lecture. (3) Editing your videos is immensely easier if you have a script. Without a script, you'll need to extemporaneously re-do either the whole video or a single slide (the latter can be done only if the software allows it and you have the skills to do basic editing work). (4) Additionally, as mentioned, the script can then become your transcript, which can be shared with your students and also used to speed up closed-captioning work.

5. ***Reinforce with visuals.*** Take advantage of the media-rich atmosphere of the online classroom by creating slides that are more visual in nature. Just as you don't want to "read" your slides when you use presentation software in the F2F classroom, you don't want students reading your slides when they're watching your video lecture. We can typically read faster than we can speak, so if you're merely repeating what is on a text-heavy slide, your students are reading ahead and likely not listening to you. (If you start to create your slide deck and can't get away from using a lot of text, consider if you should be making a handout or other written piece instead. There are many avenues for creating instructional material, so don't create a visual presentation if you want to convey something that is best done in a text-based format.) Visuals should reinforce what you are saying, as you're then able to tap two information channels for the learning brain. A visual might be a relevant diagram or chart, but it can also just be an image that causes the information to better "stick" in students' minds.

6. ***Elevate cognitive engagement.*** Lastly, consider ways to elevate cognitive engagement so that both you and your students can be active participants in your online lecture. Ideas include:

   a. *Tell a story.* You can talk through a case study or scenario or even share anecdotes and experiences from your professional work and that of colleagues. Stories "stick" because our brains are usually pre-wired to the story format, based on the foundation we received growing up with bedtime stories and books.

b. *Stop and ask.* Pause and ask a question, and give students a short time to answer. Your question during the lecture could ask them to recall, apply, or reflect on a piece of information, and the lecture could then be followed with a quiz. Or, if you have software that allows, you can put these interactive questions in the video itself.

c. *Create an intentional error.* This works especially well if you are showing and describing a process or solving a problem. If there was material, such as a textbook chapter, that students should have read before watching your lecture, include an "error" in the process or problem, and ask students to identify what was wrong and how they'd fix it (just like above, this can lead to an actual assigned activity). Another way to approach this is similar to the "two truths and one lie" game, where you might write several facts on a slide, with one of them being incorrect. These tactics are also great if you're doing synchronous lectures, and students can answer via a poll or be sent into breakout rooms to discuss the error.

d. *Provide relevant examples.* Our brains love relevance when we're learning! Especially if you're creating a lecture to augment information from a textbook or other source, provide examples that are from your students' perspectives. You can relate course information to students' everyday experiences, lived experiences, or future experiences.

e. *Create a screencast.* As another idea to promote engagement, you can include a screencasted portion or replace a given lecture with a screencast. As mentioned, a screencast records your computer screen, including your mouse movements, as well as your voice. It's a great option for demonstrating a process, walking students through how to use a software application, solving a problem, or showing how something works.

If this seems like a lot of work, you're right—it absolutely is. When it comes to creating topical lectures for an online course from slides used in in-person class lectures, consider this quote from Cliff Atkinson, author of Beyond Bullet Points:

"It's hard work to take a fresh look at your ideas, to reformat them so they connect with your audience, and to simplify them to their essence. These are not things you can do with a 'quick fix' – you have to be committed and willing to see the process through" (Atkinson, 2005). Keep in mind, though, that unlike in-person lectures that you deliver anew each semester, these shorter topical lectures, when done well, can usually be used for a few years before you'll need to update them.

Lectures in Hybrid and Online Synchronous Courses

You may be wondering if selecting or creating content looks different for hybrid and synchronous online courses, as opposed to asynchronous courses. Perhaps surprisingly, there are not that many differences in best practice for asynchronous courses versus other online modalities in terms of instructional materials. Here are some reasons why:

- For all modalities, you still build your own preferred balance of "curated" and "created" instructional materials, and you still want to choose cognitively engaging content that is aligned with your assessments and learning outcomes.
- Most multimedia can be streamed online or shown in a F2F classroom, and many classrooms are already taking advantage of web-based tools and content.
- Both hybrid and online synchronous courses (ideally) have an associated course site in the LMS. Both of these modalities can also choose to use the flipped pedagogical approach wherein students watch lectures on their own and during the synchronous components (whether in-person or through web conferencing) engage in other activities. If done as a flipped course, then, the bulk of the content would be in the asynchronous LMS course site, just as it would for a 100% asynchronous course.
- Lastly, if instructors will be using live class time to deliver instruction, the same rules of lecture best practices apply: chunk up your lecture into small, "brain-digestible" bites and pause after each portion to respond to questions, engage the class in discussion, and/or do an applied or reflective activity.

 Your Online Topical Lectures

In this Bonus Development Doc, we walk you through one way of sketching out a topical lecture.

Provide a relevant title.
Remember, each topical lecture should correspond to one major topic.

Add context and connections.
You can help students connect with the lecture by relating it to previous course topics, being clear with the related learning goal(s), and indicating which assessments it supports.

3. ***Identify the main points/ideas.***
Your lecture will likely be broken down into key points (or steps if you are demonstrating problem-solving), so note them here. This is a general, short summary of what the lecture is about.

4. ***Explain/notate each main point.***
Delineate each main point, and provide sub-points or a short explanation for what you plan to say for each one.

5. ***Identify relevant visuals.***
For each main point, identify corresponding visuals that can help make your explanation more powerful. Remember, video and slides should be more visual than text-based materials.

Your Online Topical Lectures 

1. Open the **Online Topical Lectures** bonus development document from the companion website, use the version in the Design Doc Library section of the book, or create a version that works for you.
2. Work on the **Online Topical Lectures** part as discussed above.

Faculty-ID Collaboration

Why Don't We Start with Content?

I'm thrilled that I'll finally have an opportunity to teach this course online! I've taught it face-to-face for six years now, but I have all the content you'll need already in the LMS because I upload my lecture slides there for them to review. What else do you need from me to create the online version of the course?

Oh, that's great! Thank you so much having these existing materials handy. However, I'm going to ask you to trust me a bit and to mentally just "set aside" your existing content for now. I'd really like to start with your performance outcomes for students, and then we'll discuss your ideas for assessments and activities that align with those outcomes.

OK... I've heard from colleagues that you're a great ID, so I'll put my faith in the process since design is not something I'm an expert on. But help me understand why we can't just start loading this stuff up now to save time, even as we're working on other parts of the course?

Very good question! In part, I want us to mentally "step back" from what the course is now because many course improvements come through fresh eyes and collaborative dialogue, as well as a willingness to consider the course for today's students—which may not be the same demographic you had five or ten years ago. Additionally, the online modality is very different from the classroom-based one, and even the most successful in-person courses don't benefit from "migrating" the course online—moving to the online modality necessitates a rethinking.

The other reason I'm asking you to set aside your existing content for now is that we'll likely use much of it, so there's no need to jump in now and waste the opportunity to start with a fresh perspective. We're going to focus much of our work on aligning your course design, which means ensuring that your crucial course components, like content, assignments, and outcomes, support one another appropriately. Your content supports your assignments, which provide evidence students have achieved your learning outcomes, so that's where our work begins.

Ah...OK. That makes sense to me, and I feel better knowing that we're not just going to throw away all of the content and assignments I have now. I also think I brought the content because I assumed that that's what you did: upload and organize content. But I understand that we're going to do a "real" design process, which is actually more interesting!

I think so, too! I appreciate your willingness to give the design process a chance. I promise that none of your hard work will go to waste. Just because we don't want to "migrate" or "transfer" your F2F course online doesn't mean we won't be using a lot of the materials you've already created or sourced.

Summary and Next Steps

To sum it up...

While it can be tempting in the online class to upload all the content you think is relevant and useful, we encourage you to be more selective since you can easily "overstuff" a course. Additionally, strongly consider curating some high-quality, digital, educational content and not creating all of the instructional materials yourself. Any material you use for your online course should be aligned, cognitively engaging, accessible, and inclusive/representational.

Looking ahead...

Next, we consider the role of technology and tools in your online course. We start with the standard learning management system (LMS) and then look at other tools, both general and discipline-specific, that you might need to integrate into your online course.

References

Atkinson, C. (2005). Beyond bullet points: Using Microsoft PowerPoint to create presentations that inform, motivate, and inspire. Microsoft Press.

Beer, N. (2019) Estimating student workload during the learning design of online courses: Creating a student workload calculator. In R. Orngreen, M. Buhl, & B. Meyer (Eds.), Proceedings of the 18th European conference on e-learning ECEL 2019 (pp. 629–638). Academic Conferences and Publishing International Limited.

Education and Outreach Working Group (2022, March 31). Introduction to web accessibility. W3C Web Accessibility Initiative (WAI). https://www.w3.org/WAI/fundamentals/accessibility-intro/

King, A. (1993). From sage on the stage to guide on the side. *College Teaching,* 41(1), pp. 30–35.

Schwegler, A.F. (2019). Academic rigor white paper 1: A comprehensive definition. *Quality Matters.* https://www.qualitymatters.org/qa-resources/resource-center/articles-resources/ academic-rigor-white-paper-part-one

Tanis, C.J. (2020). The seven principles of online learning: Feedback from faculty and alumni on its importance for teaching and learning. *Research in Learning Technology.* https://doi.org/10.25304/ rlt.v28.2319.

6 Technology & Tools

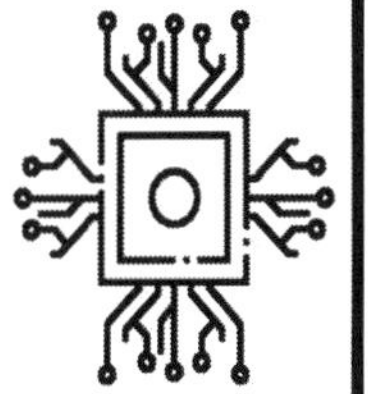

Although the HIDOC model prioritizes pedagogy over technology, technology and tools are a necessity for your online course. The purpose of Step 6 is to focus on selectively choosing aligned educational technology and tools that support both learners and your pedagogical goals...without adding confusion, frustration, or barriers.

Technology, Tools, and Your Context

In the context of HIDOC, technology refers to the software, hardware, and LMS tools that you use to support your students' learning. Most often, for higher education, online learning tools are packaged within a learning management system (LMS), sometimes called a course management system, such as Canvas, BlackBoard, Brightspace, or Moodle. Most LMSs offer similar features and functions, and we'll cover the most common tools here. You might also have options for publisher platforms (e.g., Pearson MyLab, McGraw Hill Connect), web-conferencing software (e.g., Zoom, WebEx), and proctoring options (e.g., Proctorio, Honorlock) supported by your institution. We are assuming here that you have access to tools that enable the sharing of digital content (including audio, video, and text) with your students as well as a student roster, asynchronous discussions, email, and a gradebook. You will want to determine which LMS and/or online course platforms your institution uses, as well as your learning technology support options.

While we will discuss some tools by name as examples, in general, ***we try not to focus on specific technologies***. As we all know, technology can change rapidly! If we focused on "name-brand" technology, that advice might be obsolete in a few years. For example, by the time you are reading this book, there may be a new LMS or web-conferencing platform on the scene or one of those mentioned above may have been rebranded under a different name. (Bonus points for those who remember ANGEL, WebCT, or Elluminate Live!) We also strongly encourage you to use tools supported by your college or university.

Reasons to Use Institutionally Supported Technology

- You do not want to become the Help Desk and have to do technology troubleshooting.
- Institutionally supported technology often has additional resources, such as tutorials or training.
- Using institutionally supported technology can mean free or low-cost options that save students money.
- There are privacy issues embedded with technology use, and if you are using a non-institutional technology, chances are that you (not the institution) will be liable for any privacy or security issues.
- It can also be challenging (if not impossible) to determine if a piece of technology not supported by your school meets accessibility requirements without having access to specialized knowledge and equipment, such as a screen reader.
- Technology can be a rabbit-hole/time-sink, and we've seen many faculty lose precious design time while researching and test-driving the latest web-based tool rather than using an already vetted and supported tool.

Therefore, we'll cover what you need to understand and consider when choosing technology that supports your design, and we'll highlight the most common technology tools and types while minimizing the focus on a specific LMS or software.

> ***Remember to put pedagogy before technology because technology changes constantly while good course design does not.***

Types of Technology and Tools

Below are some common technology and tools; what your students will need will depend on the specific design of your course.

Common LMS Tools

- Modules/Folders
- Content (text, audio, video)
- Assignments/Drop Boxes
- Gradebook
- Quizzes
- Discussion Boards
- Blogs, wikis, journals
- Email
- Roster/People
- Groups/Teams

Common Software

- Word processing applications
- Spreadsheet applications
- Presentation tools
- Suites inclusive of the tools mentioned above
- PDF readers
- Video recording
- Video players

Discipline-Specific Software

- Statistical analysis software
- Computer programming/web design
- Computer-assisted design
- Art and graphic design programs
- Video and audio production programs
- Apps for specific content practice and quizzes
- Virtual labs or simulations

Hardware & Peripherals

- Video camera and/or webcam
- Microphone
- Headphones
- VR Goggles
- Lab kits or equipment
- Remote access to instruments or simulators

Other Options Potentially Supported by Your Institution

- Publisher materials, activities, platforms
- Web conferencing
- Video streaming and captioning
- Proctoring options
- Plagiarism check options
- Tutoring options
- Adaptive learning systems
- Library tools and subject or course guides

Common Assessment and Activity Tools in the LMS

Here we highlight and briefly discuss the most common assessment and activity tools typically found in the LMS. The following tools may be called something else or your LMS might have different options, but most LMSs have the functionalities listed below.

- **Quizzes/Exams:** Most LMSs have plenty of options and settings for quizzes and exams so that you can enable students to take a quiz more than once (for example, retake until they get a certain score) or have extended time for completion. As discussed in Step 4, quizzes and exams can also be created as timed summative assessments or offered as open-note formative assessments or even as practice learning activities with no time limit and unlimited attempts. If your LMS provides the option for you to input feedback for answers, take advantage of this great opportunity! Wrong answers can direct students back to relevant material to review, and correct answers are the perfect place to give kudos. Both correct and incorrect answers provide opportunities for motivational feedback as well.
- **Discussion Boards:** Discussion boards are a good option for asynchronous discussions and even peer feedback and evaluation, but they are frequently misused. Discussions are best when you have an activity that requires an initial thoughtful post or question, a meaningful reply from students, and a communication exchange with a purpose. Examples of this include students sharing their thoughts and opinions with each other; collaborating to apply course material on scenarios or case studies; taking sides in a debate; or helping each other with problem-solving assignments. If a reply doesn't add to the assignment, consider another tool instead. (For more on how the discussion tool has been misused in the past, see the callout box that follows this section.)
- **Blogs:** The blog tool in the LMS is like any web-based blog in that students (or student groups) can share information, opinions, comments, ideas, reactions, and thoughts and can add new entries as the course progresses. It's also a good tool for empowering students to become content creators, as blog submissions are viewable by the whole class, and peers can add comments. Most often, commenting is optional, but if your LMS does not have this tool, you can use the discussion board

and allow for optional commenting if you'd like. This is a great tool for single/smaller assignments, group assignments, as well as a larger assignment that spans the length of the course. For example, students in a horticulture class can find plant examples in their local area that reflect that week's genus/classification and carry it out as a project that spans the entire course. Students in a political science or history class can keep a blog that relates weekly readings to current politics.

- **Wikis:** Whether through an LMS wiki tool or a cloud-based tool such as Google docs, wikis allow students to collaboratively create a paper, presentation, or other type of project. They provide a shared workspace that also provides transparency into the creation of the project, so group members and you can see who contributed, what was contributed, and when. This is a great way to reflect individual efforts, for example, in a group project grade. For larger group projects, get teams together early on and have them come together for smaller assignments or even sequential pieces of the larger assignment. This allows them to create rapport and trust among the team, while also learning the technology incrementally.
- **Journals:** Journals are a phenomenal tool for reflection and also offer a private space for instructor-student interaction and connection. Close a topic with a reflective journal analysis to provide students a way to reflect on their own learning gains, revisit their assumptions, challenge their own thinking, or even provide private feedback to you about course concerns, barriers, or remaining questions. You can also use journals for brief activities that mimic the "Muddiest Point" or "One-Minute Papers" that you might have used in F2F courses. Research has shown that depth of reflection typically increases if it's a regular activity, and many faculty use this tool to close out a module or discrete topic and end the learning cycle (Stice, 1987). If your LMS doesn't have a specific journal tool, you can simply have students turn in a reflection as an assignment.

A Note on the LMS Discussion Tool

Many of us remember the earlier days of online learning when the use of discussions was ubiquitous! In many ways, a lack of understanding about how to engage and interact with students online led instructors to think that asynchronous discussions were the best, or sometimes the only, option. However, most of us made a crucial error by using the classroom/F2F discussion as the model for asynchronous discussion. Asynchronous discussions—and the questions that generate those discussions—function very differently (Lieberman, 2019).

We'd likely never ask a question in a F2F class and force every student to answer individually, would we? We also wouldn't tell our campus-based students that their answer has to be unique from their peers (even though there weren't that many "unique" answers that could be generated). Additionally, it's unlikely that a F2F instructor would tell students that they each had to reply to at least two peers by giving a "substantive response" that wasn't just "I agree/disagree."

We wouldn't do that, because that's not how discussion works in real time. Similarly, that's also why a real-time discussion prompt doesn't work well in an asynchronous course. But, all too often, that's exactly what we do when we transfer a F2F question to the asynchronous online classroom. Campus-based discussion prompts are largely designed as a jumping-off point to stimulate a class-wide discussion, where a handful of students respond, or as small-group or paired discussion, often with a report-out to the whole class. However, when we use a question generated for an in-person discussion and try to have an asynchronous discussion with it, it most often falls flat, and is a big underlying reason why so many faculty and students dislike online discussions.

When considering discussions for your online asynchronous course, consider options like small-group discussions—you can have each small group discuss the same or a unique question, then "report back" to the larger group. This type of assignment is also ripe for reading a case study or scenario and discussing potential solutions before presenting one, along with justification/explanation, for the class. Discussions can also be used for role-playing, such as presenting a hospital scenario in a nursing class and assigning students different roles (e.g., doctor, nurse, patient,

patient advocate, hospital administrator) to enable perspective-taking and teamwork. Take-sides debates, great for political science, philosophy, history classes and more, are also great discussion board activities, as is peer evaluation and feedback on paper drafts and topic ideas.

Minimizing Cognitive Load

We already discussed the importance of privacy, accessibility, and cost in determining which technologies to use and how going with institution-supported tools is generally the best approach. Another important consideration when choosing technology and tools is cognitive load (Sweller, 2011). It can be a mistake to assume that all or most of your students are "technology fluent." New tools might have a huge learning curve for some of your students, causing them frustration, demotivation, and extra time spent on non-topical learning. Because the human brain has limits on how much new information it can deal with at once, this can impact the amount of "working brain bandwidth" students have left to spend on learning new course material. Fortunately, there are specific things you can do to minimize unnecessary cognitive load when introducing technology and tools to your students.

Ways to Minimize Cognitive Load

Offer low-tech options if applicable. When the learning outcome doesn't involve learning the technology itself, you can offer low-tech alternatives.

- For example, you might have a Mind Map or Concept Map assignment, so you seek out software that will help students create that. You might suggest software that tech-savvy students or those with time to learn new software could use, but also provide low-tech options to complete the assignment, such as using the Drawing tool in a presentation application or even completing the Map on paper, taking a picture of it with their phone, and uploading the image. This is another example of where your responses to "Who are your students?" discussed in Step 1 will come in handy! Be sure that any additional time spent learning a technology or tool has an instructional return on student time investment. Be sure to let students know that the grade is based on the content of their submission, not the "fanciness" of its format.

Think strategically about the number of tools you will use and when you will introduce them. Try to limit the overall number of new tools used in a single course. Be especially careful of third-party tools that can't be integrated into the LMS, as these often require extra effort by students to visit external websites, create accounts, manage product codes, and learn an additional navigation system. Where possible, select tools that will be used throughout the course to avoid repeatedly asking students to learn new technology.

- For example, if you're teaching a freshman class in which most students have not yet interacted with the institutional LMS, you might choose to use just the Quiz/Exam tool, the Discussion tool, and the Assignment tool. Introduce the Quiz tool early via a syllabus quiz worth only a few points (this ensures they are interacting with the tool early and that they got at least the key takeaways from the syllabus), have them do a student introduction post via the Discussion tool, and have them submit a small assignment in week 1 or 2.

Introduce new, course-related technologies with a screencast demonstration. Whether you're using a spreadsheet application in an accounting course, software for object-oriented programming in a computer science course, or a statistical software package in a research methods course, consider doing "show and tell" screencasts to help students get started with the new tools.

- For example, a research methods graduate course might ultimately require students to use statistical software to analyze data that they have collected. You can help orient them to the tool by providing sample data and asking them to follow along with your screencast demo.

Provide practice opportunities with low-stakes assignments. A sandbox or practice area allows students to perform any needed setup and get comfortable with a tool before they are required to use it for a big assessment. Low- or no-stakes assignments can serve to allay fears for students who are nervous about learning new technology and give them time to seek extra support if they're struggling. This can also reduce questions for you later, as students will not be unexpectedly confused about a tool in the middle of a higher-stakes assignment.

- For example, students in a teaching course might have an assessment for which they need to create a video lecture that is closed-captioned. Prior to this higher-stakes assignment, students would be given a demonstration of the recommended recording and captioning software, with a related practice activity of doing a 2–3-minute introduction video with captions.

Your Turn: Technology & Tools

Part 1: Technology Planning

Review your assessments and activities in your Course Alignment Map in the HIDOC Course Blueprint and start to identify the types of technologies and tools you will need. Be sure to consider instructional alignment. For summative assessments, tools should enable students to provide the evidence you need to assess their understanding, progress, and/or mastery. For formative assessments, tools should ensure that students receive the necessary feedback on their learning. For learning activities, tools should support low- and no-stakes practice. Oftentimes, the active verb from your learning outcomes will guide your choice of technology tool. For example, if students are "identifying," that might point to a multiple-choice test using the quiz or exam tool in the LMS. If students are being asked to "analyze," that might be aligned with problem analysis, such as using specific statistical software or a problem-solving tool. The following questions should help you determine which technology and tools you are likely to need in your online course. While some of these are yes/no questions, start to identify more specifics wherever possible.

What LMS tools (or web-based tools) will you select to support students as they interact with content and complete assignments? This might include tools such as a discussion board, blog, wiki, or other cloud-based interaction tools outside the LMS, such as Google Docs or Slides.

Will students need additional software outside the LMS?

This might include things like word processing software, spreadsheet software, presentation software, and statistical or computer programming applications.

Which tools will support synchronous meetings like office/ student hours?

You might use web conferencing software built in to your LMS, or your institution might use stand-alone web conferencing software, such as MS Teams or Zoom. Whatever tool you choose can be used for your web-based office/student hours as well.

Will students need a webcam or headset?

If you're teaching a synchronous online course, decide if students need a webcam and/or headset. Keep in mind that there are many good reasons why students would not want to appear on camera, including privacy, family, or bandwidth reasons. You might make cameras optional but suggest virtual backgrounds to protect their privacy. Students in an asynchronous course might also need a webcam if you want them to create webcam videos. Students in any type of online course may need a webcam and other peripherals for proctored testing as well (discussed above).

Will your course require proctored exams?

If so, find out if students will need any specialized software and/or have to connect to a web-based service for exam proctoring. Your IT office should have this information, including if students need a certain operating system or plug-in to use these services.

Will students need any special hardware or software to interact with simulations, games, and/or websites or web-based technology?

This might include virtual reality headsets and software, access to remote instruments for labs, and other remote simulators.

Will students need to download free software or plug-ins in order to access course materials?
Think about text-based and video content that they will interact with and what tools they'll need to do so.

Part 2: Technology Documentation

Because students need to know all that is expected of them in terms of technical requirements, we recommend putting the following in your syllabus or other course overview materials. (We talk in more detail about your syllabus in Step 7.) You may already have boilerplate language from your institution that you can insert.

Specifications for any software and/or hardware requirements.
Anything that you identified above that is beyond what is available in the LMS should be specifically mentioned in your syllabus. Students might need a computer with a certain amount of RAM, for example, or additional software for word processing. You will need to identify how students will purchase or access the software, including detailed instructions if they need to create institutionally connected accounts.

Browser requirements.
Your institution might have requirements for this already, but be sure to include information about what is the preferred browser for your LMS, as well as browsers that will not work for your LMS. (If you're unsure, your institutional IT office or the office who is responsible for your institutional LMS should have this information. Some learning management systems do not work with Internet Explorer, for example.).

Internet access requirements.
If your institution does not have requirements for internet access, be sure to include information that explains to students that they need consistent, reliable access to the internet.

Computer requirements.

Be clear with students that they cannot complete the entire course through a mobile device. Some parts of the course might be able to be accessed through a mobile device, such as a smartphone, so let students know if your LMS has a mobile app or how well the web-based version can be used on a mobile device. However, most courses cannot be completed entirely without a computer, as students will likely still need to work on activities and assessments using particular software, such as word processing programs.

Specifications for connecting to university services from off-campus.

How will students connect to institutional services, such as the library, from off-campus? This is also information that your IT office should be able to provide. Most online students need to use a proxy service or VPN (Virtual Private Connection) to connect to institutional services, which requires a login and password.

Your Technology & Tools

1. Open the **Technology & Tools** Design Document from the companion website, use the version in the Design Doc Library section of the book, or create a version that works for you.
2. Work on the **Technology Planning and Technology Documentation** parts in the Design Doc, as discussed above.

Now that you've thought through the technology and tools that might play a role in your course, it's time to move the key technology information to your Course Alignment Map in the HIDOC Course Blueprint.

Your HIDOC Course Blueprint

1. Open the **HIDOC Course Blueprint** from the companion website, use the version in the Design Doc Library section of the book, or create a version that works for you.
2. Go to the **Course Alignment Map [MACRO VIEW].**
3. For each module in your course, fill in the final column **Technology & Other Notes** (Step 6).

Faculty-ID Collaboration

Choosing the Right LMS Tool

In my F2F course, I do a lot of things on paper. For example, I have worksheets they fill out, we do Muddiest Point or One-Minute Papers at the end, and I also have them take quizzes and exams. How will all of this translate to the online version of the course?

Those are great activities for the F2F classroom, but you're right—they may not always translate well to an online course. So let's start by looking at your goal for the activities with fresh eyes. For example, tell me why you have students do a Muddiest Point or One-Minute Paper activity.

It's something I often do at the end of each class. It gives students the opportunity to submit questions they have without fear of asking a "dumb" question in class. Or, it gives me a sense of their big takeaways, what was most valuable to them, and what is still confusing to them. It's almost like a little private check-in with me.

I love that! OK, so it looks like you value one-on-one interaction with students and giving them the opportunity to let you know about things that they found important, helpful, confusing, etc.

There's a tool in our LMS that will help you continue all these things! We can create an activity such as this using the Journal tool, which is private by default, meaning that no one sees what a student posts except you, and you also have the ability to reply only to that student—or we could even set it up as a short-answer essay response with an assignment dropbox. Journal-type activities, though, usually have a prompt that inspires students to reflect on something, whether it be course material, barriers they're encountering, learning gains, or even struggles outside of the course that are impacting their coursework. So, it can function as a reflective activity within the learning cycle as a way to ask questions, or as a way to connect with you as a 'whole' student, sharing things that might be impacting their work, such as technological barriers or life stressors.

That sounds perfect! Let me consider which modules in the course I'd like to have these private journal activities in, and then I can create some appropriate prompts for them.

Summary and Next Steps

To sum it up...

Identifying required technology and tools is an important part of your course design process. You will first want to find out what is available, if free or low-cost is an option, and what is supported by your institution and/or department. When identifying appropriate technologies, key factors to consider include privacy, accessibility, cost, and available technology support. You will also want to think about course design to minimize cognitive load so that students don't spend precious mental bandwidth on learning several new technologies. As with all of the steps in the HIDOC process, instructional alignment should guide your tool decisions: the tools you select should match your intended outcomes for the assessments and activities. Lastly, be sure to provide students with the necessary information on required technology and tools in your syllabus or other course overview materials.

Looking ahead...

The next chapter is about the many ways you can support your online learners via course design. This will take you some time to think through as it involves tying together all of the pieces you've worked on up to this point and putting into place all of the elements you will need in your course to help your online learners succeed.

References

Lieberman, M. (2019, March 27). Discussion boards: Valuable? Overused? Discuss. *Inside Higher Ed.* https://www.insidehighered.com/digital-learning/article/2019/03/27/new-approaches-discussion-boards-aim-dynamic-online-learning

Stice, J.E. (1987). Using Kolb's learning cycle to improve student learning. *Engineering Education,* 77(5), 291–296.

Sweller, J. (2011). Cognitive load theory. *Psychology of Learning and Motivation,* 37–76. http://doi:10.1016/b978-0-12-387691-1.00002-8

Online Learner Support

Online learner support spans all elements of your course design, from sequencing and organizing your course modules in the LMS, to making sure students are informed on policies and expectations, to providing necessary avenues for help and guidance. For this reason, this chapter is one of the longest and most dense of the book. You will also see some themes and suggestions from other steps repeated here as this chapter is where everything comes together in terms designing a cohesive online course. Implementing the design suggestions here will contribute to a high-quality teaching and learning experience that is rewarding for both you and your students.

Learning Online is Different

We have discussed the primary ways in which designing and teaching an online course differs from designing and teaching an in-person course. Perhaps it isn't surprising, then, to hear that being a successful student in an online environment also differs. And, while students have now experienced some form of remote teaching due to COVID, most of them still have limited to no experience with how to be a successful online learner. For both instructors and students alike, the established mental model for teaching and learning is embedded in the live, physical classroom. This model includes the instructor standing at the front of the class, indicating when class begins and ends, and providing information, knowledge, instruction, and explanation. Students engage with their instructor in real time, participate in in-class activities such as discussions and quizzes, and do homework as assigned. Homework is typically out-of-class work that's also discussed and explained live, in class.

When students take an online course, however, things operate quite differently. Because asynchronous online learners don't have to "attend class" on a specific day and time, they lose the benefit that a set class time structure can provide and are primarily left with assignment due dates to establish their schedule. This means they need better time management skills and to be more self-directed.

Being a self-directed learner means being able to identify the resources and strategies needed to be successful in learning. Self-directed learners are also able to diagnose their learning needs, create learning goals, identify resources, create and implement strategies to spur learning, and evaluate their learning progress. Many students are not yet self-directed learners, but this is less of an issue in-person because a F2F course allows them to be physically present with their instructor, ask questions in real time, and receive live explanation of course topics and elaboration of assignment goals and criteria. Fortunately, there are key design elements you can put into place to support your online learners.

Create a Well-Designed Learning Path

One of the most important things you can do for your online learners is to create a well-designed learning path. While we generally don't recommend trying to recreate an in-person class online, we do think it can be very helpful to reflect on how things happen in a face-to-face class to identify the vital elements and learning sequences that you will need to also make explicit in your online course. Think about how new topics or units are usually introduced in an in-person class. Typically, instructors will let students know that they are advancing to a new topic. Good instructors also help students make connections to the new topic. They do this by relating the new topic to students' experiences with a prior course, professional work, social/personal lives, or any other "real-life" experiences; a previous module in the course; or an upcoming module, topic, or assignment.

Making connections to students' prior experience helps to provide an anchor for the new information, and connecting it to prior or future work/experience also adds relevance. These things are important to the brain for learning and can impact motivation, memory, and cognitive presence. After introducing the new module and making past or future connections, instructors will often highlight key ideas in the unit and related activities and assignments. They might also tie it back to course learning outcomes and describe specific things students will learn and do in this unit.

As with much of what we've talked about, however, things that take place "naturally" in the in-person class often need purposeful planning when done online. A well-designed module in an online course begins with an introduction, followed by specific CLOs addressed in the module as well as module-level learning outcomes (MLOs). MLOs are typically smaller and more discreet than

CLOs and pertain only to what students will be able to do by the end of that specific module. MLOs are usually easiest to write after you've laid out the details of your module. If your module is aligned, MLOs almost write themselves based on the activities and assessments you've included. (If you're short on time, however, MLOs are one thing to skip for now.)

Essential Module Elements

Organizing a module is simply a way for you to be transparent with your students about the learning process or sequence that you've created, and to lay out the learning path in a web-based format that is easy to navigate. High-quality online courses can look quite different from each other on the surface; however, when you drill down into their key elements, you will find that they typically include the same essential elements at the module level. These key elements include:

1. A Module Overview page that contains:
   a. A module introduction, often listing the topics for the module
   b. CLOs addressed in the module
   c. Module learning outcomes (MLOs), which reflect what students will be able to do by the end of this particular module
   d. A list of relevant readings, videos, activities, and assessments for this module (many instructors label these: "Read," "Watch," and "Do")
2. Detailed Assessment and Learning Activities prompts
3. Instructional Content and Materials
4. A Module Summary
5. Next steps or looking ahead information to preview the next module (this information might be included in the summary)

At times these elements may be called different things. For example, as previously mentioned, we use the term "module" in this book, whereas you may use "lesson" or "unit" or even "week." What's most important, though, is that you make explicit for your students the key elements of learning in each learning unit.

> ***In the face-to-face class, instructors often summarize a completed module, introduce a new one, and highlight relevant activities and assignments. Online, you'll create this important information within your module introductions and summaries. These bookend your learning units.***

Below is a real example of a module overview from a fully online asynchronous course, which shows the introduction, MLOs, CLOs addressed in the module, and the "read, watch, do" for that module. It also shows how the module is listed in the Syllabus schedule.

Module 3 Overview

Introduction

Get geared up for this imaginary scenario: You are so excited! You have an opportunity to visit the Dodge Company in Billerica, Massachusetts for a virtual tour of their facility.

You will have a chance to see a number of compounds being used to prepare all of the mixtures; you will get to see the packaging facility; you will get to ask all of your questions!

You are prepared to observe how the facility incorporates safety standards into their everyday work, including the management of vapors. The ability to produce vapors is one possible property of a molecular compound — think ammonia, alcohol, formaldehyde, and more.

But many of the compounds that are used do not give off vapors, such as salt, and sodium bicarbonate. This is an example of the way that molecules and ionic compounds have different properties. Ionic compounds, while usually very soluble in water, do not have an odor (no vapors are produced), while small molecules can be very strong smelling (vapors are produced). These properties are directly related to whether the compound is ionically- or covalently-bonded.

Let's take a look again at ionic compounds and start to study molecules. Then we will look at the properties of each.

Module Outcomes

At the completion of this lesson, students will be able to:

- Discuss the ionic bond and describe the interactions between cations and anions (simple electrostatic model)
- Use valence electron counts to predict the bonds between atoms in simple Lewis structures
- Compare and contrast the properties of ionic compounds and molecular compounds

These Module Outcomes support your work in achieving these related Course Learning Outcomes:

- Explain chemical structure and molecular orbitals

Module 3 Overview

Readings and Assignments

1. **Read pages 145 – 174, and pages 201 – 226 in Ball, Hill, and Scott (2011).** These select pages from Chapters 3 and 4 discuss ionic bonding, simple ionic bonds, covalent bonding, and simple molecular compounds.
2. **Read the List of Ions handout.** This handout is linked below and will open as a PDF in your browser. It contains the list of ions that you'll be working with in this module, and relevant information for each.
3. **Watch the Video lesson: Ionic Bonds and Interactions.** In this series of three videos which total about 20 minutes, I'll introduce you to the information that is encoded in the formula for a chemical compound and ionic, covalent, and metallic bonds.
4. **Do Lesson 3, Assignment 1: Ions and Examples from the Dodge Catalog.** In this scenario-based discussion, you'll be applying your knowledge of ionic bonds and interactions to the compounds used at the Dodge facility.
5. **Do Module 3, Assignment 2: Electrons and Lewis Dot Structure.** In this assignment, you'll explain electrons and the Lewis Dot structure in your own words, and also create a diagram as an accompanying visual.

Course Schedule

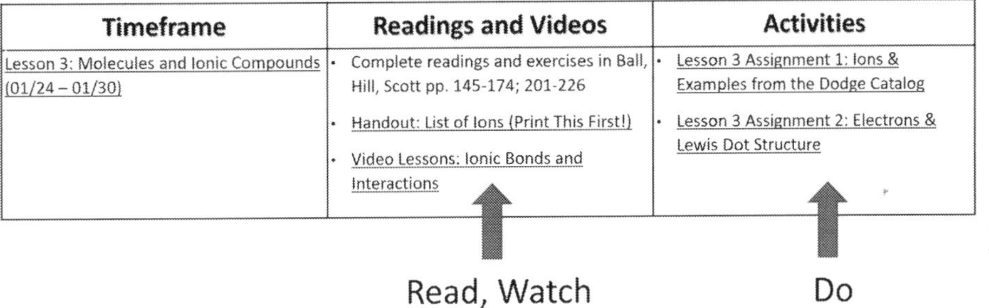

Timeframe	Readings and Videos	Activities
Lesson 3: Molecules and Ionic Compounds (01/24 – 01/30)	• Complete readings and exercises in Ball, Hill, Scott pp. 145-174; 201-226 • Handout: List of Ions (Print This First!) • Video Lessons: Ionic Bonds and Interactions	• Lesson 3 Assignment 1: Ions & Examples from the Dodge Catalog • Lesson 3 Assignment 2: Electrons & Lewis Dot Structure

Adapted with permission. Worsham College of Mortuary Science.

CLOs and MLOs

It is important to understand the difference between MLOs and CLOs as they are communicated in a Module Overview. The Module Overview would typically list only the CLOs that are addressed in that module, and it would list all of the MLOs for that module. The example below from a module in a public speaking course shows how MLOs ultimately support (and are aligned with) the CLOs addressed in that module.

CLOs addressed in this module.	MLOs for this module.
By the end of this course, you will be able to: • Write and effectively deliver a well-organized persuasive speech.	In this module you will: • Select a topic for your persuasive speech and state how you will position your argument. • Use the Toulmin Model to identify the claim, grounds, warrant, qualifier, rebuttal, and backing for your speech topic. • List the major organizational components of a persuasive speech and create an outline for your speech. • Identify credible sources that support your persuasive speech topic and construct an annotated bibliography of five sources.

Here is an example for a Chemistry course. Note that this is an example of a module in which the CLO is only partly attended to. This example module deals with mass and volume, while other modules in the course deal with temperature and pressure and would therefore also list this CLO.

CLOs addressed in this module.	MLOs for this module.
By the end of this course, you will be able to: • Accurately take and record measurements related to general chemistry, such as mass, volume, temperature, and pressure.	In this module you will: • Define mass and volume and explain how they are reported. • Identify instruments used to measure liquid volume and mass. • Correctly calculate mass and volume for various substances/objects. • List examples in your daily or professional life where it would be important to understand mass and volume and how to calculate each.

Your Turn: Detailed Module Layout

For Step 7, you will be working directly within your HIDOC Course Blueprint (rather than in a separate Design Doc). We have found it is easiest to complete the steps involved in creating your detailed, module-level view in a somewhat different order than what you will end up presenting them to students. What your students will eventually see is your "final product," whereas what you are working on here is the "work in progress." Because you will also work on detailing one module at a time, you may not yet have the information you need to construct introduction and summary material that connect to modules you have not yet developed. This process will involve some copying and pasting of previous information (from the Course Alignment Map [MACRO VIEW] to the Detailed Module Layout [MICRO VIEW]), which you can use as an opportunity to check for alignment and make improvements to your design. This will also give you a much clearer idea of how long this process will take.

Part 1: Create a Draft of Your Module Overview

To begin, go to your Detailed Module Layout [MICRO VIEW] (Step 7) section of your HIDOC Course Blueprint. You will start with your module overview, which is typically the first page of content in a module that has been built in your LMS. It makes explicit for the students much of what happens in the in-person class in terms of introductions, connections, transitions, and summaries. The first five rows of the Detailed Module Layout will ultimately make up your Module Overview.

Identify the Module on which you are working.
Here you will list the module # and module title. The module you select does not have to be the first module. Instead, we suggest you select the module that you have the clearest sense about to build your confidence and identify the process that works best for you.

List the CLOs connected to this Module.
Look at the aligned learning outcomes you identified in your Course Alignment Map [MACRO VIEW] for this module and see if they are still accurate. List, review, and possibly revise the CLOs for this module. Remember that it's unlikely that a single module will fully meet a CLO; rather, think of all the smaller,

discrete things that students will do throughout the course that are connected to that outcome.

List, then briefly describe, the module Assessments & Activities. Look at what you added previously to your Course Alignment Map for the activities and assessments students will be working on in this module and list those here. Then, determine if those activities and assessments still meet the need for this module or if you need to move, replace, or otherwise revise them. Once you're more settled on the assignments for this module, flesh them out a bit by providing a 1–3-sentence description of the assignment. Here are some example assignment descriptions:

- "Students will discuss communication in their field of study and how they can use the communication techniques and theories we discuss in the course for their own discipline/field/work."
- "Students will complete a private, reflective journal on their learning gains and remaining questions. Students will describe their new knowledge and meaningful ways they'll apply it within and outside of the course, and list any questions they have."
- "Homework problems 1–10, in Chapter 3 of the course textbook, dealing with: solving linear equations with variables on both sides, solving linear equations with unknown coefficients, and analyzing solutions to linear equations."
- "Blog post, where students report out on a theory-in-action. This week, we'll be learning about Social Exchange Theory, and students will post an example of this they experienced in real life or saw on social media/popular media."
- "Students will prepare journal entries to record transactions within their chosen fictitious company, which will use and apply the perpetual inventory system."
- "Knowledge-check quiz on new terms that students can take multiple times until they get a perfect score. Will be open-book/open-notes, and feedback will be auto-generated for each response."

List, then briefly describe, the module Content and Instructional Materials.

Look at what you added previously to your Course Alignment Map for your content and instructional materials. Then list, review, and possibly revise them for this module. Remember to look first to your activities and assessments. You only want to list the content that will support students doing well on those activities and assessments. Once your list of aligned content is more firmly established, you can flesh out each item by identifying if it's something you already have, need to create, or need to find. If it's something you already have, note if you need to make the piece accessible or if you need to explore any potential copyright issues.

Draft a Module Introduction.

This could be a short piece of text that's similar to what you might say in person when you introduce a new module. Place the module topic(s) in context of both the course and any real-world contexts in which students will apply new information, then briefly describe what students will be learning and doing. When you actually develop this, consider including a relevant picture and/or recording the intro as an audio file or a short video (either a short 1–3-minute webcam video or narrated presentation).

Part 2: Review Module Overview for Alignment & Create MLOs

Review (and revise) module overview for alignment.

Now that you've more fully articulated the specifics for this module, it is time to look critically at all of the elements in the Module Overview (first five rows in your Detailed Module Information [MICRO VIEW]) and make sure they are working together to support each other. Because HIDOC is iterative, it would be very unusual at this point if you didn't need to make revisions to your Module Overview and/or your Course Alignment Map [MACRO VIEW].

Your Course Alignment Map [MACRO] should accurately reflect your Detailed Module Layout [MICRO]. As you design and revise for alignment, you will repeatedly check and make edits between these two portions of your HIDOC Course Blue-print so that they accurately reflect each other.

Create MLOs.

Looking at all the elements of your Module Overview should allow you to organically create MLOs. This is a step that you might choose to skip if you're short on time, but it provides an additional level of transparency and clarity. MLOs describe, in discrete terms, what students will be doing in that specific module. They also provide clarity for you: are students spending their time wisely in this module such that they progress in their learning and achieve your outcomes? Is there something that should be addressed in this module but isn't? Are you clear on what students will be learning and doing in this unit and how it connects with the larger course?

Part 3: Draft Your Module Summary and Next Steps

Draft your Module Summary.

As a final step, just as you would close a topic in a F2F class or transition to the next topic, you should provide a summary of key points, ideas, and/or takeaways from the module.

Write module Next Steps.

Explain how students will build on what they learned and did in this module in upcoming activities or assessments, or even how their work in the module is translatable into future professional work.

You might choose to do your Module Summary and Next Steps together or make them separate elements.

Your HIDOC Course Blueprint 

1. Open the **HIDOC Course Blueprint** from the companion website, use the version in the Design Doc Library section of the book, or create a version that works for you.
2. Go to the **Detailed Module View [MICRO VIEW]** (Step 7).
3. Work on the **Module Overview** (rows 1–5). Review for alignment and then work on your **Module Introduction** (row 6); and **Module Summary and Next Steps** (rows 7–8), as discussed above.

Actively Support Your Students on this Learning Path

Now that we have walked you through creating a well-designed learning path for your students in your Detailed Module Layout, it is time to talk about important ways you can actively support your students on this learning path. This happens via both your course design and your active teaching (covered more in the Bonus Chapter on Design Execution).

Provide Thorough Assignment Explanations

A repeated theme throughout this book is that crucial information is often left out of online courses. It's not that online instructors intentionally withhold necessary support from students; instead, it's that F2F models for learning are entrenched with "extra" (but essential!) information that doesn't always get translated to the online course. Online students, in this context, get less information than they need to be successful, and it puts all the onus on the learner to ask questions and for clarification. This tendency applies to assignment explanations as well, and it's not uncommon to see an assignment in an LMS with little to no additional information provided beyond the minimum, such as "take the quiz on Chapter 2" or "answer the posted discussion question."

It's natural for us to assume that our online students, like our in-person students, will simply ask a question if they don't understand something. However, remember that students, like all of us, typically "don't know what they don't know." This means they often don't have a question until they're working on an assignment in-depth. Or, they feel they do understand something, even after completing an assignment, and don't realize they have confusion until they receive their grade. Research also shows that online students do not proactively reach out to their instructor as much as F2F students do—common reasons given are that they don't want to "bother" their instructor, they don't feel a rapport or connection with their instructor, or their previous online instructors have been unresponsive or unhelpful (Bork & Rucks-Ahidiana, 2013; Tolman et al., 2020).

> ***Online students are often reluctant to ask questions of their instructors. Online instructors can help with this by proactively addressing common questions, providing clear instructions and expectations, and reminding students throughout the course that they welcome questions.***

In drafting your assignment prompts, consider what you would you do in an in-person class to introduce this assignment.

- Would you pull it up on a screen and talk through the details, adding more explanatory text than what is in the assignment instructions?
- Would you show past examples?
- Would you proactively address common student questions?
- Would you talk about how you will evaluate student work and offer cautions about mistakes that are easy to make and suggestions for how to avoid them?
- Would you leave time for students to ask additional clarification questions?

If you said yes to any of these, then in your online course, you can proactively:

- Create a folder that houses examples of past assignments (get students' permission first, and remove their identifying information).
- Provide a video or screencast in which you show the assignment and talk through the details, including suggestions and cautions.
- Set up a discussion board specifically for questions and comments about the assignment.

- Designate an online office/student hours (see more information below) session to specifically talk about the assignment and take student questions.

More on Office/Student Hours

For some students, the concept of "office hours" in an online course might be confusing since they don't take place in a physical office. Others have observed that "office hours" is not a student-centered way to think about the time, as this is time dedicated to providing additional or one-on-one guidance to students. For these reasons, some have switched to referring to them as student hours instead of office hours. Throughout the book, we refer to them as office/student hours but encourage you to choose whichever nomenclature is most consistent with your philosophy.

Most importantly, however, you should begin by creating clear and thorough assignment prompts. By "assignment prompt," we mean clear instructions for the assignment, information on how students will be evaluated, and details on how to electronically submit the assignment. To help you with this, below is our second Bonus Development Doc in this book: Assignment Prompts. Just like our Bonus Development Doc for creating Online Topical Lectures, you can work through one of these now as a sample or leave it until after you've finished your course design and then start on your development.

 Your Turn: Assignment Prompts

In this Bonus Development Doc, we walk you through creating an assignment prompt. Many instructors create the assignment at the same time as the prompt, while others choose one order over the other. You might focus only on creating the prompts for now if they are associated with quizzes or exams, as writing all of those quiz or exam questions at this point can derail design progress. However, if the associated assignment is a discussion post or a journal entry, you might find it relatively easy to work on the assignment specifics and the prompt simultaneously. Please choose what works best for you: you will have to create both in the end.

Part 1: Key Segments of Assignment Prompts

If you would like to create full rubrics, those can be attached to or embedded in the assignments themselves. If you have existing rubrics from F2F assignments, those can be of use when creating your prompts. Whether you'll be using rubrics or not, you want to create an assignment prompt that does the following:

1 ***Identifies the assignment and provides a brief description.***
You should already have this information for at least one assignment from your Detailed Module Information [MACRO VIEW].

2 ***Describes what they are doing in the assignment and why.***
In this section, provide instructions for completing the assignment and explain how it connects to outcomes/learning goals/other assignments/etc. Provide connections and context by describing what students will be doing and how their work is beneficial and relevant.

3 ***Explains how they will be evaluated.***
This should reflect your own grading system and approach. You can link to a rubric here or simply explain how you will evaluate their work, including things such as what you'll be looking for, minimum requirements, and any policies for length and formatting, if relevant. This can also include portions for self-reflection and peer evaluation and can align with any grading approach, from a strict, points-based rubric to "ungrading." If your assignment prompt is for an online discussion, this section includes information for evaluating both the initial post and the reply post(s).

Specifies how they will submit their work.
Here is where you specify if you'll only accept work as a certain file type (MS Word over a Google doc or PDF, for example). Also, instruct students as to the naming convention to be used for any files they upload. (It's often best practice to have them include their last name and the name of the assignment so that if you download assignment submissions they are organized.) You can also remind students that it's important to save their work as they go to avoid emails of "the discussion board ate my homework." Finally, tell students where they will be submitting their work, such as an assignment dropbox.

Part 2: Check for Clarity

Have you ever created an assignment only to have students completely miss the mark on what they do or submit? This can often be traced back to the wording of prompts, assignment descriptions, and questions that make sense to us as experts but are confusing to students who are just learning course material. If possible, swap assignment prompts with a colleague so that you both have the advantage of getting feedback from the "student perspective" before your course runs. (You could also ask a friend or family member for feedback, as they might have a helpful "new student" perspective.) Ask them if they understand what to do and how they'll be evaluated. You can use the following checklist to determine where it might be necessary to revise your assignment prompt.

Did your assignment prompt reviewer...?

Find your prompt concise and clear?	[YES/NO]
Know precisely what they were supposed to do for this assignment and why?	[YES/NO]
Know how they would be evaluated on this assignment?	[YES/NO]
Know how, and in what format, to submit their work?	[YES/NO]

Use this feedback to revise your assignment prompt as needed and realize that thinking more deeply and specifically about your assignments will likely impact alignment because you'll now have a full and clear picture of the assignment and may, in turn, need to rethink the associated learning outcomes, edit assignments to better align, and/or re-examine what content best supports students in doing well on the assignment. (As always, make your revisions in both your Course Alignment Map [MACRO VIEW] and your Detailed Module Information [MICRO VIEW].)

Your Assignment Prompts

1. Open the **Assignment Prompts** bonus development document from the companion website, use the version in the Design Doc Library section of the book, or create a version that works for you.
2. Work on the **Key Segments of Assignment Prompts** and **Check for Clarity** parts as discussed above.

Developing a few of your digital materials during the design phase can give you a good idea of the work ahead.

Once you begin to create your assignment prompts, you will likely realize how time-consuming it is. You might even have a better idea of why we encouraged you to source and curate content rather than create all the content for your online course. Developing your online course includes creating digital materials, such as assignment prompts and online presentations/lectures, and building your course in the LMS in a logical, efficient manner.

Intentionally Schedule, Scaffold, and Remind

Because online asynchronous courses do not have the natural structure and timeline that is present in the in-person classroom, another way to actively support students along the learning path you've created is to intentionally structure it so that they can "ramp up" to higher learning. This allows you to provide assistance, reminders, and motivation along the way.

Stagger due dates throughout the week. Staggering due dates rather than having everything due on one day can help students with time management and procrastination (as well as your own grading workload).

Have a smaller assignment due during the week, and larger assignments due on the weekend. A smaller assignment might be a learning activity, such as a drag-and-drop or short-answer essay question following a recorded lecture, or a reading assignment with an accompanying quiz that students can take multiple times, receiving feedback on their attempts. It could also be a formative assessment, such as an applied discussion, timed quiz, homework assignment, or a reflective journal activity. This ensures that students are getting started on that week's content early and aren't waiting until the weekend to begin.

Scaffold larger assignments. This is something we discussed in Step 4 in terms of how you can use formative assessments to build up to the larger summative assessment. The common example is a final summative paper that also includes formative assessments along the way: a topic idea first, then an outline, then an annotated bibliography, and then a draft (which you might use as an opportunity for peer feedback). Not only will students truly have a chance to increase the depth of their learning and improve their final submission, but the final product will both be better quality and already familiar to you, resulting in less time grading the final piece.

Include assignment and content reminders in your online announcements. If in your F2F class you'd naturally say something like, "Don't forget that we have a quiz this Friday," or, "Don't forget that your research papers are due Monday." Be sure to do the same in your online course announcements.

Provide Course Supports Specific to Learners' Needs

It's also important to consider the potentially unique needs of your online learners. Revisit the Learner Analysis notes you made in Step 1 and reflect on your specifics in terms of things like how prepared you anticipate students will be for course topics and whether they may have technology or access issues. Some of the suggestions below have been touched upon in other chapters, but they are important enough to bring together here. Consider the ways your students may need additional, targeted support such as:

Optional content that provides more information. This might be preparatory or review material and/or additional content that provides additional breadth or depth. Optional material can be helpful for underprepared students, returning students, students with learning disabilities, and gifted or expert students who want to learn more.

Opportunities for student Q&A. In the next chapter we talk about more formal ways to collect student feedback, but you can also do this in a lightweight manner by having a learning activity where students share areas of confusion or questions about content. This can even be anonymous. If you are getting similar questions, especially term after term, you can create an FAQ list, which can be updated at any point during the term. You can also proactively address these questions through an announcement, a short webcam video, or a class email.

Provide Helpful and Informative Materials and Activities

We've just discussed how to support your online learners by (1) designing a clear, aligned learning path and (2) supporting your students on this learning path. To finish our discussion, we'll look at how you can (3) provide helpful and informative materials and activities that also enable you to elevate your teaching presence via guidance, support, motivation, and feedback.

Specific design elements we will discuss in this section follow:

1. "Start Here" folder
2. Instructor welcome and course orientation
3. Syllabus with policies specific to online learning
4. Course schedule appropriate for an online course
5. Course space for student introductions & general discussions
6. Content descriptions
7. Activity that allows students to share

A "Start Here" Folder

In addition to organizing your course modules, it's also a good idea to gather all the documents and activities that students will engage with on the first day and package them up to help students get started on a sure and easy footing. Your "Start Here" folder/page can include many of the items talked about in this section of the chapter, such as your syllabus and course schedule, your orientation screencast, and your instructor welcome video or message.

To provide additional context for the importance of this "Start Here" folder, think about how you begin the first day of a F2F class. You likely introduce yourself and give an overview of course topics, go over the syllabus, highlight major summative assessments, and possibly even create an opportunity for students to introduce themselves. This is a crucial class session, as it provides the catalyst for you and your students to begin to get to know one another, start to develop rapport, and thereby begin to form a learning community. It also serves practical functions, such as providing students with enough information about the course and your expectations of them so that they can determine if they should remain in the course.

Online, however, it's easy to overlook the vital role of the "first day of class." By this point, you have spent many hours designing and organizing your course and have perhaps begun to develop your activities, assessments, and instructional materials. (In other words, you're tired!) But it's so worth it to put the "final bow" on your course and to create either a folder or page that is easily locatable (or is the landing page of the course) so that when your online students "arrive" on the first day, they know just where to go and what to do. When students can't easily find something in their online course (especially on day one), research shows that they experience frustration, lowered self-efficacy, and lowered motivation (Simunich, et al., 2015). Students have reported that they develop confidence in their instructor (and their own abilities) when the course is easy to navigate.

An Instructor Welcome and Course Orientation

Create an instructor introduction, as well as an orientation screencast. Ideally, your instructor introduction is a short (5 minutes or less) webcam video so that students can hear and see you, including your tone, non-verbal expressions, and gestures. Having even one video such as this is very helpful when trying to build rapport and make a connection with your online learners. You can talk about things such as your professional background, why you love teaching this course and/or in your discipline in general, your teaching philosophy, your experience with teaching online courses, and what students can expect from you as well as your expectations of them. If you're comfortable doing so, you can also mention your personal hobbies, family, pets, and/or non-school interests.

As an alternative to a webcam video, you can do a voice-over slide presentation, especially if you use software that has a picture-in-picture feature so that students can still see you. If you teach several different online courses, consider making it an "evergreen" video, meaning that you speak in more generalities about your background and passion for the discipline such that you have one polished, quality piece for all your classes. (When creating evergreen pieces, be sure to avoid referring to times of the year, the semester, or to current events. It's also a good idea to refresh these pieces every few years.)

A course orientation screencast can be done with a program that records both your voice and your computer screen. The idea is to show students how to navigate around their online classroom to help orient them to key items as well as the organizational flow and layout. You can also highlight and preview your "Start Here" folder, as well as where students can find announcements. Additionally, talk through whatever quick links you may have placed in the course navigation, and walk students through a typical module, so they have your annotated tour of the learning path. Try to also keep this piece short (10 minutes or less).

Syllabus with Policies Specific to Online Learning

Just like with your F2F class, your online course syllabus provides key information students need to be successful. Online learning also necessitates some different policies, as well as some rethinking of existing policies that you might already have. As always, please check first with your institution to see if they have any required policies for online courses.

Attendance and participation policies. What do attendance and participation mean online? You might, for example, have verification of attendance requirements at your institution due to federal financial aid policies. In this case, attendance for an online class might mean turning in an assignment or completing an activity by a certain date. Attendance in this form might also be needed to determine when students stopped attending an online class (this is another good reason to have regular and distributed assignment due dates). Participation in an online class may mean students are required to log into the course site a certain number of times per week. This helps to ensure that students are proceeding along with their peers and not beginning to engage with content and assignments at the last minute (regular and distributed assignment due dates can help here as well). If you're teaching a hybrid or synchronous course, you'll need to clearly list the live attendance dates and any related policies for missed classes. You should also consider what active participation you're looking for during required class sessions. One good option is to have several activities during your synchronous teaching, such as polls, contributions via the chat, and breakout room activities.

Communication policies. In your in-person classes, you've likely experienced the phenomenon of students asking you questions before, during, and after class...instead of, or in addition to, coming to see you during scheduled office/student hours. Because online students don't have these "low entry barrier" options, it's important to inform them of options for reaching out and make it easy. Include communication policies in your syllabus that inform students when they will receive a reply to an emailed (or publicly posted) question (many instructors choose to do 24 hours during the week and 48 hours on the weekend). Also include information on how your students can contact you (email, phone, Skype, text, and through the LMS chat are some common options), and even consider giving them information about why they might want to contact you (e.g., assignment questions, confusion about a course topic, to discuss their grade, if they're struggling academically or personally). Also, clarify how you'd like to be addressed. Culture and background can play a role here as some students might think it's disrespectful to use your first name, while for some adult students in the workforce, it might be commonplace to reference their supervisor by their first name. Communication expectations can also be included in your instructor welcome video discussed above.

Netiquette policies. "Netiquette" typically refers to "internet etiquette" and applies to expectations for written communication in your asynchronous online course as well as for live communication in a synchronous online course. There are plentiful examples of netiquette policies available via an online web search. Items common in netiquette policies include requiring students to use respectful and professional language and your expectations for things like grammar and punctuation. Your netiquette policy might also state that you reserve the right to remove discussion posts and other public postings that do not follow your policy or use disrespectful language.

Technology requirements. Step 6 involved you identifying the technology and tools necessary for your online class as well as documentation of key elements such as browser, computer, and software requirements. Aside from having the technology they'll need to be successful, online students also need skills in using that technology, as well as the ability to troubleshoot basic technology issues. Below is a list of common minimal, basic skills that online students will need to be successful and should be stated in your syllabus as such:

- Using a web browser and opening new tabs
- Updating or installing an operating system
- Using common downloads and plug-ins, such as Adobe Reader or lock-down browsers
- Uploading and downloading files, as well as naming and renaming files
- Using a word processing program (most often, MS Word)
- Navigating the institutional LMS
- Utilizing the tools within the LMS, such as the discussion board, blogs, wikis, journals, or assignment dropbox
- Using course- and discipline-specific software

- Connecting to synchronous web-conferencing tools, whether for live office/student hours, individual consultations, or synchronous class sessions
- Taking exams through online proctoring services, if applicable to your class

Additionally, your syllabus should be explicit about:

- *What technology help is available:* Do they only have institutional help for the LMS? What if they have a computer hardware or software issue? What if they need to improve their skills with course-related software or have questions?
- *Where they can get help:* For example, the IT office, a student "One Stop," an institutional website, LMS tutorials, or contacting the software publisher directly.
- *How to get help:* List the phone number, email, and campus location for any institutional tech help services, or for non-institutional tech help, such as course-specific software. For this technology, you might list the software website, provide links to help documents, or list the phone number for questions.

Appropriate non-course supports. Lastly, be sure to connect your students with institutional support services beyond technology, such as accessibility accommodations and counseling services. Include academic support options for online students, such as online library services, online tutoring, proctored testing information, LMS tutorials, and institutionally created online student orientation materials. Additionally, include information for student support services such as advising, registration, financial aid, and career services and placement. Just like with technology support, make sure that students know how to contact the right person or office and what help is available. You might check in with your student services offices to see if there is an institutional page with all of this information that you can link to.

Because syllabi often include information that is required by the institution or even the accrediting body, they can become quite lengthy. Consider putting the most vital information—such as important policies or crucial information for completing assignments, connecting with their professor, or obtaining technology help—on a one-page handout. This helps all students but can be especially useful to learners with language disorders or issues with executive functioning, such as attention-deficit disorders.

Course Schedule Appropriate for an Online Course

If your institution doesn't require that your course schedule be part of your syllabus, consider creating it as a stand-alone item, as it's a document that students will refer to throughout the course. Unique to online schedules is that in addition to a due date, you also need to specify a due time and the corresponding time zone. As previously mentioned, consider having a mid-week (Wednesday or Thursday) due date for an activity or smaller assessment and a Sunday or Monday due date for a larger assessment. This ensures that students don't wait to engage with materials but also gives them the weekend to complete the larger assignment. Many online students work full-time and have been described as "weekend warriors" in terms of when they do the bulk of their coursework. When considering the due time to set for submissions, return to your notes from Chapter 1. If your students are primarily working adult professionals, avoid a 5 p.m. due time. Consistency in due dates and times can be helpful to all students, and 11:59 p.m. due times are a common choice in online courses. To avoid emails of "the computer ate my homework," you could also consider a one or two-hour built-in grace period. For example, papers due by 10 p.m. could have an automatic grace period until 12 midnight for any technology or life issues that happen last-minute.

You might also consider providing a suggested (not necessarily required) timeline to work through course modules. This can help students stay on track, prevent procrastination, and give them some of the structure that is embedded in the regularly scheduled, F2F classes that students are familiar with. The following example is for a finite math course that has a very structured format each week, allowing the instructor to include both a course pacing guide and a course schedule.

Finite math example: Course pacing guide

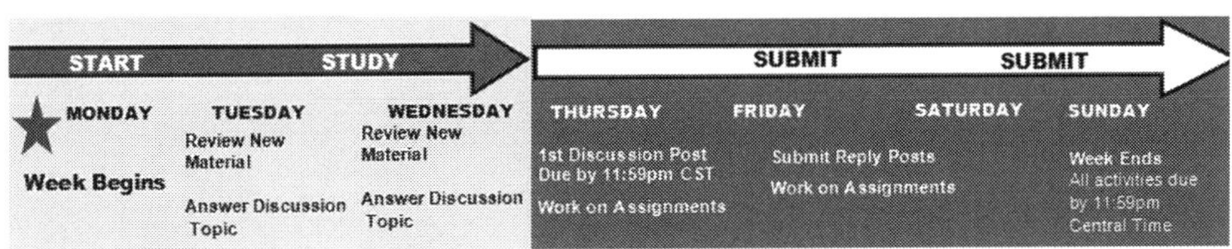

Finite math example: Course schedule

Module	Readings & Videos	Assignments
Module 1: Whole Numbers 1/10–1/16	*Read* Chapter 1: Basic College Mathematics (course e-text) *Watch* videos and study PPT lessons for the following (all in course LMS): Section 1.1: Reading and Writing Whole Numbers Section 1.2 Addition with Whole Numbers Section 1.3 Subtraction with Whole Numbers	Discuss: Study Strategies *Do:* Hawkes Learning Homework Assignments: 1.1 Reading and Writing Whole Numbers 1.2 Addition with Whole Numbers 1.3 Subtraction with Whole Numbers
Module 2: Fractions 1/17–1/23	*Read* Chapter 3: Basic College Mathematics (course e-text) *Watch* videos and study PPT lessons for the following (all in course LMS): Section 3.1: Basic Multiplication and Changing to Higher Terms Section 3.2: Multiplication and Reducing with Fractions Section 3.3: Division with Fractions	Discuss: Fraction Theory *Do:* Hawkes Learning Homework Assignments: 3.1 Basic Multiplication and Changing to Higher Terms 3.2 Multiplication and Reducing with Fractions 3.3 Division with Fractions

Group communication course example

Unlike the finite math course example above, this group communication course example varies each week, and therefore an overall course pacing guide won't work. Instead, note the suggested timeline provided for each week.

Course Schedule & Suggested Timeline by Module

Module 1 – Presence and Interaction (Monday, 9/1–Sunday, 9/7)	
Suggested Timeline	**Work Due**
Monday–Wednesday: *Read* articles A & B *Watch* recorded lecture on Elevating Presence in a Group	*Post* to your Blog: Presence & Community **Due Thursday, 9/4, by midnight ET**
Thursday–Sunday: *Read* articles C–E *Review* handout on Group Discussion Types & Approaches	*Post* to your Blog: Purposeful Discussions **Due Sunday, 9/7, by midnight ET**
Module 2 – Active Engagement (Monday, 9/8–Sunday, 9/14)	
Suggested Timeline	**Work Due**
Monday–Friday: *Read* articles A–C on Evaluating Your Communication Efficacy *Watch* recorded lecture on Group Engagement *Watch* YouTube video on Why People Become Disengaged.	*Participate* in the Discussion: "Causes of Group Disengagement" **Initial post due Wed. 9/10 by midnight ET** **Reply post due Fri. 9/12, by midnight ET**
Saturday–Sunday: *Read & Reflect* on the Communication Styles article & Self-Reflection quiz	Submit Private Journal: My Communication Style **Due Sunday, 9/14, by midnight**

The two examples are just to provide context for your own creativity. Your course schedule and suggested timeline should be tailored to your course.

Course Space for Student Introductions & General Discussions

In F2F courses, students commonly discuss weekend or campus events and common interests before and after class. Believe it or not, these conversations can actually serve a vital course-related purpose by helping students develop rapport with one another and feel connected...which can translate into how well they interact with one another during class discussions and group work. Opportunities for students to get to know one another, to connect, and to begin to feel a part of the class learning community are vital in creating social presence.

Create a student introduction activity (via the discussion board or a video-based tool), and ask students to introduce themselves; if it's in writing rather than video, have them share a picture or avatar to increase the social connection. In addition to the common prompts of sharing their major, year, and professional interests, you might ask them to share pictures of their pets (or pets they'd love to have!) or give "two truths and one lie." You can also provide prompts that give you clues about what they know, what they hope to discover in the class, and/or any aspects that they're concerned with or confident about in terms of your online course.

Similarly, you might create an open discussion forum, sometimes called a "water cooler" discussion or "coffee chat." While this discussion forum might not attract all students, it's a great way to check in and connect with students on non-course topics and allow them to connect with each other. Some ideas include asking students to share their favorite recipes (for Thanksgiving dinner, summer cookouts, or family favorites that allows students to reflect their own culture and ethnicity), doing a "pet parade" to share pet pictures, taking a picture of their backyard or the sunrise they see out of their window to share geographic visuals without revealing a specific location, or even starting a list of favorite movies or favorite coffeehouse order.

Another good discussion forum to consider is an open "Q&A" forum, where students can ask questions about course content and assignments (you might encourage students to respond to peers or even provide points if they correctly answer a peer's question). For a Q&A forum, you want to be sure to check in, however, so that students are not receiving incorrect replies from their classmates. Additionally, you might have a "Please Fix This" forum, where students can alert you to things like broken links, files that won't open, and typographical errors. You can allow students to post anonymously if your LMS has that feature.

Content Descriptions

When developing your modules in the course, you'll be uploading and/or linking to different digital materials, from lecture videos to PDFs of scholarly articles to websites. For all of these, provide students with 1–3 sentences that state what the material is, how they should use it for their learning, and how they will access it. As an example, an instructor lecture might have this text beneath a lecture video link: "This lecture is about the process of photosynthesis. You will use information from this video as you work on your photosynthesis diagram, due this weekend. Click the thumbnail image above to play the video. It is 6:20 long." Or, linked with a scholarly article might be this description: "This foundational article on the Community of Inquiry framework from Garrison, Anderson, and Archer will introduce you to teaching presence, social presence, and cognitive presence. This will be part of our breakout group discussions in our regular Wednesday class session and of your short essay due by Sunday. Click the link above, and the article will open up in a new tab. It's 17 pages long, plus references. It is a piece I'd like you to read closely, so plan to spend a few hours reading the article and reflecting on the related discussion questions before Wednesday's class."

Activity That Allows Students to Share

The purpose of this learner support activity is to get to know your students as individuals, including providing them an avenue to share important information about themselves as well as concerns they might have about the course. This can also elevate social presence as they are able to present themselves as "real people" to you. This activity can be done as a survey, a private journal, or even just as a short-answer assignment. While questions like those below could potentially be included in a student introduction discussion, sharing concerns publicly doesn't often engender honesty. When asking your incoming students to trust you with information that might be personal in nature, the best option is a private assignment.

Ask students questions such as:

- *How much do you feel you already know about some of the big topics we'll cover in this course?*
    - Answers to this question might inform optional materials you provide to students to either help them get "caught up" or to give those further along opportunities for deeper exploration.
- *Do you have any personal or professional experience related to this course and its topics that you'd like to share?*
    - This is especially useful if your course is tied to a specific profession. This information also might help you put together well-balanced virtual teams for any group projects or discussions.
- *Do you have any concerns about this course right now? This could be related to course topics, the work you'll be doing, the fact that it's an online course, circumstances in your personal or professional life, or anything that you're worried about right now.*
- *Is there anything you feel might prevent you from doing well in this class?*
    - Questions such as these allow students to share their worries and anxieties. Some concerns might be course-related, such as feeling that their peers know more/have more experience than they do. Others might be more personal, such as the fact that they're a parent, are working multiple jobs, or are dealing with a health concern.
- *How familiar are you with the LMS or the technology we'll be using?*
    - This is where it's helpful if you've listed in your syllabus all the technology skills students will need (and sent it out in advance in a Welcome Letter! We'll touch on that in the Bonus Chapter). You might even direct students to this information, then ask for feedback on the specific technology listed.
    - Students may also just have general anxieties about the technology involved in an online course. For example, this might be their first online course, and they're not certain if they're prepared, or they may not use a lot of technology in their personal life and consider themselves a "Luddite."

- *Are there things you'd like to share with me right now related to how I can best support you? This can include specific things that you know help your learning, a personal situation you'd like me to be aware of, or even how you prefer to be addressed.*
    - This question can provide you with information on teaching approaches or options that you plan to use during delivery. For example, if most of your students say that including assignment reminders in an announcement is helpful to them, then why not do it? And when you include a reminder for the first time, note that it's because so many of them mentioned they found it helpful; let them know you are listening. You may also have students who say that receiving screencasted feedback, where they can hear your tone, is more helpful than written feedback. (This is also a great question to ask on its own or after you provide feedback for the first time.) You also might have students who want to share that they're a single parent juggling school and a job, or students who choose to share their preferred pronouns or name.

Faculty-ID Collaboration

The Importance of a Detailed Learning Path

You did a great job in chunking your course up into modules, and now, as we near development and building your course in the LMS, we need to design the learning path that students will take in each module, meaning organizing each module in a detailed way that introduces the topic, lays out what students will do, and leads to the next topic or module.

Wow...really? I don't have to do any of that for my F2F course—I think students can follow things pretty naturally using my syllabus and course schedule...no?

Well, let me ask you…face-to-face, do you do things like:

- Give some intro information about a new topic before you begin lecturing on it or solving a sample problem?
- Have in-class discussions based on what you assigned students to read?
- Go over a big assignment before they begin?
- Remind them of upcoming work that is due?
- Provide an opportunity to ask questions?
- On the first day of class, do you start off by introducing yourself before you begin talking about the course?

Well…yeah? I do all of those things. Isn't that part of teaching?

Exactly—it's a big part of the guidance we give to students to help them progress successfully through the course. Online, however, all of these things need to be considered during design and must be purposefully built into the course during development.

What we need to do now is lay out your modules so that we have a guide for when we build everything in the LMS—it also gives us an additional check to make sure everything is aligned and that you've included everything in the module that you want to include.

I didn't think much about having to actually lay this out in the LMS and that it needed to be done a certain way. It makes sense, but isn't it enough to just have weekly folders with everything they'll need for that week?

You can absolutely set your course up that way—and in an emergency situation, that's usually all you have the time and ability to do. But, here's why it's not best practice: collecting everything into a folder is more like setting up "storage bins" for each week instead of actually designing a path that you can guide students along. Think of the face-to-face corollary: you'd arrive at the classroom, announce the week, then just start the lecture or assume they read the chapter or article that you listed on the schedule. Then, you'd pass out all the assignments for that week and leave.

Of course, you wouldn't actually do that face-to-face, though, because it's vital that you use your knowledge and expertise to introduce what students will be learning that week and help them make sense of it through connecting it to other ideas or showing students how it's relevant to their lives and to their learning achievement in the course. There's a 'back and forth' communication loop that happens, where you educate and explain, and students inquire and apply. Online, that happens by having that instruction as part of the module layout, so you are there in an asynchronous way to support your students each week.

Ah, OK! When you explain it that way, I can better understand what you mean. Without doing this, students are likely going to feel like they're fending for themselves, trying to figure out what to do with this whole week's worth of material and assignments. If this were the physical classroom, I wouldn't walk in and just leave handouts on a desk with no mention of what they were, or when students should pick one up, or what they should do with that information.

Summary and Next Steps

To sum it up...

There are a lot of key logistical pieces to a well-designed online course that either don't come into play in a F2F course or don't have as big of an impact because they can be easily clarified during live class sessions. Due to the spatial and often temporal separation in an online course, elements like good organization, logical navigation, and clear policies and support options are crucial. Attending to these during design and before your online class begins is vital for ensuring that students can be successful starting on day one.

Looking ahead...

In the next chapter, we consider how to build continuous improvement into your design, development, and teaching processes. As you likely know from teaching face-to-face, there are always small things to tweak and bigger things to change that you only fully realize after the course is taught. Similarly, there are likely things you know now would be great to do...but you may simply not have time to get them all done for the first run of the course. In Step 8, we'll give you a plan for how to capture, organize, and act on all of that information.

References

Bork, R.H., & Rucks-Ahidiana, Z. (2013). Role ambiguity in online courses: An analysis of student and instructor expectations. (CCRC Working Paper No. 64).

Simunich, B., Robins, D., & Kelly, V. (2015). The impact of findability on student motivation, self-efficacy, and perceptions of online course quality. *The American Journal of Distance Education,* 29(3), 174–185.

Tolman, S., Dunbar, M., Slone, K.B., Grimes, A., & Trautman, C.A. (2020). The transition from teaching F2F to online. In L. Kyei-Blankson, E. Ntuli, and J. Blankson (Eds.), *Handbook of Research on Creating Meaningful Experiences in Online Courses* (pp. 67–84). IGI Global.

8 Continuous Improvement

Continuous improvement begins by first reviewing your design holistically for both feasibility—from the instructor and student perspectives—as well as instructional alignment. This allows you to make design improvements now before you fully develop your course in your LMS. The next part of continuous improvement involves planning for future improvements, including creating a *Revision Roadmap* and identifying ways to proactively collect and prioritize student feedback.

Starting by creating a *Teaching Calendar* enables you to ascertain if your well-designed course can realistically be taught, given the other demands on your time. Even if you are designing a course that others will teach, this is still a useful activity to make sure that the course will be doable for any future instructor. As an example, imagine that you've assigned your anticipated 50+ students a ten-page research paper (summative assessment) and scaffolded that assignment to have them turn in a draft (formative assessment) one week before their final submission. Here is an example of one week of a Teaching Calendar for this course with the paper draft for the 3rd week of the course that runs Sunday May 14–Saturday May 20. You can see how the assignments are laid out as well as the expectations for grading and feedback. Seeing all of this visually will prompt you to ask yourself: *Can I really read and provide meaningful feedback on 500 written pages in a few days so that students have time to incorporate the feedback into their final paper?*

Example teaching calendar

Wk 3 (5/14–5/20)	SUN	MON	TUE	WED	THUR	FRI	SAT
1. **Student Assignments Due**	Research paper draft due (~10 pages)		Module 3 discussion post due		Discussion reply due		
2. **Instructor Feeedback & Grading Schedule**	Begin grading research paper drafts.	Continue grading research paper drafts.	Return all paper drafts with feedback.	Grade initial discussion posts.		Grade discussion replies; provide class summary on points.	

 Your Turn: Teaching Calendar

It's now time for you to create and evaluate your own teaching calendar for the course you've designed.

Create a table for the whole semester.
For each week of the semester, you will lay out the days of the week in columns at the top and then create five rows. (NOTE: In this step, we'll attend to only the first two rows of the Teaching Calendar, and in the Bonus Chapter on Design Execution, we'll return to your Teaching Calendar to complete the remaining three rows.)

Fill in Student Assignments Due.
Put assignment due dates for each week in the first row. For example, if students are to submit a discussion post on Wednesday, put "Discussion post due [topic of post]" in the Wednesday column.

Fill in your Instructor Grading & Feedback Schedule.
The second row is the most crucial in terms of planning your time and managing your workload. Here, enter the specific days and time blocks you plan to spend providing feedback. It may follow a pattern of being the day after a due date, or perhaps you typically leave your grading and feedback for the weekend.

Evaluate its feasibility.
Now...step back and take a look at your teaching calendar. Is it doable? Does the assignment spacing allow you to be present, in terms of providing feedback? If you're teaching multiple courses, you might even want to overlay them all on one calendar to get a true picture of your workload. Many instructors schedule a specific time and day that they will check into their online course(s) to see if there are questions on the Q&A discussion board, for example, or if students have submitted an assignment.

Make changes as appropriate.

After you review your teaching calendar for feasibility, you can make strategic revisions to make the course more manageable for you. When teaching online, it's easy to feel tethered to your computer and that you must be in your online course(s) 24/7. In truth, though, that will quickly leave you feeling burned out. We invite you to think about more presence, more application, more feedback, and less "work"—meaning if you need to scale back on assignments so that the schedule allows you to have meaningful interactions via active teaching with your online students, that might be a trade-off worth considering. If you make changes, though, be sure to adjust both the Course Alignment Map [MACRO VIEW] and Detailed Module Layout [MICRO VIEW] in your HIDOC Course Blueprint.

Your Teaching Calendar

1. Open the **Teaching Calendar** Design Document from the companion website, use the version in the Design Doc Library section of the book, or create a version that works for you.
2. For each week in the semester, fill out the first two rows (**Student Assignments Due and Instructor Grading and Feedback Schedule**) of the table and then evaluate for feasibility as discussed above.

Considering the Student Perspective

Your Teaching Calendar can also be used to holistically review various aspects of your course from the student perspective. You might choose to look at your own Calendar in conjunction with other key course elements, such as the course schedule.

Spacing and Rhythm

Look at the "rhythm" of each module from the student perspective. For example, if you have a smaller activity or formative assessment due during the week, have you given students enough time to interact with the relevant material, as well as complete the assignment? Have you allowed time for students to use feedback before submitting additional assignments later that week?

You also may want to consider the "rhythm" in terms of depth and the level of self-directed learning they will need. You can think of your class as divided into three time periods, based on the length of your course. (This might be difficult to apply to accelerated courses that are very short, such as three or five weeks, however.)

1st Third	2nd Third	3rd Third
Students become acclimated to the course and course topics.	Students becoming more in charge of their own learning	Students demonstrate mastery
Shorter assignments, more instructor feedback. Lower-stakes peer interaction. More overt direction from instructor.	Applied activities and assessments, more opportunities for voice and choice, individual reflection. Possible group work. Instructor provides guidance and check-ins.	Culminating projects. Instructor continues to guide, mentor, and evaluate. Students engage in more knowledge-sharing with peers.

During those first weeks, students are becoming acclimated to both the course and the LMS, and you might choose a higher frequency of shorter assignments and more feedback here. In the second third, students are becoming more in charge of their own learning, and you might include more applied activities and assessments that go into greater depth, as well as assignments that ask students to reflect on their learning—both of which require your guidance and feedback. In the final weeks of the course, students can be working on assignments that demonstrate their mastery of the subject matter and might also engage more in sharing their knowledge with peers and working on culminating projects, while you balance mentoring and evaluation. If this sounds like something you'd like to try with your students, review whether your course design provides opportunities to make this happen. You might also schedule more time for yourself early on for directing and mentoring students as they acclimate to the online environment, new technology, and/or the course topics and work.

Student Workload

While the Teaching Calendar helped determine if your online course was doable for you, you must also determine if the course is doable for your students. As previously mentioned, online courses are frequently "overstuffed" and ask students to spend more time on coursework than they would in a comparable F2F version of the course. Why is that? Well, here's where we typically go wrong: let's say that one credit hour in a F2F course equals 15 hours of instructional time and 30 hours of out-of-class work. How can we adapt that thinking to online asynchronous teaching, where your direct instruction is mostly or entirely completed before the course begins?

Consider instructional time to be the time students spend with course materials, leaving them twice as much time left to spend on application, via activities and assessments. There is no "out-of-class" work in an asynchronous online course; however, the engagement and application of materials that students do via activities and assessments is similar.

If we use the time measures given above, a three-credit online course means that students will spend approximately nine hours total per week engaging with the course...but that doesn't mean we should design nine hours of reading, watching, and doing! What we often forget is that reflection, review, and cognitive elaboration takes time, and that time spent on those activities is good for learning. We also frequently calculate that nine hours based on how long it would take us to complete the work, not our students. However, our students are not us—they are not experts, and they likely don't have the same high level of "student skills" we possess (e.g., reading speed and comprehension, cognitive elaboration, time management). Review your course from the student perspective and make some content or activities optional if necessary. (Examples of course workload calculators are available on the companion website.)

Balance of Types

You'll also want to scan through your modules using a macro-level view and note the types and variety of content and assignments. If you only have text-based materials, consider replacing some pieces with short videos, a simulation or game, or an on-topic website. Likewise, if you have a preponderance of discussions and exams, consider if some of the discussions would be better suited as short-answer essay questions or reflective journal prompts; long exams might become a few shorter quizzes and then an applied, summative assessment. Including variety and balance in the types of digital materials and assignments will give you more options to engage students.

Your Turn: Course Alignment

Now that you've checked to see if your design is "teachable" and "doable," it's time to review your design for alignment. It's best to review for alignment before you develop your course in the LMS, as it will be much easier to make revisions. As with most things in this book, we invite you to take the approach that works well for you, but below is a suggested pathway for reviewing for alignment.

Reference your updated Course Alignment Map and Detailed Module Information.
Locate this in your HIDOC Course Blueprint.

Ensure that your instructional content supports your assessments and activities.
Look first at the activities and assessments that ground each module, then look at the supporting instructional materials. Do students have the information they need to do well on the assignments? If not, edit one or the other to maintain alignment. For example, you might need to add content, alter an assignment prompt, or remove a piece of content.

Also check the following:

- *Does the amount of content allow students to spend most of their time on application?* If not, you might pare down the content or place some in a supplemental/optional folder.
- *Do you have multiple pieces that reflect the same idea without adding new information?* If so, that's a great opportunity to either allow students to choose what they'd like to read or watch from those pieces, or for you to choose the best piece and mark the others as "optional."

- *Are your instructional materials accessible?* For example, are videos closed-captioned, do audio files have an accompanying transcript, are PDFs screen-readable and not images, did you use the Accessibility Checker in MS Office files, and are images alt-tagged? Frequently, we do not have the time and resources to always create an accessible course on the first try, but it's important to be proactive and consider accessibility from the start, as doing so benefits all learners. If you have accessibility concerns, please reach out to your relevant institutional office for advice or help.

③ ***If you have them, check that your module learning outcomes (MLOs) accurately reflect that module's activities & assessments.***
It's often easier to tweak an objective than it is to edit an assignment prompt.

④ ***See if your MLOs are aligned with your CLOs.***
If the MLOs do not align with CLOs, you may need to tweak one or the other or add or subtract learning outcomes from that module.

⑤ ***Take a holistic view.***
You've just completed a basic alignment check of ensuring that the instructional materials support students doing well on the activities and assessments, thus providing you with evidence that they have achieved the module outcomes and contributed to meeting the relevant CLOs. You may also want to review your module intro and summary, just to ensure that they adequately introduce and ground students to the module topics and ideas and provide them with takeaways, highlights, and next steps.

Your HIDOC Course Blueprint

1. Open the **HIDOC Course Blueprint** from the companion website, use the version in the Design Doc Library section of the book, or create a version that works for you.
2. Go to the **Course Alignment Map** section and make any necessary revisions based on the discussion and questions above.
3. Go to the **Detailed Module Layout** section and make any necessary revisions based on the discussion and questions above.
4. Ensure that your **Course Alignment Map** and **Detailed Module Layout** accurately align.

Your institution might also provide internal or third-party course reviews, where a peer reviewer would provide the student perspective on course quality elements. This is something we encourage you to take advantage of if possible because it can offer a "fresh" perspective, insights, and suggestions.

Planning for Future Improvements

At this point, assuming you've chosen to work actively on your course design while reading this book, you've now created a full course design, started a Teaching Calendar, completed a holistic instructional alignment complete with a Course Alignment Map and a Detailed Module Layout for each module. (You may have even started to create or curate your instructional content, created an assignment prompt or two, and done some organization in your LMS.) Take a deep breath, and pat yourself on the back, because we know what a huge lift that was!

Given all that hard work, it can be tough to already be thinking about "improvements"! However, continuous improvement is something that you need to *plan for proactively,* which is why HIDOC includes it as a Step. At this point, it can help to remind yourself that ***there is no perfect course.*** Even if you already believe this, you still might want to make this your "design mantra" so that you remember it. Planning for improvement can help to lessen the burden of perfection that you might be feeling at this stage in the process.

 Your Turn: Revision Roadmap

Given that an online course is never fully "done," it's important to make sure that none of your ideas or good intentions are lost. To help with this, you can start your Revision Roadmap now and contribute to it as your course is offered for the first time.

Identify your "Fix List" items.

Here you'll list things that you know now will need to be addressed or fixed. For example, there will likely be items that will need to be attended to or corrected in the future due to current time limitations. "Fix List" items might include things like:

- Breaking up a pre-recorded lecture into shorter segments
- Captioning all your videos
- Copyediting any text-based materials you created
- Making a document, PDF, audio file, image, video, or web page accessible
- Checking for consistency and readability in font type, size, and color for all materials

Identify your "Wish List" items.

Your "Wish List" will contain great ideas you had for your course design or development that you just didn't have time to implement. Common Wish List items include:

- *Curating better content pieces.* Perhaps you found an article that meets the need but is just not the perfect fit. Record this on your wish list, and take a future opportunity to connect with a librarian to see if you can find a piece that suits better. Or, you might have predominantly text-based materials and would like to replace some of those with multimedia content. You might even have a desire to source open educational resources (OER) for the course, relieving students of the need to purchase a textbook.

- *Creating some videos/presentations.* Hopefully, you have at least one video in your course by which students can hear and see you—your instructor introduction, for example. Maybe you wish you had time to create some narrated instructional presentations, though. Make notes of any presentations or screencasts you'd like to create or even short webcam videos that extend or apply the information that's currently in the module (this is also something you can choose to do a week ahead, as you teach the course).
- *Exploring new tools or technology.* There's always some new tool or software or plug-in that will capture your attention—and going down those "tech rabbit holes" can waste precious time. Keep the enthusiasm, but postpone the investigation for when you have more time to not just investigate the software or tool, but to also connect with your instructional technology office to see how or if it's supported by the institution and to check privacy and security risks.

Add to the "Other Ideas for Improvement" section as the course is running.

Your Revision Roadmap is a running document that helps you capture both corrections and enhancements. Some of these, discussed above, will be noted before your course ever runs for the first time, while others will be collected as the course is running based on your observations of student engagement and performance as well as direct student feedback. Students will alert you to things that need to be edited, added, or eliminated via emails or posts about broken links, confusing content, or course software they need to use. You'll be cued into issues with assignment prompts/instructions when students don't deliver what you (thought you'd) asked for or ask a lot of clarifying questions. You might consider alignment issues or the balance between content and application if you don't see students using course material in their activities and assessments, or if it seems as though students are not reading/watching all the material. Be sure to note these elements in your Revision Roadmap.

Your Revision Roadmap

1. Open the **Revision Roadmap** Design Document from the companion website, use the version in the Design Doc Library section of the book, or create a version that works for you.
2. Work on the **"Fix List"** and **"Wish List"** sections as discussed above. As the course is running, you can also add to the **Other Ideas for Improvement** section.

Collecting Student Feedback

Student feedback is the single most vital piece for preparing for your future revision. Don't be so secure in your assumptions of "what's working and what's not" that you forget to verify those assumptions with your students. Student feedback is also one of the few things in online learning that actively spans design (you design the survey into your course), teaching (you acknowledge and, if possible, use the feedback during delivery), and revision (you make notes of items you'd like to attend to when you revise the course.)

Understand that this is an activity that you are asking your students to take time to do, so help make them aware of and feel invested in the goal. Take a moment to consider how very helpful this information will be to you and to the future improvements of your course. Students rarely are provided the opportunity to provide feedback on course design, even though a primary way students experience asynchronous online courses is via your design. You should acknowledge their feedback (an announcement thanking them for it and explaining how you will address it can be helpful) and respect their perspective. Make students aware that your goal for providing a feedback survey is to gain information on their perspective and experience, and that you will read, reflect on, and respond to it, with the goal of improving the course.

Many faculty also choose to give extra credit or bonus points for completing the survey or include it as a required activity for points (some LMSs and tools will allow students to complete a survey anonymously but will show activity completion), considering both the value of the information as well as how it can help to create a collegial and collaborative online learning environment. Below is a list of sample questions broken up by topic, with suggested question response options for closed-ended questions, as well as an explanation of why you might want to use the question. Feel free to modify the question type, question stem, or answer options so they are better suited for use in your course, with your students. Consider how you'll use the information from a question, and that should help guide you for what questions to include.

Module-Level Survey Questions

In general, module surveys should be relatively short (<10 questions), while mid- and end-point surveys can be a bit longer. (If this is the first time you'll be delivering the course you designed, consider a brief survey at the end of each module.) We've provided more question examples here than you should include in every module survey so that you can choose what questions resonate with you most. If you're doing module surveys, you can also vary the questions by module, as there may be one module for which you want feedback on the assignments and another for which you'd prefer feedback on any navigation issues.

Workload. Previously, we discussed assessing the workload of the course. This is something to make an estimate of, while also checking your estimate with student feedback. Questions regarding workload should be accompanied by the open-ended design questions (listed further below) so that, if you need to cut materials or assignments, you'll know which ones were most valuable to your students. These questions work best when asked after each module or week but can also be tweaked slightly and used at the end of the course to provide some level of feedback for future course revisions.

1. **How many hours did you spend on this module?**

   This can be open-ended, or you can give students options that reflect the appropriate rigor, plus several hours more, and several hours less.

This is one way to help determine if your estimated student workload was accurate.

2. **Overall, considering the amount of work in this module, was it: just right, more than you expected, or less than you expected? [the response options can also be expanded to a 5-point Likert scale]**

   This can help you determine students' expectations. For example, if most students answer "more than expected," but they also report they did, on average, five hours of work per week, then the problem is not the workload but students' expectation of the workload. Keep in mind that many students expect that online courses will be "easier" and take less time—some believe that they'll only need to do the "out of class work" of a comparable F2F class. If your students have an incorrect idea of workload, this is something you could address via an announcement or short webcam video, for example, and might be something to highlight for students the next time you teach the course.

Course Design. It's crucial to gather student feedback on the pedagogical design of your course as well, as these questions are most often not included in student evaluations of instruction. So, if you don't ask them in your course, you may not have any information from students at all as to how the design worked for them. These are best-suited for the module level, but several could also be adapted to the course level for use on an end-of-course survey.

1. **The content in this module gave me the knowledge I needed to complete the assignments. [can be True/Unsure/False, or Agree/Disagree Likert scale]**

   This is an alignment check to see if students felt the module had the right content that set them up for success on assignments. If most students disagree with this, it's a cue to do a mini-alignment check within the module and make notes of content that is misaligned. Note this content on your Revision Roadmap as potentially removable or to be put in an "optional materials" folder. You might also check future, unreleased modules, where you could proactively make design changes if necessary.

2. **I used all the content in this module when completing assignments. [can be True/Unsure/False, or Agree/Disagree Likert scale]**

This is a good alignment check for the area of alignment that students are often most aware of: are they interacting with content that they're not using? This is a common, and valid, reason for students to cry "busy work." If you know that all of your content is well-aligned but students still report they did not engage with all of it, then examine your assignments. If students did well, even without engaging with all of the content, then you likely have some content that is extraneous and could be made optional. (Combining this question with the "What pieces of content were most helpful?" question below is often very useful.

3. **Assignment instructions were clear. [can be True/Unsure/False, or a Agree/Disagree Likert scale]**

   This is a great check for whether your assignment prompts provide clear directions and are being well-understood by students. If most students disagreed with this statement, you might know why (based on assignment submissions or student questions about the assignment), or you might create a short poll or survey that asks students to anonymously report why they were confused. Acknowledge their feedback and also proactively scan future prompts for clarity.

4. **I understood how I would be graded on the assignments for this week. [can be True/Unsure/False, or Agree/Disagree Likert scale]**

   Similar to the above question, this is a great check for whether your assignment prompts provide clear information for students on how their work will be evaluated. If most students disagreed with this statement, you might know why (based on assignment submissions or student questions about their grade), or you might create a short poll or survey that asks students to anonymously report why they were confused. Acknowledge their feedback and also proactively scan future prompts for clarity.

5. **Which pieces of content were most helpful to your learning in this module, and why? [open-ended]**

6. **Which pieces of content were least helpful to your learning in this module, and why? [open-ended]**

7. **Which assignments were most helpful to your learning in this module, and why? [open-ended]**

8. **Which assignments were least helpful to your learning in this module, and why? [open-ended]**

   For each of these four questions, the purpose is the same: to determine what content, activities, and assessments were most (and least) helpful to students' learning, so that if you need to delete items in the next revision (based on responses to the workload questions), you don't end up cutting what students found most valuable.

New strategies, technology, or tools. Gather student feedback on specific strategies, technology, or tools you may be trying out or only using for one activity due to time or resource constraints. You may want to expand their use in future iterations of the course.

1. **Would you like the course to use [strategy, technology, tool] in other places? If so, where? [open ended]**

   Current students can help pinpoint where additional simulations (or other strategies, technology, or tools) would be most useful. For example, if you added a lab simulation in Module 8 and received positive results, you may choose to add more in the next offering of the course.

2. **This week [unit, module, etc.], you were introduced to [new strategy or approach, new technology, tool, software, etc.]. Did you find it difficult to [learn, use, accomplish, etc.]? [can be Likert scale of "level of difficulty" or open ended]**

   Consider including an optional open-ended response even if using a Likert-type scale. What you're trying to determine here is how steep the learning curve was, and whether (or how much) it affected either the time students had to engage with the related content or assignment or their learning performance/achievement. You could also break this into two scale questions: level of difficulty, and to what degree it negatively impacted their learning.

3. **Is there something that would've improved your experience with [strategy, technology, tool]? [multiple choice or open ended]**

   Here, you're asking for suggestions for improvement. Multiple-choice options might include: clearer instructions, more time to learn the [strategy, technology, or tool], demonstration of [X], a practice activity using [X], holding an optional Q&A live session, and "Other" (as an open-ended option).

Course-Level Survey Questions

The course-level survey questions are broader and would typically be administered as a mid-semester or end-of-semester survey. You might need to update tense depending on when you are administering the survey.

Navigation and technology. Questions like the ones below will provide you with some feedback on organization and navigation, as well as alert you to technology problems.

Disagreement here might indicate a lack of course and/or module organization. Examine whether you have layout consistency from module to module (so students don't have to learn a new layout each week), or whether you might need to create or revise an orientation screencast. Consider having a peer colleague review your course to provide feedback from the student perspective.

1. **I was able to find things easily in the course. [True/Unsure/False, or Agree/Disagree Likert scale]**

   This question provides feedback on those "first day" items, such as finding the syllabus and schedule, knowing where to find important information, and being directed to their first assignment. Disagreement here is a cue to check that you have all these important items on a home page, in a "Get Started" or "Start Here" folder, or in some way have them easily laid out for students.

2. **The course was easy for me to navigate. [True/Unsure/False, or Agree/Disagree Likert scale]**

   Disagreement here can speak to course layout, LMS layout, and/or the left-hand navigation bar. If many students disagree with this statement, check in with a faculty peer or mentor, an instructional designer, or your LMS staff to see if someone can provide expert feedback on your course navigation. Alternatively, you could invite students to share specifics with you about what issues they are having.

3. **I did not have any technology issues in this course. [True/Unsure/False, or Agree/Disagree Likert scale]**

This question is good to ask during the first week or two, as well as when you introduce new technology or tools. Early disagreement might be due to lack of knowledge or lack of support. Share relevant tutorials to help students get up to speed and also remind them where to find information within the course on who to contact for technology support, how to contact them, and what support is provided. Module-specific disagreement might mean that students need more information on how to use a specific new technology or tool, or that learning it was frustrating or time-consuming.

Online teaching efficacy. The questions below inquire about aspects of online teaching, such as timeliness, helpfulness of feedback, motivation, support, presence, and connectedness. These can inspire immediate teaching adjustments or future considerations.

1. **My questions were answered well by my instructor. [True/Unsure/False, or Agree/Disagree Likert scale; include N/A for both]**

   This question has to do with helpfulness and might point to confusing course topics or materials or the helpfulness of an actual response. If replying in a text-based format, ensure your responses use simple and direct language, and offer (via an announcement, for example) to meet with students by phone or web conference to discuss any of their questions more in-depth.

2. **I received timely assignment feedback. [True/Unsure/False, or Agree/Disagree Likert scale]**

   This question relates to turnaround time for assignments. If students disagree with this statement, investigate further to determine if the issue was timing of assignments (i.e., they didn't receive your feedback in time to use it on the next assignment), or if they had incorrect expectations about when they would receive feedback (e.g., you did not have information on this in your syllabus, and even though you returned all assignments within five days, students expected that you'd return them within one day).

3. **The feedback I received on assignments was helpful. [True/Unsure/False, or Agree/Disagree Likert scale]**

This question focuses on the helpfulness of the feedback, usually in terms of depth or whether students understood your suggestions for improvement. If students disagree with this, review some samples of feedback (or have a colleague review them to provide an outside perspective) for clarity and whether someone at the level of your average student would understand what the issue was and how to address it. In addition, if you felt students didn't thoroughly interact with the content, did you suggest pieces for them to review? If they missed the mark on their submission, did they know why, and how to improve?

Sometimes, disagreement on this item might be due to the tone of feedback, as students don't hear the tone of our voice unless we're providing screencasted feedback.

Consider whether you remembered to give kudos when warranted, to include motivation for improvement, and/or to remind students that you're available if they have questions.

4. **I felt like my instructor was invested in my learning. [True/Unsure/False, or Agree/Disagree Likert scale]**

5. **I believed my instructor wanted me to do well in this course.[True/Unsure/False, or Agree/Disagree Likert scale]**

These two sample questions are both related to student perceptions of support from their instructor and teaching presence. Essentially, you're asking students whether they felt you cared about them and their learning. Disagreement with questions such as this doesn't necessarily mean that you're not a great teacher, however! Most often, they mean that you didn't take a moment to tell or show students you care in a way that was understood by them.

In future courses, you might consider: making sure you frequently remind students you're available for help or questions, seeing if you're posting a few helpful and relevant announcements each week, reaching out via email to students who are struggling and/or not logging in, providing helpful and timely feedback that includes kudos and/or motivation, and/or posting a short webcam video of yourself so students have a new opportunity to see you and hear you as you let them know that you're there to support all of them doing well.

6. **I felt comfortable reaching out to my instructor for support/to ask questions. [True/Unsure/False, or Agree/Disagree Likert scale]**

   This question is also related to whether students feel connected and supported. If many students disagree, you might consider addressing student questions in announcements, or create or add to an FAQ in future courses. Even if you have to create questions you know they have but aren't asking, addressing questions (without identifying who asked them, of course) in public ways demonstrates to students that doing so is part of your job, that you really want students to reach out, and that there is no stupid question.

7. **I knew how to contact my instructor if I had questions. [True/Unsure/False]**

   This question is also related to whether students felt connected and supported. If many students disagree, take opportunities in future courses to remind students how they can reach you, and make sure they have at least two convenient options to do so (e.g. email, phone, Skype, Zoom, or course instant messenger).

8. **How could I [or "your instructor"] have better helped you do well in this course? [open-ended]**

9. **What other comments or questions do you have about the course? Is there any other feedback you'd like to provide? [open-ended]**

   Both of these questions allow your students the opportunity to give direct feedback on how you might better support them or to anonymously ask questions they might have about the course.

   Including at least one question such as this also helps demonstrate to students that you are interested in their feedback and in improving teaching strategies and/or course design to best help their course learning and overall experience.

Revision Triage: Prioritizing Improvements

Below is some guidance to help you use the information from your Revision Roadmap, including notes you made from student feedback, when the time comes to revise your course.

Fixes to Make While the Course Is Running

In general, these are the small-to-medium tweaks that are often doable to address as you're teaching the course.

- **Hyperlinks:** Check and fix any broken links prior to releasing them to students. You might also notice links where you did not use a descriptive title (a descriptive title is vital for accessibility). This is usually a quick fix that can be done as the course is running.
- **Typos:** Any punctuation, spelling, or grammar errors can be fixed during delivery as well. You might notice some when you preview/review the modules, but students will also help you find some issues if you've chosen to create a "Please Fix This" discussion forum.
- **Explanatory text:** When you uploaded your content within your organized module, you provided your students some information about that particular piece, including what it was and how they'll use it. You might find that you need to add a bit more explication to content pieces, or even to your module overview, based on student questions or assignment submissions. Editing this short, explanatory text is usually doable during the course.
- **Assignment prompt tweaks:** Small changes to your assignment prompts can typically be done as you're teaching, but only if the prompt has not yet been released/shown to students. Based on student performance on earlier assignments, you may realize that you want to amend the submission instructions (to exclude certain file types that you've learned you can't open, for example), or you might need to be more detailed with the instructions or the evaluation portion. You might also need to tweak a discussion question or journal or blog prompt (again, only if

students have not yet seen the prompt). This is part of "just-in-time" online teaching, as you respond to student questions, performance, and behavior, in order to improve their experience as the course progresses.

- **Course schedule:** It can be tricky to adjust the course schedule, but sometimes it's both necessary and doable. For example, you might realize that giving students a bit more time on an assessment will result in better learning and better work. Or, you might learn that the bulk of your students have part-time or full-time jobs, and you've set course due dates for 5 p.m., which means many working students need to submit that work the day before or early in the morning. Consider how changes in the schedule will impact students (you might even poll them) as well as future assignments. It's good practice to make an announcement in the LMS that changes have been made and also edit and re-upload the modified schedule.

Planning Revisions before the Next Run

Any larger items, including alignment issues, rethinking learning outcomes, or major assignment revisions can be added to your Roadmap for examination when you revise your course in the future. To prioritize changes, consider the following questions:

- Based on your general workload and time available, how much actual time can you spend making course improvements?
- Do your ideas for improvements require you to learn something new, such as new technology? Do you have time to do this?
- Which improvements will most impact your students and their learning?
- Does your institution provide supports to help? Your institution may provide resources such as training on new technology and tools or assistance with design and technology tasks. They may also provide templates, screencasts, or student-facing instructions to give you a starting point for new technology or tools you want to add to your course.

Faculty-ID Collaboration

Planning for Revision

You've done an amazing job designing your course! Before we move to developing your content and assignments and building your course in the LMS according to your Detailed Module Layout…we need to put a few more things in the design to plan for revision.

Why would I be planning for revision already, though? We just spent all this time designing the course…shouldn't we deliver it at least once before revising?

Yes, absolutely! We won't be doing any actual revising now, and you're absolutely right—it's best to teach a course one or two times before evaluating and revising, so you have a firmer idea about what's working and what's not.

However, to know what's working well and what's not, we need to set up some ways now to collect that information. For example, I've been taking notes as we go for some things we didn't have time for—like that great idea you had to take a video camera on the road with you next summer when you're out exploring different locations in the state to look at specific rock formations. You also had mentioned interviewing a few geologists in the field, so I wrote that down as well.

Oh, wonderful! I keep thinking about those pieces and how engaging they'll be. I feel disappointed we didn't have time for them, but I feel a bit better knowing they're documented, and we have a plan to include them in the future. Is that all we have to do to plan for a future revision?

Not quite, but it's a big part of it. I'm also going to have you keep a list as you're teaching and make note of what you think is working well and what's not, as well as anything that needs to be fixed, or even additions that occur to you as you're actively teaching and interacting with students.

How will I know what needs fixing, though?

You'll know in part by how students do on assignments, and also by the questions they ask. However, we're also going to build in opportunities for students to give you feedback on the design of the course, and you can also include questions that would allow for feedback on your teaching as well, if you'd like.

Why would we need to create surveys, though? Students always fill out the end-of-course evaluation, and I thought that was their opportunity to provide feedback.

You're right that course evals are one way to receive feedback and probably the way that students are most familiar with giving feedback. However, the questions on the student evaluation of instruction don't ask much about the design of the course, and don't even ask questions that are specific to online courses. It's good feedback to have, but course evaluations won't really give us the specific information from students that we'll need for a future course design revision. Course evals are also only done once—at the end of the course. At that point, you can't even make small tweaks, so students provide feedback only for future benefit, not their own. Asking for feedback while they're taking the course provides greater value for them, as well as potential opportunities for you to acknowledge their feedback and make small fixes when possible.

I suppose I never really thought about it, but you're right. I'm going through the course eval questions in my mind right now, and very few of them are about design, and none are about technology or being an online student. And maybe so few students fill it out because they think it's a waste of time—after all, they've had no indication that I read and "respond" to student feedback!

Exactly! So, that's why planning for future revisions is the last step in HIDOC, because if we don't gather the data we need now, we won't have it when it comes time to improve your course. We can create end-of-module surveys, and/or end-of-course surveys, and you can craft the questions to gather the information that you're specifically interested in. You can also use this feedback to make changes as you're teaching, which gives it a dual purpose! It's another way to interact with students and elevate your teaching presence.

OK, that makes good sense to me, and I like the idea of having this "feedback loop" with students. I think most of the time they don't give feedback because they don't see professors using it, so they think it's a waste of time. But I like the idea that I can gather data that will help me in the future, while also seeing this as a conversation I can have now with students.

Summary and Next Steps

To sum it up...

Continuous improvement involves both review (for alignment, teachability, balance, and student workload) and revision (making changes between runs of the course and, in a few select instances, as the course is running). Determining the focus of your revisions includes reviewing information from your "Fix List" and "Wish List" and combining that with your observations as the course is running, as well as student feedback.

Looking ahead...

While we are done with all eight of the HIDOC steps, we have included a "bonus" chapter on Design Execution. Because all the design and pre-planning you've done using HIDOC is what allows for active teaching, facilitating, and moderating, we wanted to support you in effective delivery as well.

Bonus Chapter
Design Execution

CONGRATULATIONS!! You've now completed the eight steps of the HIDOC model! While not part of the HIDOC model because it's not design, how you deliver your course via active online teaching requires some attention. To that end, here in this "Bonus Chapter" we focus on how you can execute your design such that you elevate your teaching presence through active interaction with and guidance of your students. This active teaching is the crux of what's behind the federal policies related to Regular and Substantive Interaction (RSI) that we first discussed in Step 4.

Being Present in Your Online Course

To make sure RSI takes place, it is vital to create a plan for how you will be present in your online course. RSI, seen as a teaching practice instead of a policy, includes building rapport and trust to support the creation of an online learning community, engaging with students as you guide their learning, and providing rich feedback to your students. Below we discuss five specific ways to elevate these various facets of teaching presence, with differentiated ideas for asynchronous and synchronous teaching. You might have noticed that this chapter is the first time we dedicate targeted, sustained attention to both synchronous and asynchronous online courses. This is because in contrast to course design, online teaching is where the big differences come into play between asynchronous and synchronous courses. The five strategies for establishing presence in your online course are:

1. Make introductions
2. Use announcements to keep students motivated and on track
3. Capitalize on opportunities for guidance and connection
4. Make it personal
5. Extend the conversation

Make Introductions

Asynchronous option: As just mentioned in Step 7: Online Learner Support, it's important to introduce yourself and the course to students, just as you would on the first day of a F2F class. This can ideally be done through a short video, so students can see and hear you and get a sense of who you are and/or a brief presentation on what the course is about; salient course topics; the basic course structure, such as due dates and module organization; and even an important summative assignment. Use inclusive language to engender a sense of "we're all in this together." Here you begin to set the foundation for building a learning community and let students know you're available for help and that you hope they reach out. While both your instructor introduction and course introduction videos are created during your design, we're emphasizing them here again since students will likely experience this as the start of your active teaching and online presence.

Also, as per Step 7: Online Learner Support, remember to create an introduction opportunity for students as well. This is often set up within the LMS discussion space, and this is one discussion where we recommend replying to each individual student to welcome them to the course. Ideally, you can also find something in their introduction to respond to or comment on to make it more personal. If class size absolutely precludes this individualized approach, however, you can still make a whole-class announcement in which you make general comments regarding students' introductions that reference commonalities (or interesting differences!) in their posts. Students want to know you are reading and watching what they post.

Synchronous option: Begin your first synchronous session in a similar fashion to what you might do in an in-person course. Introduce yourself, go over the syllabus highlighting key policies and expectations, and start to get to know your students. You can email them prior to the first session to let them know that you'll start with a welcome/introduction discussion and provide them a pathway to pre-check their audio and video. (You might even offer a practice session or open the web-conferencing room early if students are nervous and want to make sure they won't have technology issues.)

An approach to student introductions that works for any online modality is to have students introduce themselves with a video or picture via FlipGrid or similar software. Depending on your class size, synchronous students can also do a quick hello on-screen, but you might want to save the longer introduction for an asynchronous format in the LMS.

More on Cameras

During the emergency remote teaching during the COVID pandemic, ill-prepared F2F students were forced online. As these students did not sign up for an online course, many concessions about appearing on camera had to be made. For example, some could not appear on camera for religious reasons, while others could not show their background because they had foster children who could not appear on camera. Many simply did not want to show their at-home learning space to peers.

For online synchronous courses, however, which are purposefully designed for online learning and which students consciously enroll in as an online course, there should be fewer issues with appearing on camera. In general, having cameras on helps students to get to know one another and build rapport and trust—all important for social presence and creating a learning community. That being said, however, you may still have students who need accommodations and cannot be on camera, or isolated times when students need to turn their video off for technology-related reasons. Look to see if your institution has policies around webcams in online courses.

In general, we encourage you to have an open conversation about this with your students. If cameras on helps you (and them) feel more connected and less isolated, then highlight that as a reason to engage via video. If you have course policies related to webcam use, this is important to let students know before the course begins (Welcome Letter options for this are discussed later), as some students will not necessarily assume that the course requires cameras to be on. For these students, you might steer them toward asynchronous courses or you might provide a non-camera alternative, where students use a representative image or avatar. If you do require webcams and a student requests an accommodation, you might need to connect with your institutional office that deals with legal matters.

Use Announcements to Keep Students Motivated and on Track

Asynchronous option. Make good use of the Announcements tool in your LMS, and plan for about one to three announcements per week in the LMS. The "right" number can vary, depending on length of course and your students—graduate students or those taking a shortened online course may find more than one announcement per week overwhelming, while new online students might find two or three announcements per week helps them stay on track and feel connected. If you're unsure, this is also a great survey question or live poll question for synchronous classes. Along with assignment reminders, using the Announcements tool is a great way to make additional connections for students, such as linking course topics and discussions to relevant outside-of-class events or topics to increase relevance. Strongly consider making a few announcements as videos or audio files so that your students can have a chance to see and hear you.

Synchronous option. Engage students with live announcements at the start of each session to set the tone and build momentum. Consider starting your class with something fun—it could be a "fun fact" related to course topics, a course-appropriate joke or meme, or even an essential question designed to promote inquiry. Also be sure to do some "housekeeping" by making course announcements related to work that is due that week, big assignments coming up, reminders for online student resources (e.g., tutoring, library services)—or even use the time to provide kudos via group feedback for a general job well done on a recent assignment.

Additional ideas. These apply to both asynchronous and synchronous teaching options.

- Post a first-day announcement as an additional welcome and to remind students of some important items, such as the Start Here folder, the syllabus and schedule, preferred (or prohibited) browsers to use with the LMS, and technical support information.
- Post an announcement encouraging social presence by letting them know you're enjoying getting to know them better through their introduction posts and reminding them of the Q&A discussion board if you have one.

- Post a reminder the day before a major assignment is due. Depending on the course, it may be overwhelming to remind students of every assignment, but it's always a good idea to post about larger assignments.
- The first time students have a self-check quiz (or similar activity), explain what it is, how they'll receive feedback, and how it can benefit their learning.
- Create and post a screencast or handout with images that show how to view your feedback. Viewing feedback in an LMS is often not as intuitive as you think. Students who are newer to online learning (or that particular LMS) may see only their grade but be unaware that they can access additional assignment feedback from you.
- The first time students have a timed quiz or exam, encourage them to save their work as they go if it's an option. Also, explain any other key details about how the timed assessment will work. For example, will they see their numerical grade upon submission, or will you do additional grading before they receive it? How, if at all, will they receive information on questions missed? Your announcement and timed assessment setup should reflect your approach to student access to correct and incorrect answers.
- Whenever you are done providing feedback for a particular assignment, include that in the announcement so that students are prompted to check in (students may not be automatically notified of this). You might also include how they can use your feedback, such as applying it to a specific, upcoming assessment.
- If you see low scores on practice quizzes for a certain topic(s), post an announcement addressing this and suggesting options. You can highlight material that students can review and also reiterate when your office/ student hours are and let them know if you're available to connect outside of those hours.
- If you get a good question in the Q&A board or via email that you think the whole class would benefit from, post that information as an announcement.
- Have fun, too! You can post course-appropriate comics, links to fun, short videos about course topics, and more. You'll want to be mindful if

you do use humor, though, to steer away from sarcasm and potentially sensitive topics, as those can be especially tricky online.

- Share popular articles you might find that relate to class topics or discuss what you're working on in your own studies that might be related, books you'd recommend, and/or conference talks you've heard. However, be cautious of overwhelming students with too many additional sources that they might perceive as "required." It can be tempting to "overstuff" your course, so make sure your announcements are concise and helpful.
- When a new learning unit or module begins, take the opportunity to make connections to past topics, introduce the new unit in a few sentences, and/or post a critical inquiry question.
- Let students know early on that their interaction with the LMS is transparent. You can put a positive spin on this by saying something such as, "Our Learning Management System has some great tools so that you and your professors can keep on top of your progress. It keeps track of when you log in, how long you spend in the course interacting with materials, what materials you interact with, and can even help identify completed work (such as saved quiz responses), should there be a technology issue. Although it's rare, should you have a technology issue completing a quiz, please let me know ASAP so that I can examine the LMS data to determine the issue." This lets students know from the start that you can observe their interaction with the LMS and that you'll be monitoring this as one way to help keep them on track and to know early on if someone is struggling.
- If you've collaboratively designed your course with peers, or are teaching a course you did not design, acknowledge the faculty who developed the course materials by posting an early announcement explaining that. For example, you might mention that students won't hear your voice in (some or all) the lectures if this is the case. You might post something like, "Just like most F2F classes, where the textbook is usually not written by the instructor, this online class has great material that was developed by [faculty name]. This is a great opportunity to learn from multiple instructors here in the department. So, while you won't hear my voice in the online lectures, I will be providing feedback and additional

guidance, answering your questions, and helping make sure you stay connected to your learning."

Opportunities for Guidance and Connection

Asynchronous and synchronous: As discussed, online learning environments, whether asynchronous or synchronous, are best designed as student-centered environments, allowing you to guide learning and motivate your students via robust feedback, which is a prime opportunity to elevate teaching presence. For example, consider providing feedback as a screencast (great for grading papers!) or as a video to enhance the connection with your students. Providing screencasted feedback can also be a timesaver, since talking through a student paper that you've pulled up on screen is often easier than using web-based tools for markup. As we emphasized in Step 4: Assessments & Activities, feedback is especially important in online courses because you can't easily respond to the confused faces or nodding heads. Additionally, since we don't always have the opportunity to build in-person rapport with our online students, it's even more vital to remember that feedback is also an opportunity to praise students for their work and/or effort made for improvement and to motivate them to stay invested in the course. These additional feedback goals can be done during synchronous sessions as well for the whole group, or in asynchronous group feedback or announcements.

Also consider holding some targeted online office/student hours dedicated to specific topics or assignments, and invite students to submit questions ahead of time. Especially at first, be prepared for students to not submit questions, either out of fear of asking a "stupid" question or because they "don't know what they don't know." A clever workaround, however, is to prepare some questions ahead of time (you likely know many of the questions or areas of confusion they may have based on previous offerings). Present these as student questions, helping them gain confidence that they, too, can submit questions. You might even throw in a "stupid" (or more foundational) question to demonstrate that there is no such thing!

When it comes to upcoming quizzes and exams, you can invite students to submit potential questions. You might even choose to grade questions based on accuracy, inventiveness, and complexity. These student-submitted questions can then be used in a review (live for synchronous or done as a handout or practice quiz for asynchronous) or even on the actual quiz or exam. You can also use synchronous class time for a gamified review for an upcoming exam, such as a "Jeopardy-style" game or a simple polling with multiple-choice questions.

Make it Personal

Asynchronous option: Don't underestimate the power of an individual email. Online students place a high value on a personal email from their professor, as it can help them feel an authentic connection with you. Reaching out to students via email also opens the door to having them reply and/or email you in the future. This is something that many online students are reluctant to do first. To make it doable for your instructor workload, you can create planned emails to send at strategic times, such as a few days after the course begins (for example, responding to their individual introductions), during the middle of the term, and again near the end. You can create the same or similar emails for all students, then personalize a bit for those who are struggling, to give individual kudos for students, or to acknowledge their individual contributions in other ways. This "customized copy/paste" option can make this student connection opportunity more doable for you.

Synchronous option: Pay attention to student participation and personalization during your class sessions by calling on students by name. Take advantage of the modality with some fun/social questions to build connection and rapport. For example, you can encourage students to take a moment now and then to show their pets, or ask for volunteers to share their current favorite TV show or caffeinated beverage that keeps them going. For students who are low participators, reach out to them after class and ask if there's anything you can do to make them feel more comfortable—they might have technology issues or be unsure of how to speak up. Knowing more about your students and how they interact with synchronous technologies can provide you with vital information that could change your future sessions to further elevate social and cognitive presence for all students.

Extend the Conversation

Asynchronous option: Creating an "Instructor Blog" is a great way to provide a deeper dive on course-related topics, enhance the relevance of information and skills by connecting students to real-world situations, or connect students with scholars in the field and professional organizations relevant to the discipline. Some LMSs have a blog tool, while others will allow you to use a discussion board in a blog-like fashion. An Instructor Blog could be optional for students to read and can be a combination of written text, audio, and/or video. You might, for example, take a course-related topic that students have expressed interest in but that you will not be covering (or covering fully), and expand on that in a blog post, perhaps even linking a relevant article or website. If you're at an academic conference, you might report on the sessions you're attending or interview a presenter. This "optional add" might be overwhelming to try for newer online instructors but is a great advanced piece, especially once you are more comfortable teaching the course.

Synchronous option: Talk with students...not at them. When presenting information to students during a synchronous session, create a dialogue that helps them process that information. Even if you are doing a more traditional lecture, plan "pause points" during which you can ask students a question or ask them how this new information connects to past information in the course or their own experience. You can also use this time to address any questions that they've submitted in the chat or Q&A space. You could also create a scenario or construct a case study and send students to breakout rooms to discuss and report back. The scenario could be a professional work situation, or students could discuss a process, collaborate on solving a problem, or generate potential solutions to a theoretical Issue.

Your Course Timeline

In terms of when you execute specific teaching activities like those discussed above, you can think about your course in terms of the following time frames:

1. Before your course begins
2. First week of your course
3. Early weeks of your course
4. Throughout the entirety of your course
5. Final week of your course

Before Class Begins

- **Send a "Welcome Letter"**

  Send an email to students about one to two weeks before class begins, welcoming them to the course and explaining that this is an online course and all that that entails. Be sure to address key elements of required technology such as whether students can take the entire course on their mobile device and if they need a consistent internet connection or are able to download content pieces to access while in transit or otherwise not connected. Refer to Step 6: Technology & Tools and Step 7: Online Learner Support for additional guidance on anticipating and planning for technology needs. Explain key elements of the specific course structure for your course (e.g., explain that an asynchronous course has no required meetings, that required synchronous class sessions will be accompanied by asynchronous work in the LMS). Here is where you can also provide information for anything they'll need to purchase, including a textbook or lab kit, or peripherals, such as a webcam and headset. If possible, attach or link to your course syllabus as well as any LMS tutorials.

- **Open the Course**

  A week or so before the course officially begins, consider opening your course's "first day" materials. This gives students an opportunity to explore your Start Here folder items or Home Page (e.g., your instructor introduction, course overview and/or navigational screencast, syllabus, and schedule), and even potentially post their student introduction. If you will be opening these introductory items early, note this in your Welcome Letter and email students when this part of the course is available to them.

Module Release: Staggered or All-at-Once?

Technology in the LMS allows several options for releasing learning modules in your online course. The two general approaches are **Staggered Release,** where new modules are opened or "released" when they begin (or a few days prior), and **All-at-Once Release,** where all of the modules are open when the course begins. Here we talk about the two general approaches, plus a few customized options.

In a staggered release, all modules are hidden when the course begins except for the Introductory/Start Here module or folder. New modules, then, are released on their start day or a few days prior. For example, if your modules always begin on a Monday, you could open the module on a Friday or Saturday for students who want the spend the weekend looking ahead to the next week's materials. With this approach, you are ensuring that students will generally be learning together as they work through your course week-by-week. This benefits your ability to facilitate an active learning community and elevate teaching and social presence, as students move through the course as a true cohort, guided by you. A staggered release benefits greatly from a clear course overview, a clear course schedule to give students an idea of the scope and timing of work, and announcements that reference what's ahead. With this approach, you may have to make individual accommodations for active-duty military or other circumstances that require students to have access to future modules early. However, it is the optimal approach if your primary concern is moving through the course as an online learning community.

An all-at-once release, opening all modules on the first day of the course, is generally the default option in the LMS and for some instructors is, therefore, the easiest. For many students, it can give a sense of the "big picture" and allow those who like to look ahead the option to do so, which can help introduce predictability and rein in anxiety about course topics, workload, or scope. It also allows busy students juggling multiple commitments outside of the course, such as those for work, family, or the military, to better plan their time. When using this model, however, it is crucial to clarify for students that "looking ahead" for the sake of planning is not the same as "working ahead." Students who ignore this caveat may end up investing their time unwisely by working on assessments without the benefit of crucial feedback on previous assignments, or engaging with content they're not ready to tackle. If you are not clear with students about your expectations for interaction, an all-at-once release can also inadvertently suggest to students that the course is a correspondence model, and that the instructor is not that important for learning.

Additional, Customized options:

- **Conditional Release** of individual content, activities, or assessments, if it is a feature of your LMS, allows certain things to be accessed only after other requirements have been met. For example, a discussion becomes available only after students have passed a quiz demonstrating that they have done the reading and can define and apply the terms and ideas. This variation allows students to proceed on your learning path only when they're ready to move forward. Conditional release can be used with both a staggered and all-at-once release approach.
- **Limited Release** makes only the module overview (including the module introduction and clarifying what students will read, watch, and do) visible in advance. It gives a concise but clear idea of what the module is about and lists and briefly describes the content, activities, and assessments that students will engage with (assignment prompts might be accessible as well). Together with the detailed information in the course syllabus, this approach benefits students who are looking to gain an idea of how the course will unfold and plan their time.

However you choose to release your learning modules, it's vital to establish clear policies or guidelines for things such as interaction expectations, late and early work submissions, turnaround time for feedback, and accommodation requests for work or life events that prevent students from following the set schedule. Ultimately, you'll need to consider your student population and the practices and expectations of other courses in the program to determine which module-release option is most appropriate. There is a balance between respecting the diversity of your students' needs and contexts outside of your class, and ensuring that you have an active, engaged learning community rather than a correspondence course.

First Week of Class

- **Post a Welcome Announcement**

  On the first official day of class, post a course announcement welcoming students and reminding them of important items and tasks, such as reviewing the syllabus and schedule, watching any introductory videos from you, and directing them to their first activities (usually a student introduction and/or short syllabus quiz). This is also a good time to remind students of the course modality (i.e., asynchronous, synchronous), any requirements regarding live attendance, how they can contact you if they have questions or are struggling. Be sure to set a positive and welcoming tone to enhance feelings of belonging, to reduce distance and "humanize" the course, and to allay potential fears or anxieties from students who are nervous about the course and/or being an online student.

- **Highlight Technology Help and Resources**

  Sometime during the first week, make an announcement that includes or links to comprehensive technology information students will need to be successful in your course. For any of this technology information that you already mentioned in your welcome letter and/or syllabus, simply be explicit that you are reminding them of it here.

- **Email Students Who Have Not Logged In**

  Week One is a crucial time to connect with students who are struggling—you might begin by using any available LMS-based-analytics options for monitoring student performance. By day three or four, individually email any student who has not yet logged in to the course. Students may have technical issues and not know how to contact you or may not realize they signed up for an online course (both are additional good reasons to email out a welcome letter in advance!). Alternatively, some students might be under the incorrect impression that online courses, especially asynchronous ones, are passive learning experiences where they can log in when they want, work ahead, or even complete all the work at once, and that they'll have no required interaction with their professor or peers. In your email, ask if the student is having issues, and give various options for connecting with them. Remind them of how to log on, expectations for online attendance, and where to find help if they can't log in. You will likely need to send this email outside the LMS platform in case the issue is with them accessing their online course.

Early Weeks

The following actions might be done separately, or you could choose to combine some or all into one announcement.

- **Begin Assignment Reminders Early**

  Be sure to post an announcement prior to the first assignment. Remind students (or directly link to) where they can find information about the assignment, what tool they'll be using, and when they can expect feedback. This is also an opportunity to remind students where the course schedule is, and that assignments have both due dates and due times. In this announcement, you might also choose to highlight syllabus information related to your grading approach or policy (e.g. points, weighting, ungrading) and even your late-work policy.

- **Explain Online "Office/Student hours"**

  This announcement reminds students when your online office/student hours are and explains alternative ways they can contact you if necessary. Prior to your first "live" office/student hours, remind students of the focus of the session and how they can connect (e.g., Zoom, phone, chat).

- **Highlight Academic and Student Supports**

  Also in the beginning weeks, remind students of available academic and student supports, such as how to use the library and borrow materials as an online student, as well as how to access relevant online tutoring services, mental health services, and accessibility services, and what to do if they need a learning accommodation. Much of this information will likely be in your syllabus, so you can remind them of it or simply draw their attention to the relevant location.

Throughout the Course

- **Practice "Just-in-Time" Active Teaching**

  "Just-in-Time" active teaching is a way to be responsive to students' learning needs in real time, but to also be as proactive about it as possible. This means reflecting ahead of time on course topics or assignments where you expect students to struggle or be confused, either because it's complex or because past students have had a difficult experience. A short "Clarification Point" video can clarify topics with your additional explanation; you can address misconceptions and answer questions within the module in an email or announcement; or you can respond to questions in an open Q&A discussion forum. Of course, as a truly "just-in-time" response, you might also be creating or curating some material as the course is running if students struggle in a new or unexpected way. (This then becomes just-in-time material for you to have ready for the next time you teach the course.) Releasing pieces like this in a spontaneous way not only provides students with additional guidance when needed, but also conveys that you are guiding students in real time. Your teaching presence is elevated, and students experience that you are actively engaging with them and responding to their needs.

- **Focus on Robust and Varied Feedback**

  As we've discussed throughout the book, providing quality, robust feedback is a primary component of active online teaching. As the course runs, refer to your Teaching Calendar to stay on top of feedback so that students receive it in a timely manner. We also encourage you to think of feedback as a communication loop with your students. When they turn in an assignment (or complete a course feedback survey), provide acknowledgement feedback similar to the "thanks" you might say when students hand you a paper in class. For student feedback surveys, highlight some good suggestions students gave and how you'll put them to use (even if it's only possible to do so in future iterations of the course). It's also a good idea to explain why you aren't changing certain things that students asked for, such as due to technology or time limitations, or for pedagogical reasons.

- **Provide "Summary" Announcements**

  Summary announcements can be used to summarize the big ideas from a module that is ending, or to provide summary feedback to the whole class that highlights good ideas contributed in a class discussion or examples of good student work. Summary announcements provide a good way to help students focus on the big takeaways from a module or discussion, highlight the major points for an important piece of content, and/or provide closure and connection from one learning unit to the next.

- **Keep an Instructor Blog**

  As previously mentioned, an instructor blog is a blog (or blog-like discussion) that you keep throughout the course as a way to connect with students and expand the relevance of course content and activities. It's a great way to share timely information with students, provide additional insights, connect students to professional resources, make what they're learning/doing in class even more relevant, and increase your teaching presence. Again, this is another place to be proactive—have some blog posts drafted before the course begins on topics that you want to share more on but are not required information. For posts you create while the course is running, then, save those to re-post next time you teach, making edits where necessary. Pretty soon, you'll have a great series of blog posts that you can easily release at strategic points in the course, and students experience it as just-in-time, responsive, active teaching.

Final Week

- **Provide Closure**

  In F2F classes, it's very common that some type of closure happens on the last day of class. You might collect a final assignment, have students fill out end-of-course evaluations, and/or thank them for a great semester. The end of a course is an opportunity for you to close both the larger cycle of learning for the class and to connect with students in a way that closes your time with them. You can do this via an announcement, for example, that shares top course takeaways, highlights assignments that can be used for their professional portfolios, or simply offers closing thoughts or thanks. As this will likely be your final announcement, it's also a great opportunity to create it as a short webcam video, so students can see and hear you a final time.

- **Solicit Feedback**

  If you have a final feedback survey and/or a required institutional evaluation, such as a student evaluation of instruction, remind students to complete this, as well as why their feedback is important and how it will be used.

 Your Turn: Active Teaching

Regardless of what online modality you're teaching in, it's important that you keep yourself (and your students) on track by planning in advance. This is where we return to your Teaching Calendar to finish creating your plan for being active and present as the course is running. This planning is especially vital for asynchronous online courses, where you don't have any scheduled class sessions to provide a "rhythm" for the course or built-in opportunities for interaction. For synchronous courses, the Teaching Calendar can also serve as a way for you to plan how you will engage with students in person and how you will interact with them online in the asynchronous course space.

Below is an example of a completed Teaching Calendar with all five rows filled out (the first two rows might look familiar as they were previously shown in Step 8). Many of your weeks might look similar to each other, with notable differences only when there is a big assessment or tough topic, or it is the first time students are interacting with new technology.

Example teaching calendar

Wk 3 (5/14–5/20)	SUN	MON	TUE	WED	THUR	FRI	SAT
1. Student Assignments Due	Research paper draft due (~10 pages)		Module 3 discussion post due		Discussion reply due		
2. Instructor Feeedback & Grading Schedule	Begin grading research paper drafts.	Continue grading research paper drafts.	Return all paper drafts with feedback.	Grade initial discussion posts.		Grade discussion replies; provide class summary on points.	
3. Office/ student hours				Caption and post office/ student hours Zoom session to LMS.		Office/ student hours 3 – 5 pm	

Wk 3 (5/14–5/20)	SUN	MON	TUE	WED	THUR	FRI	SAT
4. Clarification & Guidance		Post handout on attending office/student hours in Zoom.				Answer any remaining questions about the research paper draft.	
5. Announce-ments		Introduce M3; remind re: 1st disc post. Explain dedicated office/student hours for research paper			Reminder for disc replies; remind about paper draft and to review office/student hours recorded		

 Your Turn: Teaching Calendar

In Step 8, you laid out the first two rows of your Teaching Calendar. In this section, you will fill out the remaining rows in the table.

List your Office/Student Hours.
List the set days/times on your Teaching Calendar. If any will be focused on a specific topic or upcoming assignment, you can indicate that as well. This is also the row where, if you are teaching a synchronous course, you would indicate the days/times of required class meetings.

Indicate times to provide Clarification and Guidance.
In this row, proactively block out time for answering questions or providing guidance when learners are tackling a tough or challenging topic. A proactive way to address this is to create "clarification point" posts or videos to be released when learners are diving into complex material.

Note when you will post your Announcements.
Here is where you will strategically plot out the timing and focus of your class announcements, although of course this can be added to or altered as you respond organically to how the class is going once it begins.

Your Teaching Calendar

1. Open the **Teaching Calendar** Design Document from the companion website, use the version in the Design Doc Library section of the book, or create a version that works for you.
2. For each week in the semester, finish your **Teaching Calendar** by completing the last three rows **(Office/Student Hours, Clarification & Guidance, and Announcements).**

Summary and Next Steps

To sum it up...

Your role as an active instructor is as vital in an online course as it is in an in-person one. Like so much that we've discussed with online learning, however, it does require advanced thinking and planning, and this chapter has highlighted several different ways to connect with and guide your online learners. Given all the moving parts of an online course, it can be especially important that you manage your teaching activities through a tool like a Teaching Calendar.

Looking ahead...

The next section of the book, Section II: HIDOC-in-Action (Course Design Cases), explores multiple case examples that address many common design scenarios, including common oversights and pitfalls. The cases span multiple disciplines, highlight successes and challenges, and show how the HIDOC model can be used to make improvements that benefit both instructors and students.

For Further Reading on Online Teaching

Ambrose, S., Bridges, M., DiPietro, M., Lovett, M., & Norman, M. (2010). How learning works: 7 research-based principles for smart teaching. San Francisco, CA: Jossey Bass.

Anderson, T., Rourke, L., Garrison, D.R., & Archer, W. (2001). Assessing teaching presence in a computer conference environment. *Journal of Asynchronous Learning Networks,* 5(2), 1–17.

Boettcher, J.V., & Conrad, R-M. (2016). The online teaching survival guide (2nd ed.). San Francisco: Jossey-Bass.

Darby, F., & Lang, J.M. (2019). Small teaching online: Applying learning science in online classes (1st ed.). Jossey-Bass.

Fiock, H. (2020). Designing a community of inquiry in online courses. *The International Review of Research in Open and Distributed Learning,* 21(1), 134–152. https://doi.org/10.19173/irrodl.v20i5.3985

Garrison, D.R., Anderson, T., & Archer, W. (2001). Critical thinking, cognitive presence, and computer conferencing in distance education. *American Journal of Distance Education,* 15(1), 7–23. https://doi.org/10.1080/08923640109527071

Garrison, D.R., & Cleveland-Innes, M. (2005). Facilitating cognitive presence in online learning: Interaction is not enough. *American Journal of Distance Education,* 19(3), 133–148. https://doi.org/10.1207/s15389286ajde1903_2

Lehman, R.M., & Conceição, S.C.O. (2010). Creating a sense of presence in online teaching: How to "be there" for distance learners (1st ed.). Jossey-Bass.

Palloff, R.M., & Pratt, K. (2007). Building online learning communities: Effective strategies for the virtual classroom (2nd ed.). Jossey-Bass.

Riggs, S. (2020). Thrive online: A new approach to building expertise and confidence as an online educator. Stylus Publishing.

Shea, P., Swan, K., & Pickett, A. (2005). Developing learning community in online asynchronous college courses: The role of teaching presence. *Journal of Asynchronous Learning Networks.* 9.10.24059/olj.v9i4.1779.

Stavredes, T. (2011). Effective online teaching. Jossey-Bass.

Szeto, E. (2015). Community of Inquiry as an instructional approach: What effects of teaching, social and cognitive presences are there in blended synchronous learning and teaching? *Computers & Education,* 81, 191–201. https://doi.org/10.1016/j.compedu.2014.10.015

DESIGN DOC LIBRARY

HIDOC Course Blueprint

Key Course Details (Step 1)

1. Course name & number	
2. Course level, e.g., grad., undergrad., dual enrollment	
3. Course length	
4. Course credits	
5. Expected enrollment range	
6. Required program course or elective status	
7. Course prerequisites, if any	
8. Courses following, if any	
9. Course modality, e.g., dual mode, online synchronous, asynchronous	
10. Other details, e.g., cross-listed, writing intensive	

Course Learning Outcomes (Step 2)

CLO #1	By the end of this course, students will be able to…
CLO #2	By the end of this course, students will be able to…
CLO #3	By the end of this course, students will be able to…
CLO #4	By the end of this course, students will be able to…
CLO #5	By the end of this course, students will be able to…
CLO #6	By the end of this course, students will be able to…
CLO #7	By the end of this course, students will be able to…

HIDOC Course Blueprint

Course Alignment Map [MACRO VIEW]

Use abbreviations as appropriate and be sure to add a row below for each module (or unit, lesson, week).

Module #, title, duration (Step 3)	CLOs (# or abb.) addressed (Step 4)	Assessments & learning activities (Step 4)	Content & instructional materials (Step 5)	Technology and other notes (Step 6)

HIDOC Course Blueprint

Detailed Module Layout [MICRO VIEW] (Step 7)

Your module overview is the first page of content in a module and makes explicit for students much of what happens naturally in an in-person class (e.g., introductions, connections, transitions, summaries). It comprises the first five rows below. The last page of your module includes a module summary and module next steps that connect the module they are leaving to the next part of the course. (Create a copy of the table below for each module and be sure to update your Course Alignment Map [MACRO VIEW] to reflect revisions.)

Identify the Module on which you are working	
List the CLOs connected to this module	
List, then briefly describe, the module Assessments & Learning Activities	
List, then briefly describe, the module Instructional Materials	
Draft a Module Introduction	
Create MLOs	
Draft a Module Summary	
Write module Next Steps	

Step 1: Learner Analysis

Part 1: Key Course Details

Enter the following key information about your course.

1. Course name & number	
2. Course level, e.g., grad., undergrad., dual enrollment	
3. Course length	
4. Course credits	
5. Expected enrollment range	
6. Required program course or elective status	
7. Course prerequisites, if any	
8. Courses following, if any	
9. Course modality, e.g., dual mode, online synchronous, asynchronous	
10. Other details, e.g., cross-listed, writing intensive	

 Step 1: Learner Analysis

Part 2: Learner Considerations

Respond to the following questions to get a holistic sense of your anticipated learners and their learning needs.

1. Who typically takes your course?
2. What knowledge & experience do students typically bring into the course?
3. What misconceptions or preconceived notions do students often have/are likely to have about the course?
4. What are some things students frequently struggle with in your course?
5. How is this course, and its topics and activities, relevant to these students?
6. What "non-content" skills must a student have to be successful in the course?

Step 2: Learning Outcomes

Part 1: Big Vision

This is a "Free Think Space" for you to use before moving to the more granular level of drafting your CLOs. Consider your vision for this course. What are its big takeaways? What are the significant ideas or provocative questions that drew you in and will draw students in?

Part 2: Draft Your CLOs

What do you want your students to know or understand by the end of the course? What should they be able to do, and/or what new skills should they have? In this draft, you can use "fuzzy" verbs that can't be measured, such as "know," "understand," "learn," or "appreciate," to begin your thinking, or you can choose to dive right in with using active verbs.

CLO #1	By the end of this course, students will be able to...
CLO #2	By the end of this course, students will be able to...
CLO #3	By the end of this course, students will be able to...
CLO #4	By the end of this course, students will be able to...
CLO #5	By the end of this course, students will be able to...
CLO #6	By the end of this course, students will be able to...
CLO #7	By the end of this course, students will be able to...

Step 2: Learning Outcomes

Part 3: Revise Your CLOs

Now it is time to carefully revise your draft learning outcomes to be measurable and student-focused (i.e., clear, specific, focused on mastery). Clarify your CLOs to describe what students will be able to do by the end of the course.

CLO #1	By the end of this course, students will be able to...
CLO #2	By the end of this course, students will be able to...
CLO #3	By the end of this course, students will be able to...
CLO #4	By the end of this course, students will be able to...
CLO #5	By the end of this course, students will be able to...
CLO #6	By the end of this course, students will be able to...
CLO #7	By the end of this course, students will be able to...

Step 2: Learning Outcomes

Part 4: Check Your CLOs

It's time to check your CLOs. Can you answer YES to each of the following? If not, return to Revise Your CLOs to make the necessary improvements.

Each of my CLOs begins with an active verb and describes what students will do to demonstrate their learning.	[YES/NO]
Each of my CLOs avoids fuzzy verbs such as "understand," "know," or "learn," or any verb that cannot be measured or observed.	[YES/NO]
Each of my CLOs is written in clear language so that incoming students can understand what they mean.	[YES/NO]
Each of my CLOs gives students a general idea of what they will be learning and doing in the course.	[YES/NO]
Each of my CLOs is broad enough that they are major outcomes for the course.	[YES/NO]
Each of my CLOs is specific but not an assignment description.	[YES/NO]
Each of my CLOs relays the desired degree of mastery.	[YES/NO]

Step 3: Course Structure

Part 1: Module Brainstorming

1. Brainstorm your learning path. Think through the learning path you will create. What will students need to learn and do first? What topics will then build on their new knowledge and skills?
2. Consider the length of your course. If you are currently teaching a shortened version of a course that you know will also be taught as a full-term course, we suggest mapping it out first as a full-term course.
3. Focus on your first and final week. Will the first week include some "introductory" material? Will the final week include some type of reflective activity?

Step 3: Course Structure

Part 2: Module Planning

It's now time to do a first draft of your course structure. For each learning unit (e.g., week, module, lesson), complete the following steps:

1. Provide the module #.
2. Give each module a title.
3. Indicate the length of the module. For example, you might have one module per week or a module that spans several weeks.
4. Capture additional information. This can include topics you know will be covered, associated assessments, and activities. These are notes that will guide you in brainstorming instructional content and assessment ideas later in the process.

#	Module title	Length	Additional module info.

 Step 4: Assessments & Activities

Part 1: Summative Assessments

1. Reference your most updated module information & revised list of CLOs. Your most updated list of course modules will be in the HIDOC Course Blueprint in the Course Alignment Map [MACRO VIEW] section, and your revised CLOs will be near the top of that same document in the Course Learning Outcomes (Step 2) section. You can copy over the most updated module information to the table below or simply reference it.

2. Describe, or simply list, each of the summative assessments you think will be in the course in the table below. Start by determining where each summative assessment falls in the context of your course modules. Remember, these are typically larger assessments that happen at crucial times (e.g., mid-term and final) or after covering crucial topics.

Module # & title (time span if helpful)	**Summative Assessments**	**Formative Assessments**	**Learning Activities**

 Step 4: Assessments & Activities

Part 2: Formative Assessments & Learning Activities

1. Describe, or simply list, each corresponding formative assessment in the previous table. Make sure that students have opportunities to be evaluated with feedback that will help them prepare for their summative assessment.
2. Describe, or simply list, each corresponding learning activity in the previous table. Reflect on assessments or concepts that students struggle with (or places you anticipate they'll struggle), then provide practice learning activities in these areas to provide additional guidance and instruction.

Part 3: Assessments and Learning Activities Check

Given your identified assessments & learning activities ("assignments"), it's time to think about voice & choice and opportunities for interaction. For each summative assessment, formative assessment, and learning activity:

1. **Identify which assignments could provide elements of voice & choice.**
2. **Identify which assignments could be made to be interactive.**
3. **Brainstorm new possibilities for assignments that might lend themselves to voice and choice and/or interaction.**

 Step 4: Assessments & Activities

Part 4: Learning Outcomes Alignment

You want to ensure that each of your Course Learning Outcomes (CLOs) is assessed by at least one summative assessment and that each summative assessment aligns with at least one CLO. Remember, you might have a CLO assessed by more than one summative assessment, and a summative assessment that aligns with more than one CLO. Return to Part 1 and review your summative assessments and CLOs. Can you say yes to each of the following?

Each of my CLOs is assessed by at least one Summative Assessment.	[YES/NO]
Each of my Summative Assessments is aligned with at least one CLO.	[YES/NO]
The cognitive level of the active verb(s) in each CLO matches the cognitive level of the corresponding assessment(s).	[YES/NO]

Based on this review, revise your CLOs and/or assessments as needed.

 Step 5: Instructional Materials

Instructional Materials

At this point in the process, you'll start to identify which specific instructional materials will best support the summative assessments in each of your modules.

1. Reference your most updated modules, assessments, and activities. (The most updated version of the first and second column below should be in your HIDOC Course Blueprint document, so you can either have that open while you work or copy it over here.)
2. Describe the learning function of the content/material that students need to be successful in this module.
3. Provide specific information about the source for this content.
4. Evaluate content inclusivity.
5. Evaluate content accessibility.

Step 5: Instructional Materials

Module # & title	Assessments & learning activities	Learning function of the content	Content source information	Content inclusivity notes	Content accessibility notes

 BONUS DEVELOPMENT DOC Step 5: Online Topical Lectures

Online Topical Lectures

In this Bonus Development Doc, we walk you through one way of sketching out a topical lecture.

1. Provide a relevant title.	
2. Add context & connections. Relate it to prior topics, be clear with related learning goal(s), & indicate which assessments it supports.	
3. Identify the main points/ideas. This is a general, short summary of what the lecture is about.	
4. Explain each main point. And, provide sub-points or a short explanation for what you plan to say for each one.	
5. Identify relevant visuals, then identify corresponding visuals that can help make your explanation more powerful.	

 Step 6: Technology & Tools

Part 1: Technology Planning

Review your assessments and activities in your Course Alignment Map in the HIDOC Course Blueprint and start to identify the types of technologies and tools you will need. Be sure to consider instructional alignment.

1. What LMS tools (or web-based tools) will you select to support students as they interact with content and complete assignments?
2. Will students need additional software outside the LMS?
3. Which tools will support synchronous meetings like office/student hours?
4. Will students need a webcam or headset?
5. Will your course require proctored exams?
6. Will students need any special hardware or software to interact with simulations, games, and/or websites or web-based technology?
7. Will students need to download free software or plug-ins in order to access course materials?

Step 6: Technology & Tools

Part 2: Technology Documentation

Because students need to know all that is expected of them in terms of technical requirements, we recommend putting the following in your syllabus or other course overview materials. You may already have boilerplate language from your institution that you can insert.

1. Specifications for any software and/or hardware requirements
2. Browser requirements
3. Internet access requirements
4. Computer requirements
5. Specifications for connecting to university services from off-campus

BONUS DEVELOPMENT DOC Step 7: Assignment Prompts

Part 1: Key Segments of Assignment Prompts

Select an assessment or learning activity to work on here. Whether you'll be using rubrics or not, you will want to create an assignment prompt that details the following.

1. Identify the assignment and provide a brief description.
2. Describe what they are doing in the assignment and why.
3. Explain how they will be evaluated.
4. Specify how they will submit their work.

Part 2: Check for Clarity

If possible, swap assignment prompts with a colleague so that you both have the advantage of getting feedback from the "student perspective" before your course runs. Did your assignment prompt reviewer...?

Find your prompt concise and clear?	[YES/NO]
Know precisely what they were supposed to do for this assignment and why?	[YES/NO]
Know how they would be evaluated on this assignment?	[YES/NO]
Know how, and in what format, to submit their work?	[YES/NO]

Use this feedback to revise your assignment prompt as needed.

 Step 8: Revision Roadmap

1. **"Fix List"**

   Here you should list things that you know now need some attention.

2. **"Wish List"**

   Here, make a note of things you wanted to do but did not have the expertise or time to carry out during this first iteration of your design.

3. **Other Ideas for Improvement**

   As the course is running, you may note other ideas for improvement, including those that come from student feedback, that don't fit the "fix list" or "wish list."

Step 8: Teaching Calendar

In Step 8, you will fill out the first two rows of this table, and in the Bonus Chapter you will fill out the remaining three. You will need to create a copy of this table for each week of the semester.

	SUN	MON	TUE	WED	THUR	FRI	SAT
1. Student Assignments Due							
2. Instructor Feedback & Grading Schedule							
3. Office/ Student Hours							
4. Clarification & Guidance							
5. Announcements							

SECTION II

HIDOC-IN-ACTION: DESIGN CASE EXAMPLES

HIDOC-in-Action

Welcome to HIDOC-in-Action: Course Design Cases!

This section reflects real-life design cases from our over 60 years combined experience working with instructors like yourselves across numerous disciplines, levels, and institutions. While these cases are based on real-life events, they are also an amalgamation and cannot be attributed to any single course, instructor, or institution. Here, we provide examples that span a wide range of disciplines, student cohort types, and instructor design choices. Most importantly, though, this section presents how ***students experience the course,*** based on the design choices made by the instructor.

All cases include some unanticipated consequences, providing both a learning opportunity and ideas for future revision. At their core, these cases reflect knowledgeable faculty who had a good vision for their online course and the best intentions for their students' success. The online modality, however, is ripe for the lesson of "you don't know what you don't know," so lessons learned by the instructors represented here may very well save you from making the same assumptions and design missteps.

Case Structure

Each case includes these sections:

1. The Case example **Title** (written mystery-novel style!) provides a clue for what the case is about.

2. The **Case-at-a-Glance** box then presents the basic course context and issue.

3. This is followed by a narrative of **The Instructor's Plan** which includes their design vision and choices.

4. Next is **The Student Experience** which reveals the successes and challenges experienced by students.

5. Each Case then presents **Using HIDOC to Revise the Course,** which provides targeted advice for revising the course considering each Step of the HIDOC model, plus bonus notes related to course delivery.

6. The Case concludes by inviting you to **Reflect on Your Course Design.** This final section provides reflective questions to prompt your thinking about whether your own course might encounter some of the issues discussed and how you might be proactive in addressing them.

HIDOC-in-Action: Design Case Examples

Case #1: The Case of the Third-Party Tool and Technology Issues

Case #2: The Case of Lab Kit Logistics and a Heavy Workload

Case #3: The Case of Assignment Choice Leaving Too Much to Chance

Case #4: The Case of a Hands-on Headache

Case #5: The Case of Learner-Curated Content Complications

Case #6: The Case of Copyright Complications and Tough Topics

Case #7: The Case of Multimedia Simulation That's Difficult in Reality

Case #8: The Case of High Anxiety and the Absentee Professor

Case #9: The Case of the Peer Collaboration Calamity

Case #10: The Case of the Dual-Mode Disparity

Case #1: The Case of the Third-Party Tool and Technology Issues

Case-at-a-Glance

An introductory, undergraduate Computers in Society course with no prerequisites was offered online. In the Communication Tools unit, students were asked to install, use, and evaluate a third-party communication tool. During the course design process, it was assumed that students had PCs rather than Macs, adequate computer experience to succeed in the activity, and minimal need for technical support.

This case explores the impact of using a tool not supported by the college or university and how the technology choice could have been better aligned with learner needs and learning outcomes.

The Instructor's Plan

Professor Vee's goal for the Communication Tools unit was for students to experience synchronous online communication and then reflect on their experiences. She chose a free downloadable tool called "Synchrony," which she felt to be superior to the cloud-based platform supported by the university. Professor Vee set up the module with a related reading assignment and the link for Synchrony, along with her directions for downloading, installing, and configuring the tool. The activity instructions specified that students should communicate with one another using the software; reflect on their experience; and then make and discuss their recommendations in the LMS discussion board as to whether Synchrony would be useful to businesses. Given this setup, the professor was confident that the students would have everything they would need to succeed.

The Student Experience

Students had many different types of computers (e.g., Macs, PCs) and degrees of experience using them. Some tried to install the software on a tablet or a mobile device, not knowing such devices were incompatible with the application. Other students didn't know how to configure their machines to work with the software or where to go for help. Some tried using Synchrony from their workplace or military base and found it blocked due to firewalls. The university help desk could not offer support since Synchrony was an external tool. Students with

Macs who contacted the software company directly were told Synchrony didn't work on Apple products. While a few students were able to install the software, they were not able to complete the discussion part of the activity because of the challenges encountered by their team members. Most students ended the week frustrated, angry, demotivated, and disappointed. Some began to doubt their ability to succeed in the class…or in any online class. Professor Vee spent much of the weekend overwhelmed with emails and confused about how something that seemed so straightforward ended up being such a challenge.

Using HIDOC to Revise the Course

To improve the course, Professor Vee could consider the following actions:

Step 1: Learner Analysis
As predominantly first-year students, remember that the class cohort will be new to LMS technology. Consider surveying students to collect information about their devices as well as their comfort level with using new technology.

Step 2: Learning Outcomes
Clarify the relevant learning outcomes so that student time is focused on using and evaluating the communication tool rather than installing or learning new software.

Step 3: Course Structure
Examine spacing and sequencing to allow more time for students to practice using the new technology, ask questions, and seek help as needed.

Step 4: Assessments & Activities
Include a non-graded practice activity in an earlier module and add associated support materials in that module as well.

Step 5: Instructional Materials
Create a screencast (or link to an existing one) showing students how to download and use the software. Consider creating an FAQ list to help with technology issues.

Step 6: Technology & Tools
Select a technology that is aligned with the learning outcomes and supported by the university. Be aware that, by using a technology not approved by the university, any breach of student privacy or data would have legal repercussions for the instructor.

Step 7: Online Learner Support

Share minimum technology requirements for the course and tell students how to find technology support. Create a Q&A Discussion forum for students to ask each other questions about assignment instructions. Be sure to monitor this Q&A Discussion for accuracy and areas of confusion.

Step 8: Continuous Improvement

After using the technology tool, have students complete a survey that provides feedback on its ease of use, its appropriateness for the learning goal, and whether they would recommend it for future classes.

Design Execution

Dedicate an office/student hours session to going over how to access and use the technology (and record this to post in the course). Remind students of the assignment due date and suggest they get started early to learn the new technology. Schedule extra time on the Teaching Calendar to address issues students may have.

Reflect on Your Course Design

Think about how this case might apply to or inform your course design work.

- Do you have activities that involve external tools? If so, are there technology, privacy, or other considerations that you need to potentially address?
- Are there additional "how-to" materials you need to create (or reference if they already exist), such as an explanatory screencast and/or an FAQ list?
- Do you provide contact information indicating whom students should contact if they need help with the technology?

Case #2: The Case of Lab Kit Logistics and a Heavy Workload

Case-at-a-Glance

A four-credit introductory, undergraduate chemistry course for non-majors, with no prerequisites, was offered online. Each week, students were asked to complete an at-home lab using materials from a course-specific lab kit augmented with "common household items." The course was fast-paced with a heavy workload, and students struggled with the lab activities.

This case explores special considerations for online labs and how course design can help students manage a heavy workload.

The Instructors' Plan

Because the course they were designing was an intensive 4-credit laboratory course, Professors Kay and Jay provided a detailed weekly schedule, listing what students were expected to do each day. They reinforced this through weekly announcements. The professors had seven assignments due each week, with one due every day, including two preparatory homeworks, the pre-lab activity and safety waiver, the lab report, two related discussions, and a quiz.

Knowing that most of their students would have minimal science and lab experience, and that doing labs from home would create safety concerns, the professors required students to complete an online safety waiver prior to completing each lab. Professors Kay and Jay created a lab kit with basic equipment that students would be required to rent from the campus bookstore. Students could pick the kit up at the bookstore or have it shipped, and they would have to supplement the kit with some common low-cost, household items that differed for each lab. Once they completed the lab-specific safety waiver, students were informed of the supplemental lab items they needed for that week's lab. Finally, the professors created a simulation for the most difficult lab so students could view the lab before doing it.

The Student Experience

Overall, students were able to navigate the course fairly easily since each module used a consistent structure and naming conventions. However, completing coursework every day of the week was not feasible for some students, especially those with full-time jobs who did coursework primarily on the weekends. These students fell behind quickly, and several dropped the course in the first few weeks.

For laboratory work, students were assessed on whether they followed proper procedure, reported the findings correctly in the lab report, and identified possible errors. The sequence students followed for each week's lab activity was:

- Read warnings, cautions, and tips.
- Sign safety waiver via a quiz with one "I accept" question.
- Read the released lab procedure and shopping list.
- Purchase and gather needed materials from the lab kit and shopping list.
- Conduct the experiment.
- Communicate findings through the lab report.
- Debrief on the experience with other students in the discussion forum.

Students had difficulty acquiring lab materials. Because the online safety waiver provided a list of supplemental items to purchase prior to starting the lab, because students were not able to access this until they took the online quiz, and because most students didn't own the "common" household items, they were not always able to plan for the time or money needed to get the additional items. They were also not able to order the items online because they only received the shopping list after completing the safety waiver for each lab. Additionally, the total cost of the extra items totaled around $100, an expense that students did not budget for. Several students simply tried to do the lab activity without all the items or to substitute items they felt were "close enough." Students who lived overseas had difficulty getting the lab kit mailed to them from the bookstore.

Students did appreciate the simulation provided for the density lab, the most difficult lab, but were disappointed that the other labs didn't have simulations. And, as laboratory activities were new to many of them, having a lab due in the first week of the course felt overwhelming. Additionally, students with no previous lab experience lacked confidence in writing the report and in sharing their experience in the related discussion. A few students eventually stopped turning in work.

Using HIDOC to Revise the Course

To improve the course, Professors Kay and Jay could consider the following actions:

Step 1: Learner Analysis
Consider that some students may not be able to acquire certain lab items. Also consider anxiety levels for students who are new to labs or have traditionally not done well in science courses.

Step 2: Learning Outcomes
Whether in the syllabus, course introduction, or elsewhere, emphasize that critical thinking and problem solving are more important than conducting the experiments flawlessly.

Step 3: Course Structure
Remember that activities requiring large amounts of time and/or complex instructions (such as labs) are best to start in the second or third module of a semester-long course. Students need time to get acclimated to the course environment before beginning complex work.

Step 4: Assessments & Activities
Provide an orientation in the first week to introduce the lab experience, and have students complete a low-stakes activity related to the procedure. Sequence the labs from easiest to more complex.

Step 5: Instructional Materials
Create FAQs for any labs that have common problems/foreseeable issues and/or where students routinely ask the same questions. Consider a pre-packaged lab kit with all required items included. If that cannot be done, provide a list (ideally before the course begins) of additional items that will need to be purchased.

Step 6: Technology & Tools
Add simulations to help students prepare for complex labs. Or, as a lower-tech alternative to simulations, create simple video recordings of someone going through the lab and include this as required content for each lab activity.

Step 7: Online Learner Support

Acclimate students to the course prior to starting lab work. Provide information in advance so that students can adequately prepare for the labs and be aware of additional expenses. Students could even share online sources for lab add-ins to crowd-source low-cost or fast shipping. Create a "Lab Help" open discussion forum for Q&A dedicated to lab activities.

Step 8: Continuous Improvement

Provide post-lab surveys asking about the level of difficulty, what barriers or issues students experienced, and their satisfaction level with the assignment. Note any questions or problems and use them to improve future labs.

Design Execution

For workload-heavy courses like this one, it is important to communicate work expectations early and often, so that students with already packed schedules can consider alternative options during the time when they're allowed to drop courses without penalty. Consider doing a live demonstration of the upcoming lab during online office/student hours, giving students the opportunity to ask questions live or submit questions in advance (or after watching the posted recording). If several students struggle early with a given lab, consider recording a short video talking through the issue, as other students will likely encounter the same problem.

Reflect on Your Own Course Design

Think about how this case might apply to or inform your course design work.

- Do you have activities that involve labs? If so, how can you best guide students as they conduct lab activities? Do the labs need to be approved by risk management?
- Are there additional "how-to" materials you need to create, such as a demonstration recording and/or an FAQ?
- Does your course have intensive projects that require daily work? If so, how can course structure, including assignment sequencing and due dates, help?

Case #3: The Case of Assignment Choice Leaving Too Much to Chance

Case-at-a-Glance

An introductory, undergraduate psychology course with no prerequisites was offered online. Each week, students were asked to create an "artifact" to represent their interpretation and understanding of the course materials. Students were provided with an extensive list of options (e.g., paper, presentation, multimedia project) or could propose their own unique idea. However, students were unprepared to entertain such a wide range of options, and there was too little guidance on the goals and evaluation of the assignment.

This case explores the unique considerations involved in activities and assessments in which students are provided with choices. It also highlights the importance of clear instructions for assignments that require peer interaction, such as discussions.

The Instructor's Plan

Professor Bee designed the course to allow students "voice and choice" and the opportunity to see course material through the lens of each other's backgrounds, experiences, and cultures. To do so, he asked students to post an artifact each week to communicate what they had learned from the week's materials and how the concepts might apply to their future professional practice.

To accommodate students' varied skills and interests, Professor Bee gave them freedom in choosing their artifact and how they presented it. The options included recording an interview, presentation, podcast, or skit; writing and illustrating a comic book; writing test questions, a summary essay, poem, story, or song; or creating a flyer, infographic, game, advertisement, painting, drawing, or a collage of images found on the internet with a paragraph explaining the meaning. Students were also free to come up with their own unique idea.

Students were instructed to post their artifact in the discussion forum, explain how it connected to the topic, and then discuss each other's interpretation of the key points of the week. They were given 20 points for their initial post and 10 points each for commenting on a post of their peers. All told, there were 14 of these weekly artifact posts, each worth a total of 40 points, which comprised a major portion of their course grade.

The Student Experience

Many students expressed excitement at having options for the weekly assignment and dove in with creative enthusiasm. They seemed to enjoy seeing others' interpretations of the material, and the sharing in the discussion forum helped the class bond.

However, as most of the students were working full-time and taking other courses, their time was very limited; also, some of the options were intimidating, requiring extra software and skills the students didn't have. Therefore, some students gravitated toward the "easier," less time-intensive options, which meant less variety and creativity than Professor Bee expected. These students worried their choices would affect their grade.

Some students also seemed confused by the assignment: "Create an artifact that represents or relates to this week's topic in some way. Then, explain how it is connected and how you can apply it to what you are learning." Not all students knew exactly how to define an "artifact" or how to explain why it was representational. "How do you apply an artifact?" became a common question on the open Q&A board.

When it came time to respond to peers, students had no idea what to say to get the full 10 points. Should they comment on the artifact, the explanation, or both? Should they comment on the creativity? Or on whether they agreed that the artifact was representational? Or should they comment on how their peer was discussing the application of course ideas and topics? For many students, the sheer amount of choices coupled with minimal instructions, especially regarding how they would be evaluated, led to them feeling anxious, overwhelmed, and concerned for their grade.

Using HIDOC to Revise the Course

To improve the course, Professor Bee could consider the following actions:

Step 1: Learner Analysis

Understand that students have different time constraints and skill sets. Frame the activity in such a way that students know it's not a talent show and that it's okay to pick the medium that works best for them. Remind students that the focus is on their interpretation of the course materials, the questions they have, and their level of understanding and application of key concepts.

Step 2: Learning Outcomes

As an assignment that spans the entire course, consider creating a learning outcome that encompasses being able to communicate, via various types of artifacts, how course topics can be understood and applied.

Step 3: Course Structure

Use structure to clearly communicate the choices available to learners in each module. Professor Bee might also provide limited options initially, then expand those options once students have some comfort level with the assignment. For example, maybe there are three low-technology options given for weeks one and two and then a new option is added each week.

Step 4: Assessments & Activities

Add time and length limits as parameters to each artifact option to be sure there is an equivalent amount of work required for each. Additionally, include an example of many (or all) of the artifact options so that students have some frame of reference. Provide examples of previous student work for each option to help clarify expectations, level of production value, and amount of time required.

Step 5: Instructional Materials

Update materials if students are missing specific key concepts in their interpretations.

Step 6: Technology & Tools

Provide one or two suggestions for software or tools that could be used for some of the artifact options to support students who want to try something new. Also, consider whether the discussion tool is the best option for this assignment; if the reply post does not add to student learning, this might be done as a blog post, for example.

Step 7: Online Learner Support

Provide clear assignment prompts that give the "what and why" of their posts, as well as how they will be evaluated.

Step 8: Continuous Improvement

Track the options chosen by students to inform decisions about which submission options to include in future course offerings. Survey students to ask them what other submission options might be effective for them. Observe concept areas where they seem to struggle so that those instructional materials can be expanded during a course revision.

Design Execution

Especially in early weeks, provide group feedback in addition to individual feedback, and offer to do live Q&A sessions via online office/student hours.

Reflect on Your Own Course Design

Think about how this case might apply to or inform your course design work.

- Do you have activities that promote choice? If so, what can you do to ensure equitable options?
- How can you motivate and engage students with choice while not overwhelming them?
- For any discussion assignments in your course, are you explicit about the purpose of the discussion, what the initial post and the reply post should consist of, and how each will be evaluated?

Case #4: The Case of a Hands-on Headache

Case-at-a-Glance

A lower-level, undergraduate geology course with a mix of majors and non-majors was offered online. The professor planned to use a lab kit containing various rock samples required for lab assignments. Students were surprised at the high cost of the lab kit, however, especially considering that it wouldn't be useful for non-majors after the course. Additionally, there was a lack of descriptive information provided for students who were blind or low vision.

This case explores various student experiences with tactile content when materials are not available, confusing to apply, too expensive to purchase, or not accessible for all students.

The Instructor's Plan

The goal of this particular geology course is to introduce students to geology and also attract new students to the major. Professor Ell chose to focus her design on building foundational student knowledge of geology that would be needed to succeed in more advanced courses in the major. She felt this would meet the needs of all students.

In the F2F version of the course, Professor Ell passes around rock specimens for students to see and feel. She felt that the best way to replicate the classroom-based experience online was to provide a lab kit so that each student would have their own set of samples. She curated samples via a geological supply company, and these were packaged for purchase by students, both geology majors and those taking the course to fulfill a general education requirement.

The Student Experience

Many students were excited about the tactile nature of the course, and even non-majors were keen to learn some basic geology, as Professor Ell had done a good job of getting students excited via her course overview video. Because Professor Ell put so much emphasis on future geology majors, however, non-majors soon felt overwhelmed.

More importantly, though, the rock samples lab kit created issues. The cost of materials and shipping charges turned out to be prohibitive for many students, as they were not told in advance that this would be an additional expense. Some non-majors were hesitant to buy the kit because they felt they would have no future use for the samples. Some wanted more guidance on how to interact with the samples in a meaningful way. Finally, students who were blind or low vision had no way to distinguish the samples besides weight and texture, as no detailed information about the samples had been provided.

Once students began to communicate these concerns, Professor Ell quickly created a text-based fact sheet for each rock, as well as a detailed written description of the physical properties of the sample. She also created three recordings of herself showing and describing various rock specimens, including detailed close-up shots. For accessibility, the videos were also transcribed, captioned, and included an audio description. Funds and time were limited, however, so Professor Ell was only able to create videos for three main types of rocks. Students appreciated the videos but wished for additional "show and tell" videos in other parts of the course.

Using HIDOC to Revise the Course

To improve the course, Professor Ell could consider the following actions:

Step 1: Learner Analysis
Consider the knowledge levels of students: geology majors will have more foundational knowledge than non-majors. Focus on relevance for all students. Additionally, consider the additional cost of a lab kit and whether having at-home samples is crucial for learning achievement or is a potential financial barrier without being wholly necessary.

Step 2: Learning Outcomes
Clarify that the course and module learning outcomes are appropriate for the level of the course (introductory-level) and are also appropriate for both majors and non-majors.

Step 3: Course Structure
Organize modules in such a way that it is clear to students which videos or 3-D models apply to each learning outcome, activity, or assessment. If the lab kit is used, give plenty of time for students to order and receive the kit, and don't begin

activities related to kit items in week one, or any time before students would reasonably receive the kit if they ordered it when class began.

Step 4: Assessments & Activities

Clarify how content related to rock specimens, including instructor videos, 3-D models, and lab kit samples (if kept), will be used for course assignments. As one alternative, engaging idea to the lab kit, students could be directed to find samples of a specific rock type in their own community or even via a web search and then share those with peers.

Step 5: Instructional Materials

Create and add more "show and tell" videos to the course as budget and time allow. Provide optional foundational materials and address the sense of overwhelm by clarifying required and optional materials and their use.

Step 6: Technology and Tools

Collaborate with IDs and campus technologists to create or curate additional online 3-D models with tactile descriptions and ensure that they are accessible.

Step 7: Online Learner Support

If using 3-D models and simulations, provide context and an introduction. Start talking about specimens early on, and be clear about the various ways that online students will interact with them, including options for students with disabilities. If using a physical kit, have a "no-kit" option for activities in case the kit does not arrive in time for students overseas. Also, provide contact information for the company preparing the kit, so students with issues have a direct link to help.

Step 8: Continuous Improvement

Survey students with questions specifically related to any tactile-focused content, including which type students found most valuable (specimen, show-and-tell video, and/or 3-D simulation). Also ask where more "show and tell" videos might be helpful to be sure limited resources and time are used for the most needed videos. Review alignment between content, assessments, and outcomes.

Design Execution

Use course announcements wisely to let students know in advance when they'll be interacting with specimens or models. If the lab kit remains an option, send out information to order the kit in the welcome letter, along with the cost and average shipping time.

Reflect on Your Own Course Design

Think about how this case might apply to or inform your course design work.

- Do you have hands-on activities or content that require tactile interaction? If so, what problems might you or your students encounter, and what can you do to ensure student success?
- Do outcomes require students to physically touch materials? Or could alternative virtual materials, 3-D models, or simulations be provided to students?
- Do you have access to resources to create customized videos, 3-D models, or other alternative materials?
- If you've created and/or curated videos for tactile or other materials, are they accessible?

Case #5: The Case of Learner-Curated Content Complications

Case-at-a-Glance

A graduate, seminar-style course in sustainability management was offered online. Students were required to create a comprehensive sustainability plan for a community that could eventually be funded and implemented. To support the plan, they needed to research topics of their own personal interest that were relevant to their community needs. The professor hoped the online course would have the same active and deep discussion of current events as the F2F version of the course.

This case explores options for keeping a course with dynamic content fresh while engaging students and allowing their voice and choice of materials to enrich the course.

The Instructor's Plan

Professor Cee designed the sustainability management course to focus on a semester-long community project in which students developed a sustainable plan for nature tourism within their community. He surmised that the online students, like his F2F students, would likely be working full-time in the sustainability industry or have some aspect of community planning in their current positions.

In addition, he wanted the course to focus on an ongoing discussion of current events, issues, and happenings in the field. To facilitate this, he planned to have regular discussions in a weekly forum with predetermined prompts he'd provide. He did his best to anticipate student needs and to find articles and news stories that related to each week's topic and would support the creation of community project plans.

The Student Experience

Students appreciated the core content that walked them through the process of creating a sound, community-based plan. Students with professional experience quickly connected to options in nearby communities and began to work on their projects. Because each week's discussion topic paralleled the project creation process, these students felt well-guided and were able to support each other.

However, as Professor Cee realized early on, the online course attracted a different cohort than the F2F course—experienced students seeking an advanced degree in the field but also students not yet admitted to the graduate program. These less-experienced students had trouble starting a project and wanted more information, guidance, and mentoring. They also felt left out in the discussion activities that were dominated by the more experienced students who often used field-specific jargon. As the less-experienced students fell behind, their self-efficacy lowered, and several decided to drop the class.

Also, more experienced students felt that some of the discussion articles were not a good fit and/or outdated. They began to find more relevant resources on their own and share them with each other. In response, Professor Cee added additional, up-to-date news stories to the weekly announcements. However, additional readings meant more work for students, and many students became overwhelmed and confused about what material was required or most relevant. Ultimately, inexperienced students felt a lot of uncertainty, and the experienced students felt as though they were consistently "leading" the discussion rather than "learning" from it.

Using HIDOC to Revise the Course

To improve the course, Professor Cee could consider the following actions:

Step 1: Learner Analysis

Continue to see the students as professionals who also have knowledge and experience to contribute but realize that an individual cohort might have a larger variance of field experience, including none at all. Use this as a design advantage to create small-group discussions that represent a good balance. Consider pairing working professionals with a new-to-the-field students on each discussion team.

Step 2: Learning Outcomes

Consider how much foundational knowledge should be reflected in the CLOs, and if the course should have any prerequisites. Revisit the discussion activities to make sure each is aligned with course outcomes.

Step 3: Course Structure

Arrange each module so that learners understand where to add their content, and have the first one (or two) not require student-curated content, giving students time to acclimate to the format and purpose of the activity before contributing their own materials.

Step 4: Assessments & Activities

For experiential learning assignments, provide general options that are location-agnostic. For example, students could work locally (provide some general types of business that could be an outlet), could connect with an "approved" virtual organization, or could even work with a fictional organization they create and describe. Create a weekly "In the News" discussion forum to encourage students to share their findings, interpretations, and experiences in a non-assessment based format.

Step 5: Instructional Materials

Ensure the course reflects the current, prevalent theories, practices, and policies of the field. Help students understand the difference between "foundational knowledge" and "current practices/trends." Use student-curated current events stories and recent articles in the "In the News" forum to keep the course content up-to-date without the need for constant course revision.

Step 6: Technology & Tools

Provide detailed instructions on how to post links and attach files to a discussion forum. If using a Twitter hashtag, explore how that works, including if the feed for the course hashtag can be embedded in the course site/LMS space.

Step 7: Online Learner Support

Provide a rubric to communicate the desired depth of discussion and quality of resources shared. Provide a model discussion as an example and participate in the discussions as a guide. Create a short webcam video to explain the concept of "Students as Content Curators" as part of the getting-started materials, so students know that this is a part of the class.

Step 8: Continuous Improvement

Provide early opportunities for detailed feedback about the discussions and the project plan, so tweaks can be made if necessary.

Design Execution

Provide more in-depth feedback early on to student submissions in the "In the News" forum to help students in identifying good sources to share. Offer mentoring and guidance (or design this in as a required activity) for the project plans, especially encouraging less-experienced students to meet with the instructor or share early ideas and drafts. Have students submit questions and project plan issues or barriers and focus some office/student hours as "Q&A" time.

Reflect on Your Own Course Design

Think about how this case might apply to or inform your course design work.

- Is the content of your field dynamic and rapidly changing? If so, does this impact the materials students need to be successful in your course?
- Do you have students in your cohort who are already experienced in the field, including working professionals? If so, how can you capitalize on existing student knowledge for the benefit of all students? What additional information or guidance might less experienced students need?

Case #6: The Case of Copyright Complications and Tough Topics

Case-at-a-Glance

A 200-level undergraduate communication course focusing on inclusion and diversity in the media was offered online. The media-rich, content-heavy course was popular with majors as well as non-majors. Many content pieces became unavailable during the course through broken links or copyright violations. Discussion of how women, minorities, and other groups are portrayed in various media resulted in either flat, one-sided conversations, or polarizing, emotional debates.

This case explores how the curation of a large number of copyrighted media examples, sensitive discussion topics, and reluctant students can complicate a course design.

The Instructor's Plan

Professor Ess, having taught the Diversity and Inclusion in the Media course F2F for many years, has a big stack of DVDs as well as a comprehensive list of resource sites and YouTube videos relevant to the subject matter. These include feature films and documentaries, as well as media reviews and reactions. In designing the course to be taught online, Professor Ess saw an opportunity to share all these resources with students. They began to create an extensive resource list for each course module and uploaded some pieces online.

To help students analyze how minoritized groups are portrayed in various media, such as films, television, and print, Professor Ess created discussion assignments related to themes of stereotypes, representation and misrepresentation, and societal implications of media portrayals of gender, race, ethnicity, disability, sexual orientation, and culture. Because the in-person class typically featured meaningful, frank, and open discussion, Professor Ess anticipated similar exchanges but thought students might be able to get deeper with their thoughts because of the asynchronous nature of the threaded discussions.

The Student Experience

Even though Professor Ess had been confident in their curated resource list and uploaded media, and had checked all the links prior the start of the course, students reported broken links each week. The professor soon realized that several pieces had been taken down due to copyright violation. As working adults, students had limited time to interact with course content and were frustrated at having to circle back to materials after links were fixed.

On one hand, having ample materials/media examples helped when there were access issues; students could always engage with a different piece of content. On the other hand, many students felt overwhelmed by the sheer volume of content. Some students complained that watching all the films, television episodes, and other resources took more time than was required for the credit hours of the course. Although Professor Ess did not intend to have students watch all the resources provided, students were confused as to which resources were required and which were optional.

Overall, the discussions went okay, but most students seemed reluctant to share divergent views or ask tough questions. Additionally, in one module a small group of students got into an antagonistic discussion and began attacking one another personally. Professor Ess was able to intervene and speak individually with the students. Thankfully, the situation was resolved quickly, and future discussion forums were without incident but also remained relatively surface-level.

Using HIDOC to Revise the Course

To improve the course, Professor Ess could consider the following actions.

Step 1: Learner Analysis

Consider the experience students will have in interacting with diverse people with different views, as well as whether all students will have the internet bandwidth to stream large pieces of media. A poll or survey might help to gather this information.

Step 2: Learning Outcomes

Revisit outcomes to ensure that developing skills in discussing sensitive topics is included. Realize that to meet this outcome, students will likely need additional guidance and mentoring.

Step 3: Course Structure

Because course discussions are centered around tough topics that ask students to be both vulnerable and respectful, design smaller "get to know you" activities early on that allow students to build rapport and the instructor to model active listening and mutual respect. This will allow the course structure to scaffold toward the more difficult discussion topics.

Step 4: Assessments & Activities

Provide opportunities for students to share their own perspectives in a safe and supportive environment by incorporating voice and choice aspects in some assignments. For example, as a first project (or even in lieu of a traditional student introduction discussion), students could create an "About Me" piece that communicates their self-identity and lived experience, with options for how to complete the piece, such as a webcam video, photo collage, or short essay.

Share (in the syllabus and as part of the assignment) information on how to have discussions about sensitive subjects, such as practicing active listening, perspective-taking, and respectful disagreement. Consider including a rubric that reinforces how negative behaviors will impact student grades and stating that the instructor reserves the right to remove any post that does not follow stated course guidelines for language and tone.

Step 5: Instructional Materials

Work with the library and/or instructional designers to provide streamed media examples to students that meet copyright requirements. Clearly define required and optional materials but, when applicable, allow students to choose from a list of aligned resources. Be sure choices are relatively equivalent in terms of length, however, or have students choose one (or more) from both a "short" and "long" list.

Step 6: Technology & Tools

Provide a reliable streaming link for students to use. If linking to streaming sites such as YouTube, have an alternate resource or link in mind in case the material is taken down due to copyright issues or the link is broken for another reason.

Step 7: Online Learner Support

Provide clear instructions and guidelines for students on how to discuss sensitive issues in a civil and respectful manner. Reach out individually to students who seem hesitant or unsure when engaging in discussions, or to those students who are not practicing mutual respect when responding to peers.

Step 8: Continuous Improvement

Keep a log of any broken links for the "Fix List" portion of the Revision Roadmap, and if any new content needs to be curated due to copyright issues, place that on the "Wish List." Build rapport while gathering student feedback by inserting relevant questions in private journal assignments, such as: "Did you have any issues with this week's discussion topic or posts?" or, "Did you feel safe and supported in expressing your opinions and asking questions in this class? Is there anything I or your fellow students can do to help everyone have better discussions about sensitive topics?"

Design Execution

Hold office/student hours dedicated to live conversations about relevant "tough topics" being discussed so that students can ask hard questions of the professor… not their fellow students. Realize that students, especially those from minoritized and/or marginalized backgrounds, will bring unique and often traumatic lived experiences to class discussions, and helping all students feel safe and respected may require an even more purposeful teaching presence during delivery.

Reflect on Your Own Course Design

Think about how this case might apply to or inform your course design work.

- Do you potentially have copyright issues in your course that you now feel you should discuss with a librarian, ID, or other staff resource?
- Does your course contain topics that are controversial, sensitive, or otherwise challenging to discuss? How might you model appropriate discussion norms for your online students?

Case #7: The Case of Multimedia Simulation That's Difficult in Reality

Case-at-a-Glance

A 100-level undergraduate Italian language course with an emphasis on listening and speaking skills was offered online. The immersive experience took students on a virtual tour of Italy to learn basic Italian grammar and conversation. Students had ample opportunity for practice using games, simulated conversations, and synchronous partner practice.

This case explores how creating an immersive experience requires resources, testing, and extra consideration for technology and tools.

The Instructor's Plan

Professor Zee was excited to expose a new group of students to the beautiful language and culture of Italy! Rather than relying on sound files and a textbook, the professor wanted students to have an immersive experience in the language and culture of Italy, as if they were tourists on a 15-day tour, with each day representing one week of the 15-week semester.

The immersive experience required a custom interface to organize and present all the course components and media. A team of instructional designers, producers, and other educational technology specialists was quickly assembled to develop prototypes of the interface, design technology that allowed interactive conversations, and produce interactive games and assessments throughout the application.

The interface resembled a trip itinerary with titles that described where students were and what they were doing. Students would page through the material watching videos, performing listening and speaking practice, playing ungraded practice games, and completing graded assessments. In terms of CLOs, students were required to master basic grammar via ungraded assignments that would allow them to practice with peers as much as needed. Recorded audio or video assessments would then measure their speaking and listening skills, while short quizzes and exams would measure reading, writing, and comprehension.

During the course design process, it became clear that the final product would end up exceeding the departmental budget allocated to develop the course, which meant the team could not do prototype testing. Because they spent so much time working on the interface, though, they were confident it would be intuitive and meet the intended goals for an immersive language learning experience.

The Student Experience

After the course opened, students were initially very satisfied with the immersive "day trip" experiences and reported that the course was easy to navigate. They appreciated the option to perform the ungraded practice as often as they liked before completing the graded work. Many shared that they learned much more than they expected in a short amount of time.

However, some students wanted to hear additional examples by native speakers and to have options to use closed-captioning in both English and Italian to reinforce their learning. Additionally, some students did not have the technology to easily record themselves speaking Italian, and several could not figure out the web-conferencing software that enabled conversational practice with peers. For these students, technology issues affected participation, satisfaction, and performance.

Further, while students reported the interface worked well the first time, it was not easy to navigate back to review information. The design team, listed in the course as a help resource, began receiving a lot of questions from students about this issue as well as requests for additional tools, such as interactive flash cards for words and grammar usage. Some students also felt that the interactive "day trips" focused much more on the sights and culture of Italy than the language itself.

Using HIDOC to Revise the Course

To improve the course, Professor Zee could consider the following actions.

Step 1: Learner Analysis

Consider how students will need to navigate the course at different points in their study—initial experience, practice, and review. Also, determine what types of technology students will need for the immersive experience to function optimally.

Step 2: Learning Outcomes

Ensure all course components connect back to learning outcomes and are relevant and aligned. Otherwise, students will be distracted by extraneous information that is not related to their immersive experience.

Step 3: Course Structure

Be more hands-on early in the course when students are first learning how to interact with the immersive experience. Structure activities so that students have more guidance and less work early on, gradually evolving to more peer interaction and evaluation as the course progresses.

Step 4: Assessments & Activities

Ensure that all modules have ungraded practice activities that support the learning outcomes, as this was reported by students to be extremely helpful. Allow students to practice again and again until they feel comfortable listening and speaking in the new language.

Step 5: Instructional Materials

Ensure that each module has a variety of materials and many opportunities to listen to native speakers in the context of the immersive story. Prepare review materials to allow students to go back through a "day trip" they've already completed.

Step 6: Technology & Tools

Add dual-track captions to all videos so students can choose to view English, Italian, or no captions. Provide options for practice including audio/video flashcards, recorded voice compared to model voice, and partner practice. Because this is a technology-rich course, factor in more time to test the prototype and gain feedback before the course begins and consult appropriate university staff early on so that a more accurate idea of time and cost for creating (and testing) the environment can be determined before the project is begun.

Step 7: Online Learner Support

Record additional model videos as needed to clarify information and pronunciation for students. Allow more time in the first few weeks of the course to support and guide students both with technology issues and language practice. Be sure students are able to evaluate early on whether or not they have the technology required to fully access and experience the course.

Step 8: Continuous Improvement

Survey students in the first two weeks to be sure they are not struggling to navigate the immersive system. Also, survey students as to where they would like to have more interactive practice to prioritize the build-out of additional questions and games.

Design Execution

Send out via a welcome letter a detailed list of the technology and technology skills students will need to be successful. Provide detailed feedback on student's recorded assignments and consider doing some of this via audio feedback.

Reflect on Your Own Course Design

Think about how this case might apply to or inform your course design work.

- Do you have ideas for multimedia that will engage students but might be very resource-heavy to create? Are there available university resources you can collaborate with to develop the multimedia? What will it cost to create the learning technology, and does the department have a budget for it? What staff need to be involved to make this vision a reality?
- How can you ensure that the technology and media will be fully developed and tested prior to the start of the course?
- What can you do to inform potential students of the technology requirements for your multimedia-rich course?
- What technology and skills will students need to be successful? Will they learn these skills in the course, or should they come in with them as a prerequisite?

Case #8: The Case of High Anxiety and the Absentee Professor

Case-at-a-Glance

A 100-level undergraduate math course with publisher-provided materials embedded in an LMS course shell was offered online. The course had a high drop rate, and students were concerned about the limited feedback received from automated homework assignments.

This case explores how anxiety can impact cognitive load and performance. It also demonstrates how an instructor can provide meaningful feedback and supplemental resources to help alleviate student anxiety.

The Instructor's Plan

For this online math course, Professor Emm selected a textbook that provides homework exercises and exam questions, as well as a "full-package" publisher course site that includes videos that discuss course concepts, formulas, and problems—and the ability to auto-grade assignments and import the grades into the institutional LMS. With all of these resources, Professor Emm felt little if any additional design and development work was needed. In truth, he felt a bit relieved by this, as technology was not his strong suit. He decided to use the institutional LMS course space only for the gradebook, syllabus, and vital course communication.

Professor Emm knew that some students think math is difficult or something they're not good at, but he ultimately believed that if they worked hard and completed all homework on time, they would do well in the course. To clarify this expectation, he added this note to the syllabus: "Math is hard, and because of this it's important that you stay on track. To help you meet the deadlines, turning in any assignment late will result in a zero, and more than two late assignments will result in an automatic failing grade for the course." He hoped this late-work consequence would motivate students.

His only concern was that the publisher resources did not allow students to show their work. While he wanted students to demonstrate that they knew all the steps in solving the problems and were focused on the right thinking, not just getting the "right answer," he assumed that since the publisher site didn't include this, it must be too hard to do in an online format.

Since students were completing auto-graded homework supplied by the publisher, Professor Emm didn't see a need to provide additional or regular feedback. He assumed that if students weren't reaching out with many questions, they must be doing okay. He relied only on the exported grades in the LMS to monitor student progress.

The Student Experience

A week or so into the course, a good number of students dropped the class. When Professor Emm reached out to ask why, a few of them responded to say that they were confused, had felt anxious about their math abilities to begin with, and that they probably weren't cut out for being an online student because it was just too hard. Some also reported being discouraged that turning in two assignments late would result in failure.

Others dropped because they felt like they were "teaching themselves," since they rarely or never interacted with their professor. Some weren't even sure how to contact him for help. By the midpoint of the course, almost half of the students had dropped, with some transferring to a different online or F2F section of the course. Professor Emm was really surprised, as the textbook and publisher platform he selected were very highly rated and seemed to provide a lot of information and guidance. Based on his experience, he started to assume that "math just can't be taught well online."

Using HIDOC to Revise the Course

To improve the course, Professor Emm could consider the following actions.

Step 1: Learner Analysis

Consider that students may have a lifelong fear of math, may doubt their ability to do math, and/or might not have done college-level math for many years. Many students will need more support and encouragement.

Step 2: Learning Outcomes

Limit each lesson to a small number of module learning outcomes so as not to overwhelm students with too much information. Emphasize the importance of being able to demonstrate problem-solving steps rather than just arriving at the correct solution. Ensure that one of the CLOs addresses the goal of students increasing their problem-solving abilities.

Step 3: Course Structure

Provide a path for students to work through, with clearly labeled supplemental materials for each lesson that will help them review and practice foundational material if they need to. Consider using publisher materials and resources as add-ins to a structured course in the institutional LMS that is designed specifically for them, rather than sending students to a publisher course site.

Step 4: Assessments & Activities

Provide non-graded practice problems to help students prepare for graded assessments. For the auto-graded exercises, provide encouraging feedback for incorrect answers that guides students on what to review, and correct-answer feedback that gives kudos for a well-arrived-at solution.

Step 5: Instructional Materials

Review publisher materials, and add additional materials to provide context, tips, and examples for students. Insert suggested pause points where students can read or watch additional content if they're confused. Model critical thinking and problem-solving for students by creating screencasts of working through various types of problems while simultaneously discussing the thinking behind the solution.

Step 6: Technology & Tools

Have students turn in selected work as video assignments, where they create a screencast of themselves talking aloud about their process for solving the problem(s), helping the instructor pinpoint where their thinking has gone wrong. Find an app or software that allows students to show their work when working on problems. For a "low tech" option, students can work problems out on paper, take a picture of that work, and upload it with their assignment.

Step 7: Online Learner Support

Consider web conferencing with students, whether during office/student hours, optional "tutoring sessions," or individual appointments, to answer questions and work through challenging problems. Listen to students who express anxiety, reassure them that they can be successful, and remind them of the various support options available.

Step 8: Continuous Improvement

Make notes on the "Wish List" for additional content to create to augment publisher materials. Additionally, consider having a few short questions appended to each homework assignment that ask: How easily were you able to solve these problems? How confident are you that you arrived at the correct answer? Which problems do you feel you need additional guidance to understand or solve? These questions will help determine what to cover in live Q&A sessions and/or short screencast videos. If using math software or an LMS site with built-in analytics, look at data on the most commonly missed question types to inform future course revisions.

Design Execution

Courses that heavily rely on publisher materials need a strong teaching presence. The goal is regular and substantive interaction with students—not just because this is federal policy, but also because this guidance matters most when it comes to your students. In addition to holding office/student hours, focus on support and encouragement in announcements and individual feedback in order to encourage a growth mindset. When struggling students improve, be sure to provide individual kudos that reinforce their new knowledge and abilities and recognize their hard work.

Reflect on Your Own Course Design

Think about how this case might apply to or inform your course design work.

- Do you use publisher materials with automatically graded exercises or homework? If so, do students receive enough meaningful feedback from the automated system to make corrections on their own and improve their own performance? If not, how can you supplement this?
- If using a publisher course site or a large amount of publisher-supplied materials, how will you plan to be present during delivery? What will your active teaching focus on, and how will you encourage regular and substantive interaction?
- How else might you coach students? Would synchronous sessions to work through problems together be helpful and feasible?
- What would make students feel more comfortable and confident with anxiety-inducing subject matter? How can you encourage a growth, rather than fixed, mindset?

Case #9: The Case of the Peer Collaboration Calamity

Case-at-a-Glance

A business and technical writing course taken by students from a variety of majors was offered online. The course incorporated online asynchronous peer review of student writing, and students struggled in the assignment. The lack of social presence was an additional barrier.

This case explores how good planning during the design stage can make collaborative student work more efficient and successful. It also describes how an instructor can guide and support students to provide and utilize constructive feedback and interact well with online peers.

The Instructor's Plan

Professor Gee knows from teaching business and technical writing in person that many students lack confidence in their own writing but also don't allow themselves enough time to do the assignments well. Therefore, in the F2F version of the course, he lets students work in pairs to improve their work prior to submitting a final draft. To be sure students are giving and receiving meaningful feedback, Professor Gee typically provides a rubric informing them of what to look for, a handout on how to give constructive feedback, and instructions for how to effectively communicate feedback to their partners. Students find a partner and use class time for the peer review. They then have two days to make improvements prior to submitting the revised work for a grade.

Professor Gee did not anticipate any problems in incorporating peer review in the online course and set it up with the same parameters in terms of the rubric, handout, and instructions. He assumed students could easily find another student with whom to work.

The Student Experience

Students who already knew others in the class connected with each other for the peer review. Students who didn't know anyone, however, felt awkward randomly choosing a name from the class roster and emailing that person to see if they wanted to pair up. Some students received more than one request to partner up, and those who didn't respond quickly had to scramble to find other people to email. For many of the students, the better part of the week was spent searching for partners, leaving them with very little time to look at drafts and provide meaningful feedback.

Students appreciated the materials on giving and receiving feedback, and most were able to give helpful recommendations to their classmates. Some students, though, reached out to Professor Gee to say that they hadn't received helpful, detailed feedback. Others reported receiving overly harsh feedback or none at all.

While a few students turned their revised work in on time, many students found the two-day turnaround time to be unworkable. They had either misinterpreted the rubric's instructions or not fully read them. Almost all students requested more time, so Professor Gee gave everyone an extra three days to make revisions. This required that he modify the rest of the schedule, which posed some additional logistical challenges.

Using HIDOC to Revise the Course

To improve the course, Professor Gee could consider the following actions.

Step 1: Learner Analysis
Survey the students to get a better sense of their writing skills and experience as well as their feedback experience. Students may have experience writing without being skilled at giving and receiving writing critique.

Step 2: Learning Outcomes
Incorporate critiquing and feedback skills into the CLOs.

Step 3: Course Structure
Carefully plan the due dates to allow time to establish social presence, form pairs, provide and receive feedback, and improve the draft.

Step 4: Assessments & Activities
Provide early, low-stakes opportunities involving giving and receiving peer feedback so that students can practice this new skill. Add criteria and points for meaningful feedback to the activity rubric and include their feedback as part of the grade. Consider creating a template for the feedback, requiring students to suggest at least one improvement and to provide an example of at least one thing their peer did well. Use a screencast to talk through the assignment, show some (past or newly created) examples, and provide feedback for the examples.

Step 5: Instructional Materials

Continue to use an introductory lesson instructing online students how to give and receive critique but also provide them with specific strategies for working in teams at a distance. In addition to providing examples of good feedback, provide instruction for how to use that feedback in making revisions.

Step 6: Technology & Tools

Select a technology that allows students to easily find their assigned partner/group or enroll in a group within the LMS. Also, select technology that will allow students to efficiently share, mark up, and return papers within their pairs or groups. Include a screencast showing how to do this.

Step 7: Online Learner Support

Foster social presence so students feel comfortable with each other. For example, Professor Gee might revise the student introduction discussion to be more engaging and/or require some interaction. Clarify rules and tasks related to giving and receiving feedback. Convey to students that the assignment is as much about providing quality feedback as submitting a decent draft. Monitor feedback to ensure students are on the right track.

Step 8: Continuous Improvement

A peer feedback rating form could be added to the "Wish List." Ask students to rate their peer feedback. How useful was the feedback? Was the feedback given in a constructive way? Did students make changes based on the feedback? Use these responses to modify the peer feedback template and/or create a video or screencast that models providing quality feedback.

Design Execution

To avoid students scrambling to find partners, pre-assign partners, pairing students according to skill level or other attributes or randomly, via the LMS tool. Consider assigning students to triads so students are not critiquing the same person they're receiving feedback from. Hold dedicated office/student hours to answer questions about partnered or group work and check in with students individually via email to see if they're having issues.

Reflect on Your Own Course Design

Think about how this case might apply to or inform your course design work.

- Do you have activities that require students to give and/or receive feedback? If so, are they adequately prepared to do so?
- Do you require students to work in small groups? What information do students need to effectively participate in their groups? How can you communicate with students to get them started on their group activity? How can you facilitate social presence so that students feel more naturally connected to each other?
- For students working in groups, will you ask them to rate the performance of their peers?

Case #10: The Case of the Dual-Mode Disparity

Case-at-a-Glance

A master's-level, math-intensive chemistry course was offered to in-class and online (asynchronous) students in a dual-mode format for the first time. In-class lectures were captured and provided to asynchronous students via email, along with related assignment instructions. While the class experience for F2F students was largely unchanged, the online students missed out on crucial information communicated before and after the recording took place, and they ended up feeling generally lost and disconnected.

This case explores providing equitable learning experiences between modalities and is relevant for dual-mode courses, HyFlex courses, as well as courses that are taught as separate F2F and online sections.

The Instructor's Plan

Professor Eff typically lectures in the F2F version of the class using NexLab software; this allows students to both learn the math and also see how to solve the problem, which is displayed on a video screen at the front of the room. When he's not using the software, Professor Eff is writing notes, creating diagrams or sketches, and solving equations on the whiteboard.

In designing the dual-mode version of the course, Professor Eff planned to record his in-class lectures, post them on YouTube, and email the link to both online and in-class students. He planned to pay an undergraduate student to record each lecture with a video camera set up at the back of the room. He would wear a lapel mic to capture clear audio and instruct the student worker to zoom in when needed to capture the NexLab video screen or the whiteboard.

Since successfully using the NexLab software is integral to the course, in his F2F class, Professor Eff always includes several NexLab practice activities before having any graded assessments. He typically provides assignment instructions to the F2F class after his lecture, so he decided to email these instructions to his online students along with the link to the lecture recording. Since NexLab assignments can be submitted within the software, Professor Eff used the course LMS for only the syllabus and assignment due dates.

The Student Experience

Some online students liked the feel of the F2F classroom shown in the videos and appreciated that the content was captured and uploaded to YouTube that day. They felt part of a “real class.” Other students, though, felt that they were “watching others learn.” It seemed unfair to them, for example, that in-class students could ask questions easily during the lecture, while online students would have to submit questions by emailing the professor after the fact.

Additionally, some in-class students were upset that their faces were on YouTube, as anytime one of them asked a question, the camera panned to show their face. Also, during Q&A, the online students could hear Professor Eff well because he used a lapel mic but could not hear students’ questions. Even though the hired student zoomed in, it was difficult for the online students to clearly see the recorded video screen, so they largely relied on the NexLab-supplied tutorials linked in the syllabus rather than the demonstration done during the lectures. The whiteboard was equally inscrutable, with the camera being so far away.

Thankfully, several online students alerted Professor Eff immediately that they were missing out on crucial parts of the lecture. In response, the professor began repeating any questions asked by in-class students, so online students could hear them. Also, he learned how to directly record the NexLab demonstrations with screen-recording software and upload the recordings. Finally, he started taking pictures of the whiteboard with a high-quality camera and posting those pictures for the online students. When he learned about the privacy issue, he asked the student videographer to only record him and not the students.

Students were thankful that there were so many practice opportunities with NexLab; however, many online students were still overwhelmed with learning the subject matter along with NexLab, as well as trying to figure out where to submit things in the LMS and how to interact with their professor. Without a course designed in the LMS, they had to wait for the professor to email recording and assignment instructions. If they didn’t get the email or accidentally deleted the link, they had to email the professor to request the link again.

In general, the online students felt disconnected from their professor—he was never in the LMS, and they felt as though everything was directed toward the in-class section. Even in his introductory video, the professor recorded the in-class students introducing themselves but did not give the online students a chance to interact with them or each other.

Online students weren't sure how to best contact him or whether they could meet with him privately online. Several students wondered why he didn't offer office/ student hours via the web-conferencing tool, where he could share his screen.

Students were also confused about where to submit work that was not done through NexLab. Should they email the assignment to Professor Eff or upload it to the LMS assignment dropbox? Technology questions and assignment instruction requests soon flooded his inbox, and Professor Eff quickly contacted support staff for help.

Using HIDOC to Revise the Course

To improve the course, Professor Eff could consider the following actions:

Step 1: Learner Analysis
Consider that in-person and online students have different needs and considerations. In-person students, for example, should be informed that their voice might be caught on the recording, and that lectures will be filmed. Online students need easy access to any text written live and ways to contribute questions.

Step 2: Learning Outcomes
With the heavy focus on NexLab, consider if a certain mastery is required, and if it should be included in the CLOs.

Step 3: Course Structure
Design a full, asynchronous online course. Create the modular structure in the LMS, but leave placeholders for the live lecture videos that will be uploaded (or create shorter, targeted recordings specifically for the online students, if time).

Step 4: Assessments & Activities
Ensure that activities and assessments are equitable between groups and that all students receive the same instructions, support, and guidance. Review spacing and sequencing of assignments, remembering that students are learning both course content and software and may need more opportunities to practice and receive feedback.

Step 5: Instructional Materials

Create shorter topical videos that can be used for multiple offerings (these might even be offered to in-class students as a way to use a flipped pedagogical approach, saving class time for applied learning). Alternatively, create context-neutral topical videos for online learners separate from live lectures, utilize institutional lecture capture options, or use web-conferencing software with a tablet to record high-quality screen annotations.

Step 6: Technology & Tools

Provide videos to students through the LMS, not email. Ideally, all videos should be closed-captioned, and include additional audio descriptions where necessary. Consult the IT and media resources within the department; multimedia staff and/or instructional designers may have more experience with lecture capture and might use alternate tools and software that will produce a better product than one camera in the back of the room. They may also be able to help chunk lectures into smaller pieces, add chapters, or even add interactive, embedded questions.

Step 7: Online Learner Support

Make sure that online students have ample opportunity to ask questions and receive help. Provide a way for them to submit questions in advance of the F2F lecture, hold dedicated office/student hours for a topic or assignment online, and create an open Q&A discussion board, which could be used by students in both modalities. Provide a list of ways that online students can connect, such as email, phone, and web-conferencing software.

Step 8: Continuous Improvement

Survey online students to gather information about how they use videos to study for the course. For example, do they view videos all in one sitting? Do they view them on their computer, laptop, or phone? Would they prefer shorter, topical videos? Can they see and hear everything clearly? Are the videos easy to review? "Wish list" items might include adding chapter markers to existing videos or editing longer videos into shorter topical pieces.

Design Execution

Especially if using the F2F recordings, consider how to establish teaching presence for the online course. Use announcements for assignment due date reminders and general feedback. Create an impromptu webcam, screencast, or document if there are any necessary elaborations (e.g., assignment, activity, topic, question).

Reflect on Your Own Course Design

Think about how this case might apply to or inform your course design work.

- Do you teach a course that is dual-mode or HyFlex? If you're teaching students in multiple modalities, are they getting equitable learning experiences? Is any modality disadvantaged in a way that could be addressed via design or teaching?
- Do your students need to view (or review) lectures from in-class sessions? If so, is the room equipped such that students viewing online will be able to hear, see, and experience everything the in-class students do?
- Do you have access to multimedia support to aid in making high-quality recordings or using classroom technologies?
- Do online students have the same opportunities to ask questions, get feedback, and interact with you? How do you try to be present and connect with your online students?

Index

accessibility 20, 21, 24, 90
  closed-captioned 93, 102, 121, 168, 272
  materials 92
  practices 93
  screen reader 93, 96, 114
  transcript 94, 104, 168
  video 93, 246
  visuals 93
active teaching 20, 21, 24, 203. See also Teaching Calendar
activities 63
  knowledge-check 65, 136
  no/low stakes 65
  ungraded 64, 257, 258, 259
announcements 190
  video 190
  weekly 99, 237, 250
  welcome 199
  whole-class 188
assessments 63
  assignment explanations 139
  assignment prompts 142
  authentic 68
  formative 63
    quizzes 65
  project-based 69
  summative 63
    learning and mastery 63
  testing 63, 70, 122, 150
  timed 64, 70, 76, 116, 144, 191
  ungrading 142, 200
  video 257–258

big vision 31
Bloom's taxonomy 36
  revised 35

cognitive load 119
continuous improvement 161
  iterations 176, 201
  planning for 169
  Revision Roadmap 170
  Revision Triage 181
course design 174
  learning path 130
  navigation 13, 120, 147, 160, 173, 177
  read, watch, do 132, 198
  rhythm 164
  scaffolding 28, 76, 144, 255
  sequence 131
  spacing 164
course orientation 146, 147, 188. See also "Start Here" Folder; See also welcome
course schedule 144, 151
  group communication 153
course structure 53
course supports 145
course timeline 195
  before class begins 196
  early weeks 200
  final week 202
  first week of class 199
  throughout the course 201

Design Docs
  Bonus Development Docs
    Step 5: Online Topical Lectures 225
    Step 7: Assignment Prompts 228
  HIDOC Course Blueprint 210
  Step 1: Learner Analysis 213
  Step 2: Learning Outcomes 215
  Step 3: Course Structure 218
  Step 4: Assessments & Activities 220
  Step 5: Instructional Materials 223
  Step 6: Technology & Tools 226
  Step 8: Revision Roadmap 229
Design Execution 183. See also Active Teaching; See also Teaching Calendar
design vs. delivery 14
design vs. development 13
diversity 20

exams 63, 64, 70, 75, 76, 81, 116, 166, 193, 258
  proctored exams 69, 70
  proctoring 69, 122

questions 68, 73, 261
screencast instructions 70
types 73

Faculty-ID Collaboration
Checking for Alignment 82
Choosing the Right LMS Tool 125
Considering Your Learners 27
Feedback, Timing, and Cognitive Engagement 80
Planning for Revision 183
Replacing "Understand" with Active Verbs 47
The Importance of a Detailed Learning Path 157
The Importance of Structure and Organization 59
Using Student-Centric Language 48
Why Don't We Start with Content? 108
feedback
auto-generated 65
methods 267
screencast 191

HIDOC 1
Step 1: Learner Analysis 19
Step 2: Learning Outcomes 31
Step 3: Course Structure 53
Step 4: Activities & Assessments 63
Step 5: Instructional Materials 87
Step 6: Technology & Tools 113
Step 7: Online Learner Support 129
Step 8: Continuous Improvement 161
HIDOC Course Blueprint 11, 26, 46, 59, 75, 79, 80, 100, 101, 102, 121, 124, 125, 135, 138, 139, 164, 167, 169, 210, 211, 212, 220, 223, 226
HIDOC-in-Action 231
High-Impact Design Practices 7

inclusive design xxiv. See also voice and choice
authors, scholars, guest experts 91
content warnings 92
examples and anecdotes 91
images 90
instructional materials 90
representation 90
strategy 71
student contributions 92
trauma-informed 21
inclusivity 90
instructional design xxvi
instructional designers xviii, xxii, 2, 5, 8, 255, 257, 272
instructional materials 87
balance of types 166
content descriptions 155
copyright 96, 137, 253, 254, 255, 256
creating 98
curating 95
instructor-created content 98
Open Educational Resources (OER) 97
"Overstuffed" online courses 88
searching for 97
sourcing 94
topical lectures 14, 87, 102, 103, 105, 106, 107, 141, 225
instructor considerations
humor 192
tone xxiii, 40, 147, 157, 179, 190, 199, 255
instructor welcome 147

learner analysis 19
course details 23
learner considerations 24
self-directed learner 130
time management 3, 129, 144, 166
time zones 20, 22, 151
learner support 129. See also workload
avoiding "busy work" 66
motivation 26, 30, 130, 144, 146, 147, 160, 178, 179
non-course supports 150
procrastination 144, 151
learning outcomes 31
alignment 8
alignment map 54
CLOs 33
MLOs 133
measurable 34
observable 5, 34, 36
LMS 116
discussion tool 117
LMS-based analytics 199

military 20, 92
modalities 106, 269, 272, 273
  correspondence xv, 71, 198
  differences f2f/online 2
  Dual-Mode and HyFlex xxi
  Face-to-Face xxi
  Fully Online
    Asynchronous xxi
    Synchronous xxi
  Hybrid xxiv
  remote delivery xvii, 2
  remote learning xv, xvi, 20
  remote teaching xvii
module
  brainstorming 56
  essential elements 131
  layout 135
  organization 53
  planning 57
  staggered release or all-at-once? 196
  survey questions 173

neurodiversity 20, 21, 24

objectives 41, 51

policies 148
  attendance and participation 148
  communication 148
  netiquette 20, 21, 24, 149
power distance 20
presence 67
  cognitive 67
  Community of Inquiry framework 9
  social 9
    general discussions 154
    guidance and connection 193
    make introductions 188
    student introductions 154
  teaching 9, 14, 53, 67, 70, 87, 146, 155, 179, 185, 187, 193, 201, 202, 256, 264, 272
proctored exams 69, 70, 86, 122, 226

regular and substantive interaction 13, 71, 90, 92, 93, 94, 96, 101, 102, 110, 114, 119, 127, 150, 168, 181, 200, 223, 224, 246
rubrics 142, 228

security 96, 114, 171
"Start Here" Folder 146
survey questions
  course-level 177
  module-level 173
  student feedback 172
syllabus 148

Teaching Calendar 161, 163, 164, 166, 169, 201, 203, 206, 207, 236
technology 113, 176
  cameras 189
  choice 113, 114, 119, 121, 127
  documentation 123
  institutionally supported 114
  planning 121
  requirements 149
  testing 257, 258, 259
  third-party tools 120
  types 115
transactional distance 10

verbs. See Bloom's taxonomy
  active 34, 35, 36, 39, 42, 45, 75, 215
  fuzzy 45, 217
  taxonomies 34, 36
video
  accessibility 246
  announcements 190
  assessment 257–258
    screencast 263
    video question 84
  "clarification point" 201, 206
  closed-captioned 93, 102, 121, 168, 272
  course overview 188, 245
  create topical lecture 103
  instructor-created 147, 179, 203
  instructor introduction 98, 147, 171, 188, 196
  interactive questions 105
  known issues 102
  lab activity 239
  lecture 98, 100, 103, 104, 121
    synchronous 106
  recorded interviews 98
  screencast 98, 105
    announcements 272
    course orientation 146, 196

demonstration 120, 235, 267
feedback, giving 193
feedback, modeling 267
feedback, viewing 191
student-created 263, 267
script 64, 103, 104
short topical 70, 98, 103, 137, 145, 174, 188, 239, 240, 251, 272
"show and tell" 120, 246, 247
student-created 255
assessment 257–258
assignment 263
web-conferencing 19, 113, 150, 188, 258, 271, 272
visual design 29
accessibility 93
inclusive images 90, 104
relevant visuals 98, 100, 107, 225
voice and choice 71, 72, 76, 77, 91, 165, 221, 241, 249, 255

welcome. See "Start Here" folder
announcement 199
instructor 147
letter 199, 247, 260
video 147
workload
heavy 237, 240
student 166
survey questions 173

Made in the USA
Monee, IL
29 March 2024

56053695R00168